A Grand Adventure

Fred Reed

DEDICATION

For every dumb sonofabitch who got conned into a damn-fool war.

CONTENTS

ACKNOWLEDGMENTS

Cover design: Violeta Gonzalez

i

1 A GRAND ADVENTURE: WISDOM'S PRICE

He grew up in the woods and rivers of the county, fishing and swimming and hunting under sprawling blue skies and driving his rattletrap car insanely and lying on the moss with his girl and watching the branches above groping the sky and marveling as the young do at the strangeness of life, and the war came in a far country. It doesn't matter which. It was just a country.

His father, an angry man emitting the foul stench of patriotism, said his duty was to become a soldier and kill whoever it was in the far country, wherever it was. His father didn't know or much care. It didn't matter. Somebody would know. A man's gotta do what a man's gotta do. It would be a grand adventure, an uncle said.

He enlisted. In the aching humid heat of a hot state he drew toothpaste and seven-eighty-two gear and green clothes from supply and learned to march in squares while a sergeant said Lef-rye-lef-rye-lef. He felt the sense of power and invincibility that comes of rhythmic camaraderie with thudding boots. He learned to use grenades and flamethrowers and the proper placement of a bayonet in a kidney. He learned obedience and various forms of likely suicide, but it was for his country, dulce et decorum est, and he sang fierce cadences on the march. If I die on the Russian front, bury me with a Russian cunt, lef-rye-lef-rye-lef-rye-lef. It was a grand adventure, calling to a young man's desperation to defy existence, to cross the mountains, to see the dragon, to overcome. The colonels at Training Command had calculated this nicely.

He felt the romance and variety and absurdity that men love in the military in time of peace, and collected the stories that soldiers tell in bars. See, we was in TJ at the Blue Fox, and Murphy was getting a lap dance from this senorita with frigging water-melon tits, I mean those hangers just wouldn't quit, and this owl flies in, some kind of freaking bird anyway, and she screams and falls on Murphy and... He felt the freedom of being away from the county, in wild bars nobody back home had ever heard of. It was the life.

Then he was on the late-night tarmac of the airfield, staging out for the remote country of which he knew nothing. Wind swirled and jet wash smelled of aviation kerosene and he was fit and hardly noticed the weight of his pack. Heavies roared in and out, taking troops. He savored a new phrase, FMF WesPac. Fleet Marine Force Western Pacific, alive with hormonal appeals of armies on the march, of foreign legions and Marcus Aurelius on the Rhine-Danube line, though he had never heard of the man, and he was part of huge events happening in the night.

On the first day in-country he went to his posting in the remote land, in a convoy of open six-bys. The heat and strange people along the road exhilarated him and he was really, truly out of the county and he took it all in with wide eyes and the mine went off under the lead truck and the driver landed screaming by the road, his legs gone. Mines do that. Marines ran to him and said Jesus, oh Jesus. Fuck. Fuck, fuck, fuck. Get a corpsman. Oh shit. Oh Jesus. The screaming stopped, that being the nature of femoral arteries.

Three months passed. He now hated the people of the remote country, though he still knew nothing of it. Soldiers hate. He killed some enemy soldiers and some who may have been enemy soldiers and then some he knew weren't but who were in the wrong place after his platoon took casualties from a sniper. It didn't affect him, not that he knew. Dead people were just dead people, so what. He hated the scuttling cockroaches anyway. Light'em up. Light'em all up. Let God sort'em out. He had never heard of the Albigensians, but soldiers vary little.

One day the platoon approached a town and a sniper fired at them. "Light'em up" said the lieutenant, who hated the locals. Ten minutes later thirty-seven villagers were dead and the reporter who had been there got pictures of it all. They appeared around the world. The platoon didn't know why they were being picked on. If villagers didn't want to get shot, they shouldn't let heavily armed insurgents come into their village. At a thousand legion halls, members said war is war, people get hurt. You gotta expect it. The press are wimps, comsymps, unrealistic idealists. We need to unleash the troops, let them win.

Officers, knowing that reporters were the most dangerous of their enemies, said that it hadn't happened, that the enemy had really done it, that it was an isolated incident, and that there would be an investigation. The commanding general in what interestingly was called "the theater" had presidential aspirations, and so sacrificed the lieutenant, who eventually received three months house arrest.

The soldier from the county almost made it. He was approaching PCOD, Pussy Cut-off Date, determined by the incubation time of gonorrhea, when his truck hit the mine. Nothing new here. Men in agony, exposed bone, crushed lungs, and the dying crying out for the trinity of the badly wounded, mother, wife, and water. This time the soldier from the county was half gutted.

It was a grand adventure, though.

On the ward where they removed a length of his intestines, he saw many things. He saw the soldier with his jaw shot away who fed through a tube in his nose. He watched a high-school girl of seventeen from Tennessee as she saw her betrothed, stone blind, his face a hideous porridge that would gag a maggot.

Johnny…Johnny…oh Johnny.

He left the hospital with a colostomy bag and instructions never to eat anything he liked. Women do not like colostomy bags, so he had time on his hands. He read. He thought. He came to hate, to hate with a shuddering intensity that unnerved his friends, who learned not to talk about the war. Like soldiers since before time existed, he learned that the war was not about the noble things it was supposed to be about, God and country and democracy, but about money, power, contracts, and the egos of the men who, on the principle that shit floats, always rise to the top. For the rest of his life, he would really, truly, want to kill.

He had come a long way from the county. It had been a grand adventure.

2 COMMENTATOR'S DISEASE

When I read columnists or listen to talking heads on the lobotomy box, they strike me as delusional. What are these decapitated crania prattling about? From what morgue did they escape? What country are they from? Certainly not the America I grew up in.

I conclude that they suffer from Commentator's Disease, which consists in the confluence of several disabilities, the first being high intelligence. Washington, being a center of power, politics, graft, and corruption, attracts the very bright. An acquaintance once said, "Inside the Beltway, you assume that everyone is in the ninety-ninth percentile." She meant that in the circles in which she moved, this was true. The city is rife with the very bright, most of them being invisible: campaign planners, pollsters, lawyers, scientists from NIH. The class includes many of the talking heads, the Pat Buchanans and Charles Krauthammers. They may be liberal or conservative, depending on their individual defects of character, but they are way smart.

The exceedingly intelligent form a social class seldom mentioned but inordinately influential. They are not recognized as what they are because they do not append IQs to their by-lines. As a quite ordinary example, consider the magazine *The American Conservative,* with many of whose writers I have some familiarity. The publisher, Ron Unz, studied theoretical physics at Stanford after graduating from Harvard. Bill Lind, Pat Buchanan, Taki, Steve Sailer, Kara Hopkins, John Derbyshire—I doubt that there is an IQ below 140 in the bunch. The same could be said of many other political slicks, left or right.

These people are not intellectual snobs. In the crowd they run with, they are average. The problem with them is that they hang out together. People tend to associate with those with whom they have things in common. At a hole-in-the-wall in DC like the Zoo Bar on upper Connecticut you may find a table of eight people in jeans and running shoes—Washington is about power, not style—consisting of a biochemist, an editor of a technical newsletter, a talking head you've seen, and so on, all highly educated. This clustering together by intelligence is sometimes called "cognitive stratification." It exists, big time. The clusterers are by and large decent people, not full of themselves, and mean well.

But.

But they don't know what they are talking about in important respects. They think the Beltway contains America.

The second symptom of Commentator's Disease is relative prosperity. The nature of Washington is that the very bright usually do well financially. I don't mean that they are rich, though some are, but that they manage to find secure jobs in government or with law firms or they invest wisely or, in the case of commentators, angle for well-paid gigs with syndicates or networks. Usually there is nothing crooked in this. They are simply smart enough to work the system, and they live where the system is.

The aggregate effect of their brains, security, and isolation is that they are out of touch with the country as it really is. They do not know the bleak strip-development of Route 1 South toward Fredericksburg, the red dirt and franchised cholesterol chutes and roaring traffic. Here the diabetic veteran lives in a decayed residential motel and makes his way on crutches to the down-scale diner where he drinks beer and waits to die because he hasn't got anything else to wait for. (The example is not hypothetical.) Here the aging waitress gets to the diner somehow, aching with arthritis. "Too tired to work, too poor to stop." I knew this woman. She is much of America. You don't see her at the Zoo Bar. She has never been to such a place.

I often see victims of Commentator's Disease arguing against the minimum wage on abstract grounds of economic theory. It is what commentators do—bandy abstractions, railing for or against Keynes, assaulting their ideological opponents with pointed phrases. They have never had to do the arithmetic of forty times the minimum wage minus taxes minus bus fare minus rent and gotta pay the cable because it is the only thing they have after work. They have never had to choose between the electric bill and a new coat as winter comes on.

The commentators don't realize that not everybody is like them. Those with IQs of 140 and up (130 gets you into Mensa, I think) unconsciously believe that anything is possible. Denizens of this class know that if they decided to learn, say, classical Greek, they can. You get the book and go at it. It would take work, yes, and time, but the outcome would be certain.

They don't understand that the waitress has an IQ of 85 and can't learn much of anything.

Conservatives think in terms of merciless abstractions and liberals insist that everyone is equal. Not even close. Further, people with barely a high-school education and low-voltage minds regard any intellectual task with utter discouragement.

Some commentators urge letting people invest their Social Security taxes in the stock market. To them it is a question of abstract freedom and probably the Federalist Papers. The commentators are smart enough to invest money. I'll guess that at least half the population isn't. Go into the tit bar (does it still exist) in Waldorf, Maryland, and ask the dump-truck drivers and nail-pounders what NASDAQ is.

Liberal commentators want everyone to go to college, when about a fifth of people have the brains. Conservatives think that people can rise by hard work and sacrifice as certainly many people have. Thing is, most people can't. Commentators only see those who made it.

The tendency of the Beltway 99th to live in an imaginary world, of conservatives to think that everybody can be a Horatio Alger, of liberals to believe that inequality arises from discrimination, guarantees wretched policy. Those who can do almost anything need to recognize the existence of those who can do almost nothing. Few of the latter are parasites. The waitress has worked all her life, as has the truck driver. They ended up with nothing.

Which is easy to do. A girl marries her high-school sweetheart in Busted Hump, Tennessee and he goes to work for the local pickle-bottling plant, which switches to hiring people as independent contractors to avoid paying benefits. Neither of the pair is real bright, just ordinary Americans trying to make a living. They live paycheck to paycheck because they don't know how not to. Neither is lazy. They just don't know how to start the next Microsoft. He dies of a heart attack at 45, she can't make the mortgage, and...she is well and truly screwed.

At the Zoo Bar, they have great wings and some really good walk-in blues bands, and what you have to understand about

Keynes is….Commentator's Disease.

3 CONSERVATIVES

I am trying to understand conservatives. The word has got to mean something, unless of course it doesn't. For years I thought it meant someone like my grandfather, a professor of mathematics at a small college in the South. He embodied courtesy, respect for learning, personal responsibility, compassion for those in the town who found themselves in distress, dignity, a love of the language, a morality opposed to promiscuity and bastardy, and a quiet Christianity having nothing in common with the cruelty and hostility of today's unlettered evangelicals. I thought it a pretty decent package, though I had problems with the part about avoiding promiscuity.

Over my years of writing this column, I have received a great deal of mail from people, entirely male so far as I can remember, calling themselves "conservatives," yet having nothing in common with granddad. (I use quotation marks, though I will omit them in what follows as being annoying, because there are many people who regard themselves as conservatives but are decent people.)

These email conservatives are a specific type of person, characterized by:

(1) Hostility to other groups—blacks, Mexicans, homosexuals, and Jews for example. In earlier times they would have detested the Irish, Italians, Asians, and Slavs;

(2) A view of life as conflict, struggle, and war. We must arm, arm, arm. Commerce also is a fight to the death in which we must prevail by any means. We must not become soft and weak, as only the strong and resolute will survive in this red-fanged world; this finds philosophical support in Social Darwinism, which says let them starve if they can't keep up. Further, we must breed like incontinent oysters or the Chinese (Muslims, Africans, etc.) will overwhelm us. This often shades into:

(3) Subclinical paranoia. The (pick one) Jews, communists, Russians, Chinese, Muslims are insidious, fiendishly patient— waiting, waiting for us to falter so that they can take over and enslave us. You have doubtless heard this sort of thing: The gates

of Vienna, what Lenin said about probing with a bayonet, the Protocols of the Elders of Zion.

Strange shapes twist in the inner fog. Spies are everywhere, traitors await their chance, dissent is not dissent but a prelude to treason.

(4) An obsession with profits and economic growth for their own sake. "For their own sake" is a key qualifier. They do not ask "How much growth of what kind where for what purpose?" Nor do they ever use the phrase "quality of life." They want more housing starts, more construction, more population to buy the houses without regard for anything else. People exist to serve the economy, not the other way around. On libertarian sites this sometimes approaches belief in capitalism as a supernatural force: The Invisible Hand of the market. This view is facilitated by:

(5) A lack of esthetic sensitivity. Where other people see a towering redwood forest as a place of contemplation, of solemn ancient beauty and God's handiwork, the conservative (of the type I am talking about) sees timber suitable for making weatherproof decks for yuppies (at a good profit). Whales? Dog food. The Grand Canyon? A potential tourist bonanza needing only a four-lane highway, several malls with five-star hotels, and a Disneyland park with an Old West theme and mechanical-burro rides.

For them, everything is raw material for making a buck. They honestly seem to have no idea why anyone would object to killing everything and bulldozing everything else since there is money in it. Thus they hate enviro-wackos as perverse and irrational. This save-the-spotted-owl business is lunacy, they figure it's just a freaking bird, for god's sake, and we could put a subdivision where it nests. And then a mall. Tied into this view is a tendency to regard people likewise as raw material, a view underpinned by:

(6) A lack of empathy. Suppose that squishy bleeding-heart do-gooders object to the employment of children, often for twelve hours a day in Indonesian sweatshops, making pricey running shoes for people who don't run. This will infuriate the conservatives (again, of this type). The factory makes money, doesn't it? Photos from war zones of children with their entrails hanging out? The communist media are trying to sap the public's will to fight. These conservatives just don't care, and can't care.

Now, by the foregoing I do not suggest that they are always

wrong in their prescriptions. Sometimes there are enemies abroad (chiefly because other countries also have their martial paranoids). Immigration by incompatible groups may well be inadvisable. And so on. Yet these same people will find enemies where they are and where they aren't, oppose immigration whether it makes sense or not, because it is how they think.

Whatever the wisdom in a particular case, I believe that most of politics can be explained by friction between those who have the above-mentioned traits, and those who don't. Emotion determines policy, and the mind provides a window dressing of plausibility.

Consider empathy and its lack, perhaps the most profound dividing line in politics. Do you remember the uproar over exploitation of migrant workers in California? One side was willing to pay ten cents a head more for lettuce so that the migrants wouldn't have to live in hovels; the other side wasn't. Similarly, the Pentagon is perfectly willing to bomb cities and kill indiscriminately, to torture prisoners; the other side cringes.

A recurring example is the dispute over national medical care. The conservatives oppose it because they say it would become a bloated federal program, as it probably would. (They do not oppose bloated federal programs that produce profits, as for example the military, but have a deeply principled aversion to anything that might require them to pay taxes. Note that they favor private charity over public welfare, because they don't have to pay for the former.) They simply can't care what happens to others.

I have noticed that women are scarce among this group. They by nature do care. I have never heard a woman talk about the need for a pre-emptive nuclear strike against China. Many men do, all of the type who call themselves conservative.

What happens of course is that conscienceless, amoral men dress themselves in whatever ideology suits their purposes. Stalin was no more a socialist than he was the Tooth Fairy. However, since socialism requires that the state control the economy, it appeals to dictators. Thus the Union of Soviet Socialist Republics. "Free enterprise" appeals to those who want no interference with their rapine, who want to run sweatshops, starve sharecroppers, and make billions on subprime mortgages. Same people, different scaffolding.

4 LUNATICS TO THE LEFT, LUNATICS TO THE RIGHT, AND NOT A DROP TO DRINK

God. Oh God. Oh God, God, God. It is getting worse. Maybe I'll take cyanide.

I find this inspiriting headline polluting my inbox like rotting road-kill. It's from Broward County, Florida:

"Child Still Expelled for Toy Gun - a Year Later:

Parents want their child back in school. School board says no way"

See? Florida collectively is out of its tiny little mind. What if this crepuscular pathology spreads to other countries? Or planets?

"School board officials said the rules are quite clear and that the toy gun constituted a weapon."

Me, I figure the school-board officials constitute a pack of priggish low-Board simians who ought to be swinging in trees instead of trying to run a school. But then, I'm a curmudgeon.

Think about it. Kid—he's eight—shows up with toy gun after watching 12,000 hours of shoot'em-ups on the lobotomy box, Luke Skywalker blasting funny-looking milkmen like a pretty little mollycoddle turned psychopath. Kid sees war coverage with heroic GIs in Afghanistan killing anybody they can see. He watches recruiting ads for the Marines, who carry guns and want A Few Good Persons. Why would he possibly be interested in a toy gun?

And why would nominal adults, even the barely educated variety characteristically found on school boards, want to wreck the kid's life? Actually of course it is passive aggression, an attack on the tyke, said attack masquerading, or perhaps marauding is the better word, as high moral endeavor. See, they're protecting Western Civilization.

The US these days rolls in passive aggression. The country grows daily more mean-spirited, more wrapped in a miasma of diffuse anger, but you still can't just go up to a child and hit him with a ball bat, or throw acid in his face. No. Instead you find a smugly righteous way to set him back two years in school, thus making him into a guaranteed social misfit. How very...I don't think "intelligent" is an adequate word. Perhaps "sublime" is better. Or "supernal."

As tensions grow in America, as divisions flourish, and the nation leads up to something unseen but ugly, prissy vindictiveness and moral sadism become normal. We have become a gotcha culture, watchful for transgressions meaningless but forbidden, so that we can make the malfeasor squirm. How we enjoy the squirming, the writing on camera, the heavy punishments inflected for nothing.

The other day I was watching television, which I do in the spirit of Margaret Meade investigating her primitives. It's an electronic Petri dish. Anyway, a story aired of excruciating importance, At any rate it was excruciating. A politician had been discovered to have forwarded an email containing a picture of a woman copulating with a horse. Delight erupted, disguised as horror: A chance to make him squirm! His election could depend on revelation of this vile perversion, this sickening transgression against, and so on. All waited expectantly for him to whine and beg and lick feet. This reaction by the public strikes me as kinkier than the horse and its tart.

Let us dive, or perhaps wade for reason of long drought, into Truth. We are all adults here. Let's have a show of hands: How many readers have never looked at porn online?...Ah, I see that I am writing a blog for amputees. How many have never looked at anything more robustly exotic than Presbyterians in the missionary position? (Raise your stumps.) How many are genuinely shocked, appalled, disgusted etc. by the thought of the dread equestrian email, of whose contents most fourteen-year-olds have probably heard? Tijuana used to be internationally famous for such erotic vaudeville. If it is erotic.

The likelihood that the pol is amorously interested in horses is of course zero. Sheep, maybe. Horses, no.

Back to the eight-year-old. "He made a mistake, but why the severe punishment? I don't understand that," said Miguel Burgos, Sam's dad."

What? The child did not make a mistake. He's freaking eight. He brought a toy to school. Since eight is too young (at this writing) to be made to snivel on camera in delicious auto-humiliation, his parents per force do it for him.

The correct solution to the problem, if there were a problem, would be to tell the kid, "Hey, you aren't supposed to bring stuff like this. Don't, OK?" When he is a little older, he might be told that the entire scholarly (which it barely is) establishment constitutes a dry run by Darwin, which he judged a failure and meant to discard, but forgot.

There is something wrong, something fetid and cruel, about anyone who will so treat little boy. It gets stranger:

"The school board said they would admit Samuel into a correctional school for problem children who have been expelled located in Hallandale Beach."

Oh joy! Reform school! What better way to turn him into a happy and stable boy? (Which he is anyway.) Why not Leavenworth? We could try him as an adult. I recommend solitary, to protect the other inmates. And don't let him bring his teddy bear. He has to learn that actions have consequences.

I thrash about in search of understanding. It cometh not. Perhaps the explanation lies in physics: The stupidity of a closed system tends to remain the same or to increase. Usually, increase.

This sort of neurotic theater has gone on for years. I remember the boy expelled for pointing (so help me) a chicken finger and saying "Bang!" Another for bringing plastic soldiers to school, another for drawing a picture of a soldier with a gun, another for swatting a girl on the butt on the playground. This last resulted in the calling of cops, a handcuffed kid, and compulsory psychiatric treatment instead of an admonitory, "Don't do that again, Bobby. Do you understand me?" How does a society come to this?

I can make guesses that sound vaguely plausible. The United States is not a happy country. People waste their lives in meaningless jobs, trapped by the credit card, the mortgage, the student loan. They know they are wasting their lives. Racial anger runs high. Women resent men. Divorce screws up kids. There is the two-hour commute to the cubicle and back to the sterile box in the anonymous subdivision, the lack of influence over their lives, life from paycheck to paycheck. And anger at affirmative action, either because they suffer from it or because they need it. Life is just flat stressful.

People get spiteful, mean, like mistreated dogs. They want to make others as miserable as they secretly are themselves. So they torment a little boy. I'm going to change my phylum.

5 A REQUIEM FOR REASON: OH WELL. IT NEVER AMOUNTED TO MUCH ANYWAY.

Much hoorah, there is, over the mosque that may or may not be built in New York. I don't give a tinker's damn (whatever precisely that may be; I presume that tinkers' oaths were thought more efficacious than others) whether they build it or not. The matter does however put to rest for me any hope of rationality in human affairs. This, I grant, could be accomplished with a very small bed.

At this writing, the government's war for oil and AIPAC has more or less solidly metamorphosed, among the rubes at least, into a war against Islam. Men of thunder and portent peddle the notion like starving encyclopedia salesmen. No less a political howitzer than Pat Buchanan says that the mosque should not be built, because of the religious motivation of the Saudis who attacked the towers. His view has been eagerly received by the populace. Now it seems that yahoos at some fourth-grade church in Florida plan to burn a Koran to commemorate 9/11.

Splendid, this. We are telling 1.3 billion Muslims that America is not fighting Al Qaeda, or the Taliban, or Terror. No. It is Islam itself we hate. How very wise. This will make it so much easier to win hearts and minds in Afghanistan and Pakistan. Those security forces that GIs are supposed to be training—the ones with the AKs—they will know that their trainers are their enemies. Curiously, this is just what bin Laden tells them.

Glands again trump minds, if any. Consider that ten minutes before the first tower got hit in New York, the thought had occurred to practically no one in America that Islam constituted a mortal threat to all that we hold holy, chiefly chain restaurants and iPods. But Islam afterwards offered to fill this void that the Russians had wimped out on. For a brief period after the implosion of the Soviet Union, Americans had no threat to worry about. They found it deeply puzzling. Weren't we supposed to be afraid of something? It didn't feel right.

Then came New York, and suddenly we saw it: The Clash of Civilizations. Islam was out to get us. Why hadn't we noticed? A roaring hatred for Muslims sprang up from people who had never met a Muslim, who had a garden slug's grasp of history. A deep satisfaction came over the land. We had been made whole again.

Battling Mohammedans quickly became an industry. The government at first tried to peddle Terrorism as the enemy, not Islam, but it didn't stick. Something more robustly flackable was wanted.

I find Buchanan, of the American Conservative, proclaiming that Islam is a Culture of Jihad, and most militant. No doubt. Very. Would it be poltroonish of me to note that just now Christian armies are busily annexing and wrecking Afghanistan and Iraq, having recently bombed Somalia? That they use robotic aircraft to murder Yemenis, that they hunt down Muslims in the Philippines (where after 1898 Americans engaged in atrocities that would win the admiration of the Japanese), encourage Israel to ruin Lebanon and to run a concentration camp for Muslims in Gaza, enthusiastically murder Pakistanis from the sky, and threaten Syria and Iran?

Those Muslims. Militant, they are. The bastards.

The Islamic countries listed above are only those currently attacked by America. Let us look at the matter in another way. I append here a list of all Christian countries conquered by militant Muslims since 1529:

Next, a partial list of Muslim countries conquered by Christians: Morocco, Algeria, Tunisia, Libya, Egypt, Sudan, Lebanon, Syria, Palestine, Jordan, Iraq (the first time), Iraq (again), Iran, Pakistan, East Pakistan, Indonesia, Saudi Arabia, Kuwait, Yemen, Oman, Abu Dhabi, Dubai....

This list does not include such minor Christian conquests as North, South, and Central America, India, China, Southeast Asia, black Africa, and such. Unconscionable, Muslim aggressiveness is.

Buchanan regards the events of 9/11 as no end grievous. So do I. Yet perhaps people who live in glass pots and kettles shouldn't call names. The UN's figures give 600,000 Iraqi children dead because of the American embargo, which didn't allow, for example, chlorine to sterilize water. This is equivalent to 6.4 million dead children in the United States. Hmmm: If Muslims had killed this trifling number of our sprats, might we wax grumpish?

Yes, I know, the UN is a commie Marxist socialist anti-

American conspiracy, and not as trustworthy as the American propaganda apparatus. All right. Let's assume that the UN lied by a factor of ten, and thus only 60,000 Iraqi children died thanks to us. Thus, if 3,000 Americans died in New York, we owe the Muslims some 57,000. No?

If I may sally briefly into unloved seriousness: What puzzles me, as one who has lived extensively abroad, is how little Americans are able to see things through the eyes of others, how little empathy they have (this latter defect being characteristic of both psychopaths and narcissists).

Consider a headline from Anti-war.com of a sort appearing almost daily: "US Drone Strike Destroys House Full of Children in Pakistan."

Apparently no one in the Great Rubber Room north of Mexico has an inkling why this might arouse hatred in Pakistanis. Can you imagine the fury that would ensue if a Muslim blew up a house full of American kids in, say, Queens? But when we kill their kids, no one cares. "Yeah, well. Tough. Giv'em a few dollars." Buncha dirty raghead larvae. No better than cock roaches, right?.

Now, we're going to have a pop quiz. Take out a sheet of paper. Question: Can you think of any reason why Muslims might be unhappy with America?

Right! They hate our freedoms.

In which case they daily have less to hate us for.

It doesn't pay to underestimate an enemy, I hear. All right: Muslims are so very dangerous not just because of their many extremist groups—Salamists, Al Sushis, the Falafel, and the Wasabi for example—but because of their immense industrial strength, which doesn't exist. With the possible exception of Turkey, not one Islamic nation is in the First World. I picture bearded, turbaned warriors wading ashore on aquatic camels, causing no end of panic in Atlantic City. I mean, what do camels eat?

The horror.

Herewith a searing insight for the ever-puzzled State Department: Actions have consequences. If you support Batista, you will engender Fidel. If you support the Shah, you will get Khomeini. If you attack Muslims, you will get bin Laden. It might be better to stay home and read a book.

6 SOBER THOUGHTS ON AFGHANISTAN

I get a certain amount of email saying that I am arrogant and dismissive of the intelligence and political knowledge of certain groups, most notably Tea Partyers and the audience of Fox News, but also of the American public in general. Supposedly I talk to them as if they were ignorant when in fact, I am told, they are not. Some critics have compared me to Mencken with his disdain for the Booboisie.

Perhaps they are right, and I have underestimated the knowledge and attention span of the citizenry. I hate to admit it, but, well, truth is truth. With respect to the wars against Islam, I tend to think in military terms, and then write (I confess) in vague generalities. This may appear to be condescension to Sean Hannity's viewers. If I have done them wrong, I apologize.

All right. Let me try to discuss the wars intelligently, not giving ideological solutions but just stating the problems from the standpoint of those who actually have to fight and manage the wars.

(1) The American command wants to run raids across the Afghan border into Pakistan and Kazakhstan to attack Al Qaeda guerrillas who currently enjoy safe havens in those countries. This is needed, say officers, to save American lives. But in Islamabad, Benazir Bhutto's Falafel Party—she was assassinated, but the party lives on, as intensely nationalistic as ever—says it wants the Pakistani Army to fire on American troops if they "invade" the country.

What now? While the Falafelists are not in power, they are strong in the military. Fighting very nearly broke out during a US helicopter raid against Herat in the Federated Tribal Territories. Do we pursue Al Qaeda at the possible cost of war with the Paki Army? Tough choice.

(2) We are all familiar with the Predator and Raptor drones used to target Al Qaeda suspects in Pakistan and Afghanistan. The Pentagon wants to replace the Hellfire missiles fired currently by the drones with the new Mk 48 ADCAP ("Advanced Capability") missile which, while much more accurate, also has a larger blast

radius—meaning that more civilians will be killed. Is it worth it, given the anger aroused among civilian populations by the extra deaths? This is the kind of question that commanders on the ground must decide.

(3) Then there is the difficult question of cultivation of opium poppies. When the Taliban took over following the withdrawal of the Russians from Afghanistan in 1989, they forced farmers into the production of the drug, thus making the rural population dependent on the (small) profits the extremists allowed them. The Americans of course want to eliminate the poppies, but this would do nothing to win the hearts and minds of the growers. (What are the farmers doing to do? Grow potatoes instead? College kids won't pay $500 an ounce for sin-semilla spuds.)

So what does the military do about towns like Hecuba and Priam, in Sulawesi Province on the southern border with Iran, which are transshipment points for drugs crossing Iran en route to European markets? Eliminate them, and lose the population? Or allow the traffic to continue in order to further the war effort? The present solution, if so it is, is to uneasily ignore the question.

Somebody has to make a decision. And it will be denounced in the press as wrong, either way.

(4) Apart from Black Hawk troop-carrying helicopters, the workhorse chopper of the war has been the AH-78 Comanche gunship, now equipped with the BQQ-6 submillimeter-wave radar for detecting the movement of metal armaments (e.g., rifles) at night. The radar is highly classified.

The State Department wants to transfer six of the craft to the Afghan "air force" (actually a few helicopters) to show faith in the Karzai government. The Pentagon says the technology would be in Taliban, and thus Chinese, hands within a week. Worth it? Somebody has to decide, and both answers are wrong.

The (accidental) damage to the Al Aqsa mosque in Kandahar by a drone strike aroused fury among the militant Sufi tribesmen of the region. These have a tradition of almost constant war, dating back to the rule of Peshmurga I, and of Sufi control over the silk trade through the Khyber Pass to Rawalpindi and on to Bukitinggi.

Again, it's hearts-and-minds versus military objectives. If you restrict bombing near mosques, you give Al Qaeda safe havens. If you damage (or, as some have proposed, even deliberately bomb) mosques, you infuriate the locals and, so say some commentators, produce recruits to Al Qaeda and the Taliban. A? Or B?

(5) Iran. According to Infantry Weapons and Light Armor, the bible of the military small-arms world, Iran is making available to the insurgents the AK 16"-54 (the NATO designation of the long-barreled Iranian knock-off of the AK47, which fires a heavier and therefore longer-ranged bullet). This has long been known.

More worrisome, some of the explosives used recently in roadside bombs show the chemical signature of manufacture at the Iranian arms complex at Bucephalus. These substances, used in shaped charges, can penetrate the side armor on M1 tanks. Tehran wants a stable environment for Bucephalus, since it derives considerable revenue from arms sales, and thus might stop shipping explosives under American pressure. So far it hasn't.

Should the US bomb the plant, widening the war? Or, instead, accept the additional losses in Afghanistan to avoid stretching forces already spread thin? Not an easy question.

(6) Then there is the tricky matter of Hamid Karzai, the Afghan president in Kabul. The US knows he is corrupt, but has to pretend that he isn't. Such fictions are part of diplomacy. NATO would like to replace him if it could dig up a suitable candidate—Ahmad Shah Massoud is mentioned, though he is said to be good for splashy photo-ops and not much else. Another suggestion is Yusuf Sala al-Din, but despite his lack of recent political activity he is suspected of hostility to what bin Laden calls "Crusaders," meaning European invaders of Islamic lands. Who, then? What it comes to is that Afghanistan is not brimming over with democratically-minded leaders.

Anyway, how to get rid of Karzai? He could die in a car accident, but that would be a tad obvious even for the CIA.

(7) Finally another, seemingly minor, instance of what many see as the military's lack of concern for the feelings of Afghans: General Stanley McCrystal, before being fired by Obama, flew to the town of Augea in Helmand Province—in a Lockheed C-130 Hercules cargo plane. The Herc is designed for unimproved or nonexistent runways, which explains the choice—but it terrified the herds of the villagers, which stampeded into the countryside. Then McCrystal, walking through the town, said audibly that Augea was "full of shit." True in a sense: any town relying on

donkeys for transportation will fit the description. But the village headmaster knew enough English to understand the slur. Net result: another several hundred Afghans who don't like the US.

Solution?

Enough. My point is that "the devil is in the details." It is fine to denounce Islamofascism. Yet, while I do not doubt that the foregoing matters are understood by the better minds on Fox News, for example Bill O'Reilly and Sara Palin, their viewers may have trouble distinguishing truth from fiction. I have not meant to talk down to them, and neither should the folk at Fox.

7 THE FANTASY OF DEMOCRACY

They are going to lynch me. Already they gather at the gate, and they have a rope. Maybe I can plea bargain down to tar and feathers. I doubt it, though.

Some time ago I discovered Fox News (Honest: For the preceding ten years I didn't have TV). Fox seemed to me politically dangerous, being, as I thought anyway, the voice of a huge, angry, and badly uninformed lower middle class. From such, in times of economic decline, come Brown Shirts.

In particular, talking head after talking head berated Muslims, urged support for our troops, and promoted American exceptionalism, meaning that the United States, like a Tennessee revival preacher in 1925, had God-given authority—specifically to meddle everywhere in the world in the name of virtue. I kept thinking: Do these people have the foggiest idea what they are talking about?

To find out, I wrote last week's column, above, which I filled with every political, geographic, military, and historical error I could think of. For example:

The Falafel Party doesn't exist, falafel being a snack sold on the streets of Tel Aviv. Herat is in west-central Afghans tin, not the Federated Tribal Territories, which don't exist. Afghanistan doesn't have a border with Kazakhstan. There is no Raptor drone, the Raptor being the F22. The Mk 48 is a naval torpedo.

Hecuba and Priam are not towns, but the queen and king of Troy in the Iliad; Sulawesi doesn't have a border with Iran, being an island in Indonesia.

The Comanche helicopter was never built. The BQQ-6 is a sonar suite on Trident submarines.

The Al Aqsa mosque is not in Kandahar, but in Jerusalem; Sufis are pacific mystics, and Bukitinggi is a town in Sumatra.

Infantry Weapons and Light Armor doesn't exist. The 16- inch-54 was the main gun on the Iowa class of battleships in WWII, and did indeed have a heavier bullet than an AK. Bucephalus was Alexander the Great's horse. The Peshmerga are a Kurdish militia in Iraq, Bukitinggi a town in Sumatra.

Ahmad Shah Massoud was assassinated by enemies posing as photographers; Sala al Din, Saladin, was a Kurdish leader fighting invading Crusaders (who lost, the Pentagon might bear in mind) in the 12th century.

Augea was the town with the famed and almost uncleanabe Augean stables, which Hercules nonetheless cleaned.

The response to the column astonished me. I had expected many readers to recognize it as a spoof, but almost none did. A lot caught an error or two—for example, army guys knew that the Comanche was never built—and one reader noted that I had the politics of the Taliban bass-ackwards. Far more took the column seriously.

Which gave me much to think about.

The failure to recognize classical allusions made me realize that I am a fossil squared. Apart from my being a bit long in the tooth myself, my cultural heritage is that of the rural gentry of Southside Virginia. These were people who valued polished writing, who brooked no bad grammar, for whom a knowledge of classical literature from Homer onward was simply assumed in civilized people. Times have changed and people direct their attention to other things. I didn't realize how other.

Of course nobody can be expected to know the details of everything. If someone wrote a similar spoof on the politics of Algeria, the intricacies of dentistry, or the workings of the Department of Agriculture, I would be easily taken in.

But...Afghanistan? The place is of crucial importance to the United States, costing billions, contributing to the national bankruptcy, killing large numbers of people, making America the new Nazi Germany in the eyes of the world and, very likely, signaling the end of the American Imperium. You would think—wouldn't you?—that people would have at least a feeble grasp of such matters as where Afghanistan is. But few do. I suspect that I could have referred to the Al Tadpole party in the province of Clorox, and no one would have noticed.

I thought, How can this be? From my email I know that readers of this column are intelligent, as indicated by literacy, clarity of thought, and the number who sign themselves as things like "Head of Technology Development, Applied Bio-Physics Inc." So what goes?

Lunging about, I reflected on people like, say, a neurosurgeon in Kansas City. He would necessarily be bright, that being an entry requirement for neurosurgeondom. He would spend at least eight hours a day in his hospital, plus commute and, in such free time as he had, he would have to read endless journals to keep up with the field. Throw in time with his family and a bit of television to turn his head off for a while—and maybe he just doesn't have time for a couple of dozen books a year on international cavortings.

Moreover, human beings are intensely local animals. Afghanistan is not very local, being intensely Somewhere Else. It has little to do with getting the kids through school, planting the flower garden, shoving the software project out the door on time, or getting drunk at Bobby-Lou's Rib Pit.

And of course we are herd animals with a formidable tendency to attach ourselves to groups—it doesn't much matter what groups—and fight other groups. Thus football teams, bowling clubs, political parties, and wars. Patriotism is exactly the instinct that makes people cheer frantically for the Steelers against the Packers, and armies are just Crips and Bloods with more elaborate switch-blades.

All of this I suppose explains why so many are either flatly uninterested in the war or, a la Fox, very interested but without knowing anything about it—where it is, who is fighting whom and why, how the place got that way. Emotionally it is the Bulls vs. the Lakers. Intellectually it is an empty jar.

And yet it remains, or seems to remain, that the public, almost all of it, has not the slightest grasp of the war—and, by easy extension, of anything else outside the borders. When I listen to Bill O'Reilly, I want to hold up a placard behind him, asking his audience: Where is Yemen? What is the capital? Have you read a single book on Afghanistan? Read any book on anything? Heard of Eric Margolis? Can you distinguish Sunnis from Cathars?

This of course is why the US is not a democracy: a country whose population consists chiefly of baffled gerbils cannot be a democracy in more than form. Instead we have the televangelists of ersatz patriotism shilling for policies of benefit to remote lobbies, while a catastrophically ignorant public shrieks approval. Gorgeous babes on Fox counsel war. The audience roars. Ricky, Ricky, he's out man, if he can't do it nobody can. Show your support for Central High. God almighty.

8 LIFE IN A MAHOGANY BUBBLE

HOUSTON—The remote outskirts of this city stretch forever across featureless land under gray skies, endless parking lots mostly empty, nasty malls, elevated highways roaring and almost uncrossable by pedestrians, of whom there are almost none. It reminded me of hell designed by a concrete manufacturer. High-rise office buildings erupt like square thumbs, one like another, home to god knows who or what. The weather is chilly.

For embarrassing reasons we needn't explore, I have just spent five nights in an isolated hotel in this cement waste. Nice enough place, friendly people—Texas being Texas—on one side of a parking lot. Everything in these parts is on one side of a parking lot, or in the middle of one. Across the asphalt in an undistinguished building, beneath the howl and blatt of the elevated highway, preposterously, was a gorgeous Italian restaurant, all lovely dark wood and good design. I could never figure out what it was doing there. For five days I oscillated between wretched television in my room and this improbable elegance.

Business was slow, as the restaurant had just opened. On long empty afternoons I was usually the only customer. At night things picked up.

When trapped in a small world, you get to know people. A couple of waitresses in their early twenties, white, high-school grads I'd guess, waited. Customers would appear later. We chatted. They reminded me of people I had grown up with in the rural South. Their grammar ran to "If he don't come by three...." They are not bad people, nor bad citizens. None descends to the moral level of a congressman. But they are not polished.

Lives at the low end of things run to the complex. One had two children by an earlier husband, now in the slam for assault and robbery, and a third by a boyfriend whom she planned to marry. She spoke with pride of her sprats. Her three-year-old knew her letters and colors and could count to twenty and learned her story books by heart in nothing flat—indicating that her mother was reading to her. Strange as it may seem, intelligence exists outside of Swarthmore, unschooled mothers are not necessarily bad mothers, schooled ones frequently are, and grammar does not always cohabit with responsibility. These girls were not the shiftless reprehensibles beloved of conservative politicians. They were pulling their weight as best they might. It was just hard going.

Hour after hour of nursing a Bud at the empty bar, watching the drizzle on the parking lot. Back to the room and the television. You learn a lot about professional wrestling under these circumstances. The notion that we evolved from great apes gains plausibility, although one comes to suspect that it was not a large step. Apparently there is a new form of this athletic soap opera involving folding chairs and metal ladders in the ring. Large primates in Halloween masks hit each other with the chairs, and climb up the ladder to jump on each other. The purpose of this is not clear. I don't think I'm making it up, unless the waitresses were adding mushroom juice to the Bud.

Being dropped into the bubble was strange after a week in Washington. In our nation's curious capital, people know nothing of uneducated young waitresses who juggle long hours and children, without having even one illegal nanny. DC is a world of secure jobs and money, where everyone has been to university, often to a Calvin Klein universities like Harvard, and brains in the ninety-ninth percentile seem unremarkable. We are making three hundred grand a year; why can't they? This otherworldliness accounts I think for a certain surreal quality to Washington's debates. For people with high-end Blue Cross, health care has something to do with Keynes and free enterprise and ideological cat-fights. For a young mother with a sick kid and no money, it doesn't. But Washington doesn't know this. Let them eat cake, but is there cake?

Twice I went by public bus to Houston's center. To reach the bus stop I walked and walked and walked across bleak parking lots with few cars and occasional chain burger chutes. I almost never saw a human. The bus then ran along a highway through this blasted heath to a region of towering blocky office buildings downtown. Architectural gigantism seemed to rule. People were few, traffic light. I wondered whether the citizens were abandoning Houston. Such people as I found were extraordinarily agreeable and helpful, Texas being Texas. Civility and concrete, with wet snow.

On a weekend night there occurred in the restaurant what I believe to have been the convention of a black scholarship fund. The crowd grew, starting in late afternoon. I wasn't the only paleface, but it was a near thing.

In Texas, as in the South in general, relations between the races are greatly more amiable than in the North. Certainly in the Yankee Capital there exists a self-consciousness, a sort of invisible glass wall between the colors. At a reception on the Hill you see black columnists and such, be-suited and be-tied and practicing white manners. It doesn't look right, somehow. I don't think their hearts are in it.

In the bubble it was "Whuzzup, bro?" Socially, when you get away from the Crips and the Bloods, blacks are warm and funny and idiosyncratic, and splendid company. A friend says, "They burn at a higher emotional temperature than we do." I think so. When they apply to whites words like "stiff" and "uptight," it is description, not vituperation.

The bands showed up.

There were three of them, the musicians being as far as I could tell entirely black, and all jazz. The third seemed (I couldn't see that well in the dimness) to have twelve or fifteen instruments, thirty of them being horns, and was just flat dynamite. I ingested shrimp from the buffet amid explosions of horns and a great keyboard and wished that there were more of it in the country. American music lost something when it went so heavily to small-band stuff. The big bands croaked, blues became museum music like harpsichords, and, well, it wasn't a good thing.

Back to the room. More professional wrestling, hulking beeves pirouetting in a sordid ballet, thump, wham, whack. The quality of television would be much improved if they succeeded in killing each other, but they never quite manage it.

9 BAREFOOT AND PANTY-SCANNED

OK, this goofy guy gets on an airplane with an at least somewhat explosive jockstrap and the entire earth goes wacko and orders porn-scanners and everyone has to watch Obama being Leaderly for hours. He is becoming tiresome to watch. A mahogany president with large white teeth. He looks like a goddam piano. Blacks have achieved racial equality. They can produce presidents as bad as the white ones.

What suckers we gringos are. How wonderfully amusing all of this must be for Al Qaeda. So little effort is needed to manipulate the decreasingly Great Satan into doing all manner of comic and expensive things.

For terrorists, the return on investment in phenomenal. They drop those office buildings in New York for not much money, and the US undertakes a war against Islam on which it spends a trillion dollars. Yes, Bush and Cheney and Israel wanted to invade Iraq anyway, but New York made it inevitable. Slick: Bush II couldn't not invade some Muslim country. Leave your enemy with no choice but to do what you want him to do.

So little is necessary to terrorize the world's hyperpower. A free-lance dingaling secretes a bomb of sorts in his shoe, whereupon the US goes into convulsions and long lines of Americans stand comically barefoot in airports. Dingaling Two popularizes liquid explosives, and so Washington frenziedly confiscates toothpaste. Yes, the world's hyperpower is afraid of Colgate, with fluoride. Dinglaling Three hides the infernal machine in his skivvies, so Obama makes Firm Pronouncements, and we will now have to undergo examination by panty scanners. Always, over and over, the terrorists have the imitative. The country reacts hugely and predictably.

Won't the panty scanners be wonderful? Now some affirmative-action federal retard can look at nekkid women all day. (Actually, as a guy, I can see the appeal. And, potentially, all else.)

Of course taking security pubic has its charms, and not just for the TSA guys who get to look at all those unwrapped cuties. Companies in the electronics racket are going to make out like

Wall Street looters. How much does a panty-scanner cost? Multiply it by the number of security gates, and someone is going to swim in gravy. Throw in training contracts, maintenance, and upgrades. The federal teat remains a bounteous spigot.

How much does this have to do with security? Not much. On the evidence, TSA couldn't stop a two-year-old from waddling across a living room. Note that both the Underwear Bomber and the Foot Bomber were stopped by passengers, after TSA let them board. The current bomber's father told the US government about the guy, just as various sources warned of the New York attack. The feds can't stop terrorism even when someone else does their homework for them. And a few weeks ago TSA managed to post its very secret screening manual on the web. It's good to have security in the hands of experts.

Now, who is winning the War on Terror? They are. The United States spends ungodly amounts on wars in Iraq and Afghanistan, killing people right and left in Pakistan and getting sucked in ever deeper, bombing Somalia, widening the war on Islam into Yemen, threatening Iran. From Al Qaeda's point of view, this must be peaches. The US, already in a grave recession, bleeding jobs to Asia, having become the world's foremost debtor nation, now spends itself to death in a widening gyre.

New York was genius. Evil, but brilliant. A few guys with box cutters, a bit of training, and voila! Thousands and thousands of GIs dead or ruined, America dives into a half dozen wars, and there is no end in sight. As strategy, the terrorists have been masterly. They have perfected induced suicide. We have been Kevorkianed.

Further, and implausibly, Al Qaeda has transformed America into exactly what it was intended not to be: a frightened police-and-surveillance state. Wars subvert freedoms, and subvert the desire for freedoms, and then the memory of them. If this is what bin Laden and the gang set out to bring about, they have succeeded splendidly.

The Bill of Rights is largely defunct. Americans now accept random searches in public places, and NSA monitors everyone's email. So much for the Fourth Amendment.

Police powers grow. Cops increasingly are militarized, ninja-ed out, jackbooted and unaccountable. Habeas corpus is doubtful.

American embassies abroad cower behind bars, afraid to allow women to enter with a lipstick. (The world's hyperpower is afraid of lipstick.) The ever-present loudspeakers in airports and subways urge us to watch each other: We are to be a nation of snitches. Carry-on bags on airliners are being forbidden. The FBI can pull your library records, and the library can't tell you. As the twilight deepens, journalists hesitate to criticize the government. (This latter, amigos, is happening.)

Ours is not the America it recently was, and it gets differenter by the month. Who would have thought that so little effort would be needed to wreak such internal havoc on the world's hyperpower, fearful of gel deodorants? The success of the terrorists is deplorable, but in strategic terms it has been magnificent. Never have so few done so much to so many so easily.

The down-stream consequences may be amazing, tipping the US over the cliff. The prospect is real, methinks, that Al Qaeda will have brought down the world's hyperpower, afraid of shampoo, for less than a million dollars. You think I am a raving lunatic? Consider:

Things are getting shaky abroad. America's title of top dog has become questionable. While the US hemorrhages money in strange wars, China grows like kudzu. Economic power eventually, usually quickly, engenders diplomatic and military power. Signs abound. Japan talks about ejecting American forces, apparently not wanting to be used by Washington as a sepoy spearhead against a huge neighbor. The wind is blowing.

I find it interesting to hear the BBC speaking casually of Japan as the world's most technologically advanced nation, of China as "the world's factory." It looks as if Asia will soon be dominant economically. The "war on terror" pushes America toward bankruptcy and, when lost, will leave the Pentagon unable to pursue new adventures for, probably, a couple of decades. Another decade or so of war followed by a withdrawal will leave the United States impoverished, isolated, out of Islamic countries, and with its teeth pulled. Isn't that what bin Laden or somebody said he wanted?

10 A GILDED PEASANTRY

On the website of WLOX 13, "The Station for Southern Mississippi," I find the story of Gabe Stabler, eight years old. Because he came home crying from the first grade every day, his parents put a tape recorder in his back pack to see what really went on in class. From the tape we learn much about his teacher, a Ms. Williams, and about affirmative action, and about the United States today:

Gabe: "I don't know what to do on this."

Ms. Williams: "Well, you'd better find out. It's not hard. Nobody else didn't have to ask no questions bout it. You know what to do, you just want somebody to just sit there and pet you about it, but I ain't gonna do it. You know how to go in that lunch room and tear that food up every day. Ain't nothing hard bout that sheet."

Following this Miltonian eructation, we have:

Ms. Williams: "No, do your work. She ain't goin to be sittin up in here wanting somebody to help her every time she, cause she don't wanna apply herself to her work. You know how to go in that cafeteria and enjoy that lunch and breakfast every morning."

Then, waxing ever more lyrical, even Ciceronian,

Ms. Williams: "Where this go?"

Child: "I colored that yesterday."

Ms. Williams: "It shouldn't of got changed at all, that ain't nothing to be proud of."

Ms. Williams clearly is barely literate, and should be in the first grade instead of teaching it. Gabe speaks better English than she does. In a country not sliding into degradation, a restraining order would keep her from coming within a hundred yards of a school.

Why do we permit this sort of thing? Ms. Williams is black. The story carefully doesn't say so, but it doesn't have to. Only the black uneducated speak as she does.

The proper response from parents would be fury. The discovery that this creature is attempting to turn their children into the equivalent of farm animals ought to result in the lynching of the school board of Mississippi. A civilized people with backbone will not allow their their offspring to be made into gurbling iPodded peasants. But we are not such a civilization.

Why is it happening? "Affirmative action." Since Ms. Williams does not speak the language of the country, the only possible reason for hiring her is that she is black. She is not just slightly unqualified, allowing an expectation that she might catch up—this being the founding fantasy of "affirmative action"—but absolutely unqualified.

The pattern repeats endlessly. Today I have read that the Chicago police contemplate eliminating their entrance examination on the grounds that not enough blacks pass it. Firemen of my acquaintance tell of women too weak to handle a hose, of female paramedics who can't carry a stretcher. While I was on the police beat at the Washington Times, I encountered a tiny policewoman who never had to drive the paddy wagon because her feet didn't reach the pedals.

On intercity buses there once were signs, and probably still are, saying, "Seating is without regard to race, creed, color, sex, or national origin." Today everything seems to be with regard to nothing else. Anything, everything, must be done to keep the affirmative-action classes happy.

This rush to degradation is not new. In 1981 in Harper's I wrote, in a piece on race in education, "The bald, statistically verifiable truth is that the teachers' colleges, probably on ideological grounds, have produced an incredible proportion of incompetent black teachers. Evidence of this appears periodically, as, for example, in the results of a competency test given to applicants for teaching positions in Pinellas County, Florida (which includes St. Petersburg and Clearwater), cited in Time, June 16, 1980. To pass this grueling examination, an applicant had to be able to read at the tenth-grade level and do arithmetic at the eighth-grade level. Though they all held B.A.'s, 25 percent of the whites and 79 percent of the blacks failed. Similar statistics exist for other places."

If you think it desirable to have black teachers, as I do believe it desirable, then get those who are fit to do the job. Plenty of blacks speak English. If you can't find enough, then do without. The same applies to women who can't carry stretchers. Fat chance, though.

What price do we pay for this total abnegation of responsibility, civilizational self-respect, reason? One price is a quiet contempt for blacks, and hostility toward them. Competent blacks are no problem, but "If he doan be eatin dis sangwidge..." doesn't cut it. Women make perfectly good paramedics, but what is anyone, fellow crewman or patient, supposed to think when she can't lift the stretcher? (Answer: Scorn, anger.) What does a patient think on seeing a black doctor come his way? "Oh god...." The doctor may have gotten through medical school on ability but, given affirmative action, you figure he probably didn't. Blacks know this of course, and resent it. Knowing that they are despised, they say the hell with it, and content themselves with just getting by. This is useful?

The suspicion of affirmative action pervades American life. After Katrina, a friend in federal employ visited FEMA. It was, he said, very heavily black, on which fact he blamed the disastrous performance of the agency in New Orleans. Was he right? I don't know. In the absence of affirmative action, the question would not be asked.

Thus the defining principle of American politics arises: If you don't think in racial terms, if you look only to ability, you are a racist. Count me in.

This leads to another question, seldom asked and never answered: how much does affirmative action really cost the country? If you hire someone to do a job who can't do it very well, it doesn't get done very well. This doesn't strike me as a profound thought, but it seems to elude many people. In the case of Ms. Williams, the damage is great and clear. It isn't always so stark. When you regularly pass over the first 135 people, all white, on a test for promotion to sergeant in a police department, so as to get to the blacks and Latinos, what kind of police department do you get? If you hire reasonably good female engineers because they are female, instead of very good males, the consequences are less obvious, but there.

And when it becomes a firing offense to notice, the result is a permanent, irremediable drop in the quality of the work force. I don't suppose it really matters though. The only serious economic competitors the US faces are, oh, Japan, Korea, China, India, Taiwan, Brazil, and the European Union. Piece of cake.

11 COMMUNING WITH THE GREAT PURPLE FATHER

I can't stand it. I'm going to have a nurse set me up an IV Padre Kino machine. You've heard of a morphine drip? Cheap Mexican wine is a better deal. The supply is more dependable. DEA is trying to eradicate poppies, but hasn't gotten to grapes. Yet.

I'll stay sozzled for the rest of my life, dulled to the ongoing hallucination to the north. It's getting bad up there. Worse than blotter-acid gollywoggles in a shopping mall full of cops.

See, everything is coming unglued al norte, and everything is for sale, like a garage bazaar when somebody dies. You've heard that Mexico is corrupt? Nah. Little leaguers, small frijoles. It's not that its heart is in the right place. Nobody's seems to be. Thing is, Mexico couldn't organize a backyard barbecue, but the US…ah, zat ees anozzer sing. In the US corruption is systematized, orderly, massive. Gringos go about national putrefaction with Teutonic efficiency. But only the big boys get the boodle.

It's like Violeta says: In the US, corruption is only for the rich. Mexico is democratic about it.

Washington, I tell you, is nothing but a cloud of looters swirling around the country's fly-encrusted cadaver. Ain't it so? I ask you. Everybody wants to drain money from the federal udder, from the sour dugs of the great hydra-titted monster that dwelleth all bloated within the beltway. All you have to do is think up some crackpot scam, sell it to an affirmative-action bureaucrat with glazed eyes, or pay a commoditized Congress to buy it, and the lucre flows.

Do you know about the Pentagon's spy-bot bugborgs? A swell rip. The colonels are going to grow insects—you know, wasps, beetles, crawly things—with circuitry inside them, so you can control them, maybe with something like a TV remote, to spy on terrorists. Or us. Do you think the little chitin-packaged horror buzzing around your window is just looking for whatever it eats? No. Some psychopath with a joy stick at Langley is watching you through its glittery eyes.

You think I'm kidding, don't you?

Come on, 'fess up. You were just thinking that's where you

wanted your money to go…weren't you? Can't fool me.

Something is wrong with my office. Things don't seem as vertical as they were a moment ago. I'll have to talk to the contractor.

These days in the great squirrel cage north of the Rio Bravo, everybody hates everybody else. How is that? Not long ago America was sane and agreeable, given the dismally low base line for the human race. It was my favorite country. You had slingshots and BB guns and monster-block Detroit iron punched out to more cubes than Rubik's wettest dreams, and sock-hops and happy simple-minded rock-and-roll. And Wild Irish Rose. It was a pretty good America.

But somebody has pulled its cork. Now blacks hate whites hate browns hate women hate men hate Christians hate Musselmens. High-school girls either starve themselves or vomit right and left, and the boys come to school with semi-autos to design adolescent hecatombs. It will probably be an event in the X Games before long. The country has gone wigged out. I figure somebody must have put something in the drugs.

The world is swirling strangely about. Maybe I'm at the focal point of some galaxy-wide gravitc anomaly. I can't be held responsible for what I write. Everything is somebody else's fault. A verse come to mind from a song somebody wrote. Me, actually.

"I'm a metrosexual, meek, mild, and ineffectual/My girlfriend takes karate, stands up to use the potty/

We're gender-confused to the tips of our shoes/The all-new American couple."

Hey, I think it's great. Copyright applied for.

Maybe it's a good thing John Wayne is dead. He'd have to wax his chest and talk in a squeak.

I was in Nepal a month ago hoofing it in the Himalayas. Them's gret big mountains. A guide pointed to a herd of monkeys and asked did we have them in the US. Yes, I said, chiefly in the White House but many in Congress. Oh, he said, here too.

This is good booze, is Padre Kino, cost-benefit wise. Only the extremely poor here drink shaving lotion. I wonder whether anyone shaves with Padre Kino.

But here's the real problem. America has ceased being exactly a country. Instead it is like a professional-wrestling grudge-match with no rules and everybody throwing everybody else into the audience. Think about it. The place is going broke enough to live under a bridge, but the military spends like a drunken corporal on yet more clownish wars against pissed-off peasants. The military contractors grow fat. Corporations, supposedly American, bolt for China. Wall Street pillages what is left like Tamerlane on a roll. Universities, no longer much more than enablers for loan companies, rape the young. This is going to last?

We're gonna pay for this. Like Milton Friedman said, there's no such thing as a frijol. If he didn't say it, he should have.

But corruption. Take the drug racket. In Mexico it's messy and splashes a lot, with narcos gunning each other down and spraying hemoglobin everywhere because they don't have the brains to cooperate. In the States, druggery is organized and peaceful and everybody gets his cut.

The train ain't got no driver and no tracks. Congress is a subcommittee of the Knesset and crooked as kite string in a ceiling fan, the Supreme Court an unlicensed morgue, and the president a shiny ball with pretty teeth bouncing around in a corporate pin-ball machine.

What's really slick is how the criminal element in DC has fogged the alleged mind of that vast, sprawling, larval critter, the public. Tell those salt-of-the-earth suckers out there that some hideous danger crawls ever closer, tell them you are going to protect them, and you can pick their pockets till there's not an ounce of meat left on their bones. Think buzzards circling a dying horse. I don't think there's enough Padre Kino in the world.

I mean, I keep reading that half the population believes that Iraq dropped those tower things in New York. So much for an informed public. (I've never understood why conservatives are so upset about the towers, since they would happily nuke New York if they could.)

There's no hope. A staff-weenie McSoldier named McChrystal is running the War on Islam, and Hillary, who speaks nothing but English and has never lived outside the country, is Secretary of State. Alligator mouth and hummingbird ass, both of them, as we used to say down South.

I'm going to send out for another liter of the Padre. Or maybe switch to chloral hydrate.

12 KATMANDU (DOG WOMAN DON'T)

We caught the seven-o'clock goat-and-chicken out of Kat, my daughter Macon and I, two porters, and our trusty guide Karna. A Nepalese rural bus is not the Stork Club. It is much better, depending on your nerves. For eight hours we bounced higher into the Himalayas with the tires a centimeter from precipices that would have given us time to write our memoirs on the way down. At least three hundred chattering Nepalese were stuffed into that bus. I swear it: three hundred. They aren't used to motorized vehicles, so much of the time one was hanging out the door and vomiting enthusiastically. Nice people, though. Not too inhibited. On several occasions children detached themselves from the compact mob and sat casually in my lap. Why not? Everything has to be somewhere. It's a law of physics.

We passed the night in one of those agreeable unfancy tea-houses that punctuate the trails and feed you tea and dolbaht, which means lentils and rice with seasoning. In the morning we set out on foot for real into the mountains. Nepalese have a robust understanding of "mountain." They think 10,000 feet is practically sea level. They would giggle at those sorry speed-bumps west of Denver.

Up and up and up we humped into the rumpled landscape, tea houses growing sparser, mountains just freaking huge and green and waterfalls everywhere roaring and glowing white and throwing spume and gloomy forests that had never eaten in a chain restaurant, trunks all yellow with damp golden moss. For twelve days we never saw a road or anything with a motor. Whatever finds its way to those little villages comes in on someone's back or on a horse.

Having a porter carry your stuff seemed a bit wimpy, but had its charms, such as not having to carry your stuff. The capacity of a 140-pound Nepalese to carry things is astonishing. They would make excellent astronauts, as they don't need air, and the merest of them could carry the Space Shuffle to its launching pad. So we tramped along, upward, very upward, and occasionally flung everything down and lay back in the vastness and just were. I recommend it.

If there is a prettier country in the world, I haven't found it.

Nepal abounds in miracles. At one point we crossed a long cable-suspension bridge over a gorge that you could have put Massachusetts in and had trouble finding it the next day, and plodded up to a sizable village where we sat at an outdoor table of a tea house. Three children, aged nine to eleven, wandered up inspected us, and asked, "Where have you come from?"

Gretgawdamighty: English. I mean real English, not pidgin, not phrase-book, but verbs and tenses. Whole high schools in the US can't do it. Where did you learn, we asked. "Oh, in school. We have two classes a day in Nepali, and the rest in English," responded this brown implausible mite. I'm not manufacturing the grammar.They speak actual, real English, however preposterous the idea may seem.

Trees grew few as we approached 14,000 feet. Brooding forest gave way to rocky flats and thin grass with interspersed ascents. You find a pace that balances air intake with energy output. At that altitude gringos don't sprint and gambol. I have heard that at slightly higher villages the elders keep a sacred oxygen molecule in a jar of rare red jade, and show that molecule to the young, so that they won't be astonished when they descend. However, I never saw the jar.

We drew to within two days march of the Tibetan border, which meant that for practical purposes we were in Tibet, but without the Chinese army. That is the best way to be in Tibet. In fields of pale green grass, fog drifting in ragged patches, we sometimes found water-driven prayer wheels turning, turning, splash splash clink, splash splash clink, loud in the silence of fog and emptiness.

I wondered what it must be like to grow up in a remote Himalayan village. The people are not poor. Or maybe they are. Or maybe we are, but go at it differently. These things are hard to judge. The villagers are not hungry certainly, have adequate clothing, and sleeping on a good mat next to the kitchen stove is neither uncomfortable nor lacking in dignity. The contrivances and nuisances of what we regard as civilization are perhaps not as crucial as we tend to think.

But what must it be to live all of a life under the looming quiet mountains, horses wandering free and yak ambling through, with people known since birth? They live.

There are no roads to here.

The high mountains are not altogether safe for those who don't know them, which makes a competent guide a splendid idea. Altitude sickness is real and can kill you. Your lungs ooze fluid and you drown in it. Why some people get it and others don't is a mystery.

One morning at 14K Macon made a strenuous ascent to see some lake or other. When she got back, she wasn't hungry. Symptom one. Normally she is voracious and would gnaw the varnish off a table if permitted. Karna didn't like it.

All she wanted, desperately, was to sleep. Symptom two. Karna didn't like that at all. Did she feel short of breath, he asked? "Only a little." Symptom three. Bingo, discussion over. Ten minutes later, wrapped in everything warm she had, she headed down the trail with Karna and a porter. Operative word: Down. Into a pitch dark, fog-blurry night on a wickedly treacherous trail.

I wasn't invited. Karna didn't elaborate on why. Being Nepalese, he is polite. We both understood that he didn't need a half-blind guy falling over every available precipice and generally making life complex. He meant to travel fast and I didn't fit that profile.

The porter didn't go to carry her gear, which stayed with me. He went to carry her if she collapsed, entirely possible. If you think that small Nepalese porters can't carry a large gringo in fifteen-minute shifts, you have reason on your side, but not the facts. They can, do, have, and will.

She didn't collapse, being bull-headed, and six hours later, having passed through herds of yak appearing like dark hairy ghosts on the trail, was safe maybe 1500 feet lower—whereupon the porter walked back through the night to tell me in the morning that Macon was fine. That is service. Next day we heard of a Japanese girl with a less alert guide who had to be helicoptered out.

Herewith a blatant advertisement: Should you need a topnotch guide in them parts, ask for Karna Magar and his partner Balu. Their English is good. You won't find better people.

Onward into the fog....

13 LA RUBIA Y LA DROGA

I read with horror that Hillary Clinton, posing as the Secretary of State, has been in Mexico talking with Felipe Calderon, Mexico's president, about "the problem of drugs." Horror is the reasonable response whenever an American official is allowed to pass beyond the beltway. Or stay within it. They never know what they are doing. Oh god.

In fairness, I have to concede that Ms. Clinton is well qualified to talk to Calderon, since she speaks…English. Further, I concede that she does have a grasp of things Latin American, engendered by many years in…Arkansas. Aaagh.

May I suggest that the former First Basilisk had no idea where she was or what she was doing? Oh god, oh god. Oh god.

To show that utter futility can, if not be fun, at least serve to pass an idle hour, let me express the common Mexican and indeed South American view of the, oh god, War on Drugs. It goes thusly:

Latin America does not have a drug problem. It has a United States problem. The problem is that Americans want drugs. The US is a huge, voracious, insatiable market for drugs. Americans very much want their brain candy. They will pay whatever they need to pay to get it. All the world knows this.

Why, Mexicans wonder, is America's drug habit Mexico's problem? If Americans don't want drugs, they can stop buying them. Nobody forces anyone to use the stuff.

Ah, the rub is that Washington doesn't want Americans to have drugs. All right, say Mexicans, that is a problem between the American government and the American people. Let America solve it.

Why, Mexican's ask—read this sentence carefully—should Mexico tear itself in pieces, lose thousands of dead annually, and turn into a war zone to solve a problem that America refuses to solve?

Think. Why doesn't the American government run sting operations at, say, Berkeley and Stanford, and Rice and George Washington U., and put those students caught using drugs in the slam for two years per? How about a sting at your daughter's high school, with a year in some nasty reformatory, which is to say any reformatory, for those caught? It could be a family sort of thing. You could visit her and hear what fascinating things she had learned about compulsory Lesbian sex.

The reason of course is that any effort to punish large classes of politically influential people would result in a revolution. You can't jail Harvard. So Washington doesn't. Instead it expects Mexico to do something about drugs.

Now, on the off-chance that you live in an impermeable bubble, and don't know who uses drugs, I will tell you. I note that I am not speculating about this. I spent eight years working as a police reporter from Anacostia to South Central, and know whereof I speak.

Blue-collar people use drugs—crack, for example. I've spent whole days arresting down-scale beauticians in rattletrap Chevys as they bought the stuff from black dealers in the grubby satellite towns outside Chicago. High rollers in Houston use as much powder as they ski in (and it happens to my certain knowledge on Capitol Hill). White professionals have bags of grass in the garage. So, most likely, do their children: In the suburban high schools of metro Washington, e.g., Yorktown and Washington and Lee, kids have easy access to Mary Jane, acid, shrooms, nitrous, Ecstasy, crystal. Good ol' boys in Texas make, grow, and use drugs. Country kids in Virginia have a few plants out in the woods. And so on.

Don't I remember that Hillary's husband used to smoke chunky interns—marijuana, I meant to say, marijuana—but didn't inhale?

Which is to say, as Mexicans know, drugs are about as illegal in the US as is the downloading of music. It is punished by very light sentences for first-time users (which of course means first-time caughters). High-school kids get a week of "community service," perhaps, which they regard as both amusing and a badge of honor. In general, little real effort is made to apprehend respectable white transgressors.

In short, the WOD is a fraud. In America the drug racket is a mildly disreputable business, tightly integrated into the economy, running smoothly, employing countless federal cops, prison guards, ineffectual rehab centers and equally ineffectual psychotherapists, and providing bribes to officials and huge deposits of laundered money to banks. Narcos in the US do not engage in pitched battles with the army because they have no reason to. The government barely inconveniences them.

So why should Mexico fight this war for Washington?

In a column, Pat Buchanan addresses the violence in Mexico, and asks:

"Which is the greater evil? Legalized narcotics for America's young or a failed state of 110,000 million on our southern border? Some choice. Some country we've become."

Some country indeed, on many grounds. And the WOD might be a good idea if it did anything beyond keeping the price of drugs up. But it doesn't. I suggest two things to Pat:

First, Mexico suffers narco-violence only because Washington expects Mexico to do what Washington won't. Failed state? Take away the narco wars and Mexico is a reasonably successful upper-third-world nation. If it fails, it will be because we pushed it into failure.

Second, America's young already have almost unlimited access to drugs. Many students experiment with them. Few become addicts. Why? Because they don't want to. How is that for simple?

It is common sense (the young actually do have some of it) and not the DEA that prevents addiction. Do you think that few kids become alcoholics because they need an ID to buy booze?

(Wild thought: Maybe we ought to give America's young credit for not being complete morons. Nah, never fly.)

Mexicans know all of the foregoing. Remember that there is a steady flow of Mexican nationals in both directions across the border. Americans are out of touch with Mexico, but Mexicans are not out of touch with America. They also know, as Americans seem not to, that corruption runs wide and deep north of the Rio Bravo. (A common story: when you cross the border illegally with the coyote, you wait behind a bush until the Border Patrol guy who has been bribed comes on duty.) They know that when narcos can offer bribes running into the millions, American officials will accept them as readily as anyone else. Would you refuse a million inflating green ones to unobserve a truck crossing the border? I would.

A business with that much money isn't going to be shut down, obviously, which is why fifty years on, the WOD have accomplished exactly nothing. And South America knows it.

The Latin American attitude toward the largely imaginary War on Drugs could be summed up thusly: "Solve your own problems, gringo. We aren't your mother. Leave us alone.

14 MOUNTAIN ROADS, TAKE ME HOME. IN THE UNLIKELY EVENT THAT HOME STILL EXISTS.

It may have been the summer of '85, or may not have been, when I hitchhiked out of Washington, DC, which is the left ventricle of the heart of darkness, toward the coal fields of West Virginia. I was then on the low end of respectability, as I hope I still am. As a veteran of the long-haul thumb in the Sixties, hitchhiking seemed a reasonable way to travel.

As the sun dropped low the land grew rumpled and stood on edge, green and forever with the blue undercast of the mountains. I saw a man with a lawnmower on a rope, which he paid out to mow a front lawn sloping at a steep angle. He'd pull it back up, step sideways, and let it roll back down for another swath. West Virginia is a whole 'nuther place, with respect to anywhere.

Deep in the mountains we pulled into Bluefield, where I was born. I forget who "we" was. A hitchhiker's memories are made of snapshots, visions, anecdotes, and oddballs, none associated with time or each other. Bluefield was poor and bedraggled, a city more at home in the Forties that had never quite left them. Coal dust lay over wooden houses, or maybe it was just the ghost of coal dust past. For someone who didn't like the modern world, it felt right.

I found the hotel. It was old, old and plain, and maybe it didn't really smell of coal. It didn't belong to a chain. I checked in and walked to a bar nearby, where a couple of men in work clothes were drinking: tall, gaunt, angular, with the facial planes of the Scots-Irish. They reminded me of crab fishermen on the Potomac when I was a kid.

We talked. They were with the railroad. I told them I'd come into the world in Bluefield and gone with my mother back up the holler from North Fork to Crumple. She was living with her father, the coal camp doctor, while my father killed Japanese in the Pacific.

They accepted the foregoing as credentials. We got along. Their job was inspecting the railroad tracks for cracks, which they did with a magnetometer aboard a caboose, in which they lived for long stretches. That caboose was home for them. It sounded like a pretty good life to me, better than being another sorry-ass lawyer in the cubicle orchards of Washington. The city is like a damn crossword puzzle, with little squares you fill in with people.

They asked if I would like to join them in the caboose for some serious drinking. I calculated the angular dispersion from the rails back to the hotel, figured I'd probably make it, and said hell yes.

The tracks lay in gray industrial tundra, smelling of coal and the creosote of the ties, the caboose rust-red and soot grimy and showing the dents and abrasions of a hard life. I decided I wanted a caboose. Maybe I'm attracted to trains because as a wee kid of four I watched the big steam locomotives pull out of Crumpler with loads of coal chuff...a...chufa...a...chuffachuffa. I can never hear a train whistle at night, sad and mournful as a lost dog, without wanting to climb aboard.

For hours we drank raw vodka and they told me train stories. The blue-collar and the crazy can tell stories because they have lived them in wild variety. Having spent time in truck stops at three in the morning with a dozen eighteen-wheelers brooding outside, with cops and commercial fishermen, I conclude that a misspent life is the only well-spent variety.

A natural camaraderie exists among people who work for a living and don't have much. I didn't exactly work, but I had grown up around people who did, and knew how to fit in. It wasn't surprising that they offered to share their vodka with a stranger. Talk to anyone who has hitchhiked extensively. He will tell you that the likelihood that a car will stop is inversely proportional to the price of the car. People who have needed help are inclined to provide help.

They talked of the diners and beer sluices, the miners with black lung and the waitresses in the diners and diabetic retired railroaders common in an obese state. Yeah, they said, the doctors had to cut Suzie's feet off, diabetes does that, and she died not long after.

They weren't unhappy. They drank because they liked to drink, not because of despair. They made enough to feed their families and pay for beer, and they liked to watch football and sit on the porch. Desperate consumption never occurred to them. Not having the money to engage in the competitive purchase of things they didn't need, they lived with what they had. Vacations to Europe?

An idea from another world.

And they told a common tale. They had been born in the mountains, and pretty much stayed there, depending on where the caboose got sent. But nowadays, they said (remember, this was mid-Eighties) most kids left. West Virginia didn't have anything the young wanted. They went to Dee-troit to make cars, or went into the military. The old folks stayed, lived as best they could on Social Security until they died.

Content with enough: A radical mind-set, I guess. The crab fisherman I mentioned—they didn't have much, nor certainly were they in want, but…They had the self-respect that comes of being big kids who could take care of themselves. They built their own lapstrake crab boats, converted junked car engines to marine, made the crab pots, pulled them, sold the crabs to Popes Creek, changed their own oil, built their porches, and wired their own houses. They were grown-ups.

In Washington nobody can change a flat tire, and they spend long days working on lawsuits between rival parking-lot companies. I'll go with the caboose.

Even in the Eighties, West Virginia was changing, whether for good or bad I don't know. Malls came. Some say that Walmart is a good thing because people can buy cheap power drills. Perhaps so. They certainly buy them. The price is that the state would soon look like every other state, all shopping centers and chain stores. America was becoming, has become, a nation of homogeneous consumers with tastes designed at corporate. This is progress, say some. Perhaps. I could do without it.

But this is rambling. I got back to the hotel. I never saw the men again.

15 OH HELP. OH HELP. OH HELP. OH HELP.

Reality and Sing Sing have in common that those who can escape from them do. I'm sitting in the living room drinking Padre Kino red and scratching the ears of Long Dog Silver, our low-slung tubular dog who crawled into the yard as a tiny unhappy mange-scab. Occasionally something good happens, probably by mistake. The best-laid schemes o' mice an' men. gang aft agley, but mange dip works like a charm. (That's today's wisdom.) Long Dog Silver now has the energy associated with Hoover Dam and, because of her length, can be in two places at once.

The original Padre Kino, first name Eusebio, abandoned Spain and came to Mexico too, where he became a brand of wine. The stuff is definitely hallucinogenic, usually productive of nightmares. Sometimes I wake up sweating ice water and imagine that a huge squid is sucker-glued to the plate glass window, craving fresh flesh, or that Barack Obama is president. The only thing to do is hide under the bed with a gun until the gollywobbles relent.

Maybe I'm turning into a curmudgeon. The phone rings. I pick it up and say, "Spit it. This is Babe the freaking Blue Ox. I guess you want to speak to Johnny Inkslinger. He's gay, you know." A hang-up. I can't imagine why. There is no longer a sense of community.

All will be well, though, because we have democracy. Yes. Democracy: A splendid system astutely crafted, according to some, by malignant arthropods from the wilds of Virginia. Democracy is the highest form of tyranny. It keeps people from noticing that they have no power over anything. Democracy means "rule of the people," usually by Wall Street looters and blockhead generals with the minds of giant clams and all sorts of feathers and colored tinsel stuck to them. They look like Byzantine mosaics. And lobbies, never forget the lobbies, draining the treasury in the manner of bloated leeches on a suppurating udder. People in democracies have the freedom of molten plastic being poured into a mold, but they probably think less than plastic does.

The world is swirling like water in a toilet bowl. I'm hallucinating again. The television seems to be saying something about a war in Afghanistan. This is impossible. The squid, maybe, but Afghanistan? I mean, why not French Guiana, or Lichtenstein, or maybe Yemen? Wait. The box says we are bombing Yemen. Maybe some beneficent insect cross-fertilized Padre Kino's vineyard with peyote pollen. The old bedroom-window routine.

Fat. The babble box says that three quarters of American youth are too fat and flaccid for military training, so the Army is having them do yoga instead. In advanced training they probably learn flower therapy. I say put the porcine darlings in catapults and launch them at the enemy. What think? A rain of gelatinous protoplasm and fatty acids would discourage even an Afghan.

Actually, democracy works best when the population consists of near-catatonic morons drifting in a dense Prozac-induced fog, preferably in drumming circles where they process their issues—boomathump, bongeddybongo. Hypnotic video games like Sergeant Hemorrhage the Avenging Splattermeister help. These keep the public from interfering in public policy. The schools produce these cretins with the profusion of breeding oysters.

Surveys show that half the public never reads a book, and probably wouldn't recognize one. If you ask these mouth-breathing suet globules "What are the three departments of government?" they say, Uh, JC Penney's, Monkey Wards, and, well, I think, Office Depot. The whole ingenious machinery of democracy aims at keeping them calm, calm, calm, since cattle, even Elsie the Borden Moo-cow, can fall into an uproar, or perhaps climb into a downroar—these are mysterious matters—and trample their trainers.

I'm keeping an eye on that squid. With his suckers stuck on the glass he looks like a determined bath mat. Determined to do what? Maybe I should move to another room.

The pollsters, charged with convincing the masses—good Marxist word, seems to fit—that they are Taking Part, and maybe even Sending a Message, carefully frame questions so that there is no wrong answer: "Do you think the war in Iraq makes America safer?" This allows the interviewee to give a witless answer with the air of Socrates. "I feel that those Muslims want to kill everybody…."

Pollsters don't ask, "What and where is Iraq?" ("Well, Iraq is what you put a car up on to lube it, and there's one across the way from Jim Bob's Rib Pit.")

I don't think you lose anything by hallucinating. It's cheaper than airfare, the destinations more interesting, and I'd rather have a mutant squid on my window than the State Department trying to do foreign affairs.

True heart of darkness stuff: I twiddle the knobs on the blinking Left Eye of Hollywood and see nothing but unsmiling sexless female detectives waving guns, and delicate hairless men with feelings. What would Davy Crockett think? The men's voices are an octave higher than in 1950, and the women sound like kazoos.

I'm telling you, a decent, God-fearing cephalopod is a better deal. I notice that it's fiddling with the door lock. Maybe a little more Padre Kino. It makes me lyrical.

"Of arms I sing, and the man, for malt does more than Milton can, where Ralph the sacred river ran, to leash the dogs of Peter Pan." Maybe el buen Eusebio is affecting my mind. I doubt it though.

I figure the human race is some sort of cosmic mistake. Obviously mankind can't govern any farther than it can see on an overcast day, and when things get more complicated than a Border Collie can grasp, it's all downhill. Take money. How many people can understand fractionated debentures, declivities, and marginally flensed capitalization? Complexity beyond a certain point boggles the rubes and lets the lobbies play. Most of government just does what it wants, in plain sight, and nobody sees it because there is too much of it, in too many places, and who has time?

I must be having visions again. A gal on the box says the US is foundering in debt, so the government is going to borrow more money from China and spend it. Even when you are tripping hard, you can tell the delusions because they don't make sense.

I mean, now she is saying—she looks pole-axed: Maybe she's a computer-generated effect—that horrendous floods have devastated Pakistan, so Washington is sending weird Darth Radar drones, piloted by wet-lipped CIA psychopaths in Florida, to blow up those who haven't drowned. It's gotta be a mind movie. Even wozzed out on god knows what they put in cheap Mexican red, I can tell that you don't do flood relief with Hellfire missiles. I mean, they don't float.

I'm told that mid-term elections approach, a premonition much like the fugue state before a migraine. Change is in the air. Excited people join movements and talk about bringing the country back to its principles, getting America back on track, watering the American Dream, and throwing the rascals out. Wait: I'm the one who's supposed to be hallucinating here. The elections will decide little or nothing, spending will remain exuberantly profligate, China will rise and America sink, and in two years we will again hear about Getting America back on track, the American dream, and the rest. The hell with it all. I'm going to give the squid a bottleof the elixir of the good Padre, and see if we can coexist.

16 WHY WE OUGHT TO THINK ABOUT JUAREZ, BUT WON'T

Things change. They change. I arrived in Mexico some seven years ago amid dire warnings from all and sundry that I would instantly die of foul disease, trampling by burros, and splashing sanguinary crime. All of this I regarded as nonsense, because it was. The State Department issued travel warnings and similar alarums, but State would regard Massachusetts as hazardous. There was little to fear. Expats traveled at will and walked the streets without concern.

Things change. While crime is hardly epidemic where we live, and in most places mostly involves narcos killing narcos, and takes place mostly away from the agringada regions rife with Americans, these days there is more of it. Before, you could walk home from a watering hole after midnight without worry. Now, no. There's not a lot of worry, but more than before.

The local people remain as decent as always, small towns tending to be law-abiding everywhere on the planet. The problem is the growing reach of the drug cartels, causing a weakening of the fabric of law. When one variety of violent crime gets out of control, every other kind more easily flourishes.

If Mexico were not next to the world's most ravening drug market, it would be a corrupt, but functioning and reasonably successful upper Third-World country. If this were not so, Mexico would not have the huge number of American who have come here to retire. But the country cannot withstand a drug business that, by a common figure, brings the traffickers forty billion dollars a year. The money means that the cartels can buy heavier armament than can the government, as well as buy heavier officials on either side of the border. (It is an American conceit that corruption exists only in other countries. Tell me another story, Grandpa.)

It is getting out of hand. The killing of policemen, judges, and mayors is now common. Journalists die in droves. After the murder of another of its reporters, El Diario, the major paper of Ciudad Juarez, published the following editorial, addressed to the drug lords:

"We bring to your attention that we are communicators, not mind-readers. Therefore, as workers in information, we want you to explain to us what you want of us, what you want us to publish or stop publishing, what we must do for our security.

"These days, you are the de facto authority in the city, because the legally instituted authorities have been able to do nothing to keep our co-workers from continuing to fall, although we have repeatedly asked this of you. Consequently, facing this undeniable fact, we direct ourselves to you, because the last thing we want is that you shoot to death another of our colleagues."

This is astonishing. It is worse. A blue whale singing Aida would be merely astonishing, but here we have the editors of the major newspaper of a substantial city stating candidly, with perfect clarity, that the narcotraficantes, not the national government, exercise sovereignty over the city. The federal government understandably denounced the editorial. No capital wants to be told that it does not control its terriroty. But this is exactly what the paper said.

Why is this happening? The root of the chain of causation is plain enough: that Americans want drugs, want them intensely, at almost any price—but the federal government doesn't want Americans to have drugs. Lots of gringos want dope: We are not talking of a few ghetto-blasted crack-heads and William Burroughs types sticking needles in their arms in rat-infested alleys. These don't have forty billion dollars. The users are college students, high-school kids, Ivy League profs, pricey lawyers, Congressmen, bus drivers, cosmetologists, and American presidents (though they don't inhale). All God's chillun wants drugs. Or at least enough of them do to make fortunes for those who sell the stuff.

Let's admit it: Americans are drug-mad. Legal, illegal, smokable, injectable, edible—hit don't matter. They would inject plaster of Paris if nothing better were available. When I was in Washington, at least half—at the very least, half—of the single women I knew for whom the clock ticked were on lithium, Depacote, Prozac, Xanax, Zoloft, all the gobbled M&Ms of the quietly unhappy. Shrinks regularly prescribed drugs for high-school girls miserable over divorce and uncertainty. Boys were forced to take Ritalin. My parents generation survived on Miltown and Equanil. In the Sixties, hippies took drugs. Now it's everybody. We have democratized chemistry.

But Mother Washington doesn't want Americans to have drugs. Nor does it want to imprison half of Yale for droppin,' poppin,' and tokin,' as we once said. In effect the feds protect the consumption (through low penalties and slight likelihood of being caught) while penalizing the sale, thus keeping prices high.

The War on Drugs is of course a farce, having accomplished less than nothing over a half-century. Somewhere the other day I saw a story saying that consumption in the US has just risen by seven percent. This is not surprising since, as a society decays, the escape market prospers. And, despite excited hype about having killed this or that drug lord, there is no hope, no hope at all, of eliminating a business that lets impoverished third-worlders drive BMWs.

None of this would matter if it weren't causing copious bloodshed in countries like Mexico, and threatening the anarchy that is often called "destabilization." Absent this creeping hecatomb clotting in the streets, everyone would be happy. The narcos would get their money, consumers their drugs, officials their bribes, and DEA types their salaries. All good. But the bloodbath exists.

Intelligent Mexicans of sound mind, to the extent that humans can approximate the condition, worry that all hell may break loose. Not "will," but "may." There is a sense here, as there is in the United States, that something is wrong, and that something will happen. Mexico cannot defeat the traficantes. These are bad, bad boys, willing to ambush police convoys, kill federal judges, and rule towns. By comparison the Italian Mafia was a basket of puppies.

The US had better think about what it wants on its borders. As long as drugs are illegal, they will flow and the gringos will buy and the narcos will roll in dough. Nothing will stop or impede this. American colonels with steely gaze and firm handshakes and the comprehension of flatworms have told me that the Merida Initiative will rid Mexico of corruption, and then the Federales will clean house on the narcos. Is there an adult in the house?

I understand that Americans have no interest in Mexico other than to give jobs to illegals and then complain that they have them.

And of course to buy drugs and then complain that Mexicans sell them. But a bit of attention, even of realism, might have its virtues. Afghanistan is somewhere else. Mexico isn't.

17 WIKILEAKS

Two ways exist of looking at Wikileaks, the site that publicizes secret military documents and videos. The first is held self-interestedly by the Pentagon and by Fox News, the voice of an angry lower-middle class without too much education. These believe that Wikileakers are traitors, haters of America, who give aid and comfort to the enemy and endanger the lives of Our Boys.

Implicit in the Foxian view is a vague idea that the leaks give away important—well, stuff. You know, maybe frequencies of something or other, or locations of ambushes or, well, things. Important things. The Taliban will use this information to kill American soldiers. The notion is vague, as are those who hold it, but emotionally potent.

The other view, held usually by people who have some experience of Washington, is that the Pentagon is worried not about the divulging of tactical secrets, but about public relations. Wikileaks doesn't endanger soldiers, insists this way of looking at things, but the war itself, and all the juiceful contracts and promotions and so on entailed by wars.

Which is obvious if you look at what the military (the president, remember, is commander-in-chief) actually does. Remember the military's frantic efforts to suppress the photos of torture at Abu Ghraib, photos of prisoners lying in pools of blood while grinning girl soldiers play with them? These had zero tactical importance. They did however threaten to arouse the Pentagon's worst enemy.

The American public.

In recent decades the military has almost achieved its wettest dream, the separation of wars from the American population. The fielding of a small volunteer army prevents the riots on campus that helped to end the adventure in Asia long ago. "Embedding" reporters with combat units pretty much prevents coverage that might upset people. The media for whatever reasons are now complicit, declining to air what really happens on the ground. All of this allows ghastly behavior, which is what wars always produce, to go forward with little opposition.

Ah, but leaks, YouTube, holes in the wall of silence—these

pose real threats to the flow of contracts.

If you don't think that contracts—money—have a great deal to do with wars, reflect that all those hundreds of billions of dollars end up in pockets, and those pockets do not belong to soldiers. Makers of body armor, boots, ammunition, helicopters, on and on, are rolling in gravy. All this half-watched loot flows in cataracts at the price of at most sixty dead American kids a month (and lots of brain-damaged droolers, but what the hey). A bargain. Afghans don't count.

Note that the Pentagon's orchestrated screaming has not been about technical data that might in fact get GIs killed, but about revelation of the ugly things the US is doing to people. Consider the footage of an American helicopter gunship killing pedestrians in a city street, and apparently having just a swell time doing it. This didn't reveal military secrets. But it showed the gunsnip crew as the butchers they are. Bad juju for the military. PR is all.

The pattern holds. Remember when the White House furiously suppressed video of torture? The Taliban would have garnered no tactically devastating details. But men screaming, choking, crying, bleeding, begging—even the patriotic might gag.

Why are the fun and games at Guantanamo kept secret? Watching a man die under torture does not make it easier for the Taliban to ambush Marines. In no way would it endanger American forces. But it would endanger the war. The golden goose.

Then there was the photo of the hideously wounded and dying GI that was (miraculously) published in the New York Times. SAD Robert Gates (Secretary of Alleged Defense) said that the publication was "irresponsible." Oh? How so? The Taliban could have gotten no militarily useful pointers from seeing an expanse of red gushing meat (the leg looked to have been nearly severed). But people in Kansas might look and think twice about the war.

The whole profitable circus rides on keeping things abstract. The war isn't children looking at their entrails in brief puzzlement as they bleed to death. (Just what do you think happens when you bomb a village?) No. It is about Islamo-fascism, the Gates of Vienna, national security, the War on Terror, and it is done with precision weapons that kill only the evil ones.

Remember when Bush II forbade the photographing of coffins

coming back into Dover AFB (I think it was)? That lamentable president said the prohibition was to "protect the privacy" of the dead. (The inside of an anonymous coffin isn't private?) Those photos contained no military information—but they could have made the public think. Bad. Very bad.

The Taliban can keep the war going, which is fine for the military, but they can't end it. The American public could. No more contracts.

Can you think of a single instance in which the information to be revealed was of military value? The detailed workings of an IED detector? The name of a Talibani secretly working with the US? The date and place of an attack by a team of Special Forces? Or is the suppression always aimed at keeping Americans in the dark?

There is of course a great deal to hide in any war, but particularly in one such as that in Afghanistan. In any guerrilla war, the soldiers quickly come to hate the locals. In Afghanistan, as in Viet Nam, virtually no American speaks the language, the "intelligence" outfits are clueless, the troops don't really care who they kill, and pilots bomb according to their own or some intel weenie's guess as to who they see on the ground. Atrocities, intended or not, occur daily. All of this has to be lied about, concealed, papered over. Concealed from the American public, I mean. The Afghans already know about it.

It works. A decade into the war, Fox cheerleads onward, interviewing former CIA thisses and military thats, generating a warm glow of togetherness aimed perhaps more at liberals than at the Islamo-whatevers. The Wickileakers are putting Our Boys in danger as they risk their lives for Freedom and Democracy.

Next to sex, the strongest human instinct seems to be to form groups and hate other groups. I have long suspected that the bulk of humanity has more glands than neurons. It never changes. I need a drink.

18 GETTING WHAT YOU WANT, WANTING WHAT YOU GET: AN UNBIASED STUDY OF FEMINISM

I see where women, or college girls anyway, are honking and blowing most fierce about how they don't like the way sex works nowadays. Yeah. It seems that the hook-up is in flower. This means that the girl meets some guy on a bus or in a remedial-reading class in college or finds herself in the same elevator, and he says, "Let's screw," and she does, maybe right there in the elevator, and then she's all mad because she did, and because he did, men, the bastards.

I was born too soon.

What seems to get their panties in an uproar is that they offer their favors to passersby like soap companies handing out shampoo samples, but without the intimacy, and then grouse because the guy doesn't call them back. Why would he? Give me one reason.

What I don't get is, why are gals bitching? This is the world they wanted. They clawed and scratched and burned their bras and had court cases and threw fits to get exactly what they have. They hated men because, they said, men weren't letting them copulate frantically like men had always wanted them to. Men, or more likely their mothers, didn't let them make themselves unattractive by dressing like hod-carriers and swearing like sailors. Finally men gave in and now women hate them for that. Whatever happened to gratitude?

When I was a young stud—well, young anyway—in high school, girls were still oppressed, which meant that a guy knew he probably wasn't going to get laid, so he might as well find a girl he really enjoyed being with. The idea slowly leaked into his hormonally disabled psyche that girls were kind of special. You could actually like one. Sure, a guy made pawing motions because he was expected to, and she went along to a minor extent. But that was it.

So she didn't feel used or hooked up with because she hadn't been, and he thought he was damned lucky to have her. It was a concept of sorts.

But then came fem-lib. A torrent of really nasty dykes with

politically-significant hairy armpits started yowling about how it wasn't fair that men could cat around and women couldn't. Then the Pill shifted the paradigm into high gear. Girls could now Do It in relative security, and abortion, also championed by feminists, provided sure-fire back-up. There was now no reason why a woman shouldn't say Yes.

Which meant—Oh bliss!—that she had little excuse for saying No. Sally Sue might have teeth like pearls and brains and perky tits and a wacky sense of humor and actually be quite a prize, but sex trumps art. If Sally didn't say Yes, she knew that Greta would. Women had commoditized themselves. It was a marvelous thing for the testosterone wads we think of as college boys.

It quickly came to the old country saw with fangs: Why buy the cow when you can get the milk for free? Guys learned that they could say, "Check your oil, lady?" and it worked. Praise de Lawd! Gloria Steinem and Andrea Fire-Plug-with-Leprosy Dworkin had done what men had failed to do in millennia: produce a race of obligately loose women.

Women, never happy, discovered that they didn't like this either. They wanted the right to rut, but not the duty. Unfortunately the two were a package. What they really wanted was to…get married. Being less adept than men at getting outside of their own heads, they didn't understand why a lot of men were happy single. For a guy, serial monogamy was fine. So was hooking up. Soap flakes are soap flakes.

But it was what women had deliberately brought about.

Not being too good at abstraction, they didn't understand that a man can be perfectly happy with casual sex, scuba gear, and a Harley Sportster. Left to himself, he would never think of having a Volvo station wagon, a boring McMansion with a backbreaking mortgage, or a wedded termagant who wouldn't let him go out with his friends. He doesn't see himself as exploiting his one-nights. He didn't tell them he was looking for a soul mate, and may well have told them he wasn't. (Fortunately they never believe it.) He probably isn't contemptuous of them. He just wants a shot of leg, and figures she must have been taken by the idea, since she did it.

Certain dialogs become common:

"All you want is sex!"

"Uh…what else have you got?" or "So what?"

Or, "Marriage? Why? Would sex be better? Would food taste better? I don't get it."

Or, "Marriage doesn't make sense. Do you want to eat in the same restaurant all your life?"

Marriage of course has only the function of getting the woman's legal hooks into the guy. It's a set-up aimed at child support and nothing else.

Anyway, it was the world women crafted, but somehow it didn't suit them. Nothing does. They relapsed to their default position: Furious.

To make matters worse, women decided that they wanted to be men, or like men, or one of the guys, or some equally awful thing. Enter Anti-Viagra: the little blue blazer with shoulder pads, and the floppy pants-suit suitable for a trailer park outside of Las Vegas. These had the appeal of truss ads and alone would have dropped the birth rate below ZPG, but then came the Chip. As women entered what had been a male workplace, they found that they didn't much like it, precisely because it was male. Angry as always, they set about neutering all things male, with wild success.

The Chip was the view that they weren't going to take any crap, accompanied by a constant search for crap not to take. Hating men gave them a horsepower unavailable to males, who didn't hate women but just wanted to get away from them.

Here again, women got what they wanted. Much favored them. Though they knew less about politics than do men, they voted in larger numbers and, since they did the shopping and liked buying things, they discovered that they had tremendous economic clout. They couldn't compete well with men, but didn't have to: Affirmative action worked just fine.

Except somehow it didn't. One triumph after another somehow didn't make them happy. They chased boys out of college, providing the satisfactions of vengeance for a crime never committed, but it engendered the hook-up culture, and they hate men for it. They pressured the divorce courts to rape men, and now hate men—the beasts—for not marrying them.

I dunno, Brothels and Cisterns. It seems to me that the feminists got just what they wanted. They made their bed. Now let them lie in it. But quietly. Oh please, quietly.

19 FREEDOM AND ILLUSION. MOSTLY ILLUSION

When I was a kid long, long ago, before time began, or anyone had thought of why time ought to begin, or what it might be good for, I lived in rural King George County, Virginia. The county bordered on the Potomac River and was mostly woods. Dahlgren Naval Proving Ground, on which my family lived, sloped down to Machodoc Creek, perhaps three-quarters of a mile wide.

Things were looser then. When I wanted to go shooting, I put my rifle, a nice .22 Marlin with a ten-power Weaver, on my shoulder and walked out the main gate. At the country store outside the gate I'd buy a couple of boxes of long rifles, no questions asked, and away my co-conspirator Rusty and I went to some field or swamp to murder beer cans.

Today if a kid of fifteen tried it, six squad cars and a SWAT team (in all likelihood literally) would show up with sirens yowling, the kid's parents would be jailed, the store closed and its proprietors imprisoned, and the kid subjected to compulsory psychiatric examination. Times change.

In King George if a buddy and I wanted to go swimming, we might go to the boat dock, which was for public use, and jump in. We did this by day or night. Almost never were there other people around, certainly no lifeguard. Or we might take my canoe, bought with paper-route money, and paddle out into the nighttime water and glory in being young and free and jumping overboard to swim. No one thought anything of it. It was what kids did.

Today, unsupervised swimming is everywhere forbidden. Worse, swimming at night, hundreds of yards from shore. In a canoe without floatation devices approved by the Coast Guard. No supervising adult? No proof of having taken a governmentally approved course in how to paddle a canoe? Impossible in these over-protected, vindictively mommified times.

We saw no need of floatation devices because we were flotation devices. We could swim, easily, fluently, because we had been doing it forever. I don't think I knew anyone who couldn't have swum the width of Machodoc. Nobody supervised us. Nobody thought we needed supervision. And we didn't.

If we wanted to fish, an urge frequently upon us, we just got our poles and did. We caught mostly cat, perch, and bream and the occasional wildly combative eel. Adults had nothing to do with it. We didn't need fishing permits. Nor did we need help.

What I didn't notice then, but remember now, is that we didn't look nervously about to see whether our elders might disapprove. We knew they wouldn't. We were fishing. So what?

The whole world worked that way—unsupervised, unwatched, left alone. In winter the Cooling Pond on base froze deep, and way after dark fifty of us would sail across slick new ice on skates, unsupervised. Adults skated, but they were skaters, not Mommy. And if you wanted to stay late till you were the only one on the (huge) pond, sailing fast, ice hissing under blades, not tired because you are sixteen and don't know what the word means—you did. No supervision.

The boys had cars. The county being mostly empty, we spent endless nights driving, driving, to Fredericksburg to get Might Mos at Hojos, or just putting miles behind us on winding roads through the woods, alone, with friends, with our girls.

What I remember is how free we were. Solzhenitsyn once told of stopping on some desert desert highway, getting out of his car, and marveling that no one knew where he was, or cared. That's how it was in King George. You parked with your girlfriend for endless hours on some blind pull-off into the woods. No one asked where you had been or what you were doing or, more likely not doing. Parents didn't care because they didn't need to care.

In retrospect, it felt unregulated. And was. In today's world of over-policing by militarized hostile cops, of metal-detectors and police in schools and compulsory anger-management classes and enforced ingestion of Ritalin or Prozac, King George sounds, well, dangerous. I mean, how can you let kids run around as they like, with…with….guns, (eeeeeeeeeeeeeeeeeeeeek!) and beer, and unregistered canoes without supervision by a caring adult, and…?

The answer of course is that we supervised ourselves. Within limits, anyway. I do remember lying on the roof of my father's station wagon and looking up at the brake pedal because I hadn't taken that unbanked downhill S-turn on Indian Town Road quite as well as I had planned.

But, being Southern kids, we boys knew how to handle guns, and the girls knew how to handle us, and though the country boys were physically tough from doing real work (consult a history book), we were not crazy in the head, as the phrase was. To the extent that adolescents are willing to be, I guess we were happy. We just didn't know it.

The wretchedness we see today—the kid who shoots ten classmates to death, the alleged students strung out on crystal meth, the suicides, the frequent pregnancies—just didn't happen. Why? Because (I strongly suspect) we were left the hell alone. The boys were allowed to be boys and the girls, girls. We grew like weeds, as our natures directed, and so did not have anorexia or bulimia or the sullen smoldering anger that comes of being a guy kid forced to be a girl or androgyne or flower.

I cannot speak well for the girls, except to say that they were sane, good-natured, and splendid. I do know that the boys needed, as plants need sunlight, to take canoes up unknown creeks, to swim and bike and compete—without a caring adult. In fall we used to play hours of pick-up basketball at the base gym—unsupervised. The brighter of us read voraciously. Some took up ham radio or read physiology texts. But we needed physical exertion, adventure, and freedom.

We had them. The consequence? Our heads were screwed on right. We probably even thought that the world looked to be a good place for a while. Although the entire high school had easy access to fire arms, nobody ever shot anyone. The idea would have seemed lunatic. In rare fights, boys might punch each other in the nose. Pick up a tire iron? Kick the other guy in the head? Not a chance.

The foregoing will enrage the whole sodden bolus of therapists, psychological beard-scratchers, counselors, feminists, fruit-juice drinkers, and congenitally insecure promoters of sun block. But it worked.

20 THE CASE FOR HUMAN EXTINCTION: HOW DO YOU START AN ASTEROID STRIKE?

For technical reasons I'm not much good at email just now. Denunciation can best be done through billboards perhaps. Many find burning in effigy satisfying.

I have walked by night on the wild empty beaches of Michoacan when the moon, at its full, aimed a silver path at me over the restless waters, when the wind blew chill and strong from the sea, and the waves, come from China perhaps, rose and roared and crashed and ran up the sands, over and over, over and over, and I have thought, do we know what the fuck we are doing? Is there nothing our sorry species, dirty as monkeys, will not make worse?

I wonder whether we are not on the earth by accident. We have no love of it, no reverence, no restraint before things we do not understand. I do not think we belong here.

The wind has always enchanted me. I hear in it…I hear in it…what? Something larger, older, apart, something that does not care about us, pro or con. How does one say this to a thoughtless rabble twiddling video games? To them the beach is prime real estate for development into tee-shirt emporia, boardwalks, and jet-ski rentals for ill-mannered adolescents.

What is this? We live, we die. We destroy, we strut and fret, we burn, we live apart from the world. We are fools, imbecile children, a disease on the earth, a brief noise. We do not belong here.

Others belong. On the porch in the outskirts of our small Mexican town, La Coyota sleeps. She is a street dog, a starveling puppy when we took her in. She flourished, grew deep of chest and long-legged and when opportunity arose to the dry brown hills that rise a hundred yards from our door. She is domestic because it suits her, ours because she wants to be, but there is a savage streak in her. She is the color of the parched earth, fast, well fanged. She doesn't need us. By night she runs through the matorral and broken rock, content in the darkness, fearless for it is her world, scenting on the wind things closed to our dull senses, hearing wisps and traces of sound beyond the high edge of our hearing. She does not wear shoes, need spectacles, require packaged food from a market. She belongs in the world. We force ourselves on it.

Soon she will not run in the hills. They are putting a road through to relieve the pressure of population. It is thought urgent that people be quickly able to get to CostCo, which in a large parking lot where one may buy crates of tomato catsup for bargain prices.

I do not understand. We breed incontinently as flies, spread like impetigo, and burn and cut and poison and bulldoze. To what end? Why is a lake, solitary and wild, made better by a subdivision of six thousand units, with unnecessary children littering the pavement with plastic bottles while their parents gawp at televisions? Yes, I know. It is Progress. I just don't see why it is.

I wonder what the world must have been a million years ago, before our sordid race of moralizing apes arose to invent the sewage outfall, before we learned to perforate the floor of the floor of oceans and poison whole seas with the bile of the inner earth. Yes, I know of property rights and the desperate need for the economy to grow, though to what end I cannot imagine. It seems to me that we should strive to shrink the economy. Pelicans and seals do not grow their economies and, I think, seldom use bulldozers. Yet they prosper.

We lack respect. There is more to the world than parking lots, much that would inspire reverence in a race less boorish. There are things in heaven and earth. But how does one explain this to a corporate magnate who believes that we must increase tithe birth rate to compete with the Chinese?

I have dived a hundred and twenty feet below the tropic seas, where light fades to wan blue and color dies, myself an alien creature depending on tanks of air, and seen the rays. Oh yes, the rays. As we finned along a deep wall, encrusted with nightmare shapes of mushrooms that were not mushrooms, tangled wires that were not wires, in a realm not ours yet not hostile, just not interested in us, the rays winged by. There were four, almost in formation, chill wings rising and falling, fast, at home in the depths. I wondered where they were going.

A million years ago they did this, and a million years hence, they will again, unless we poison them. Above us our bubbles rose and broke, rising and rising. We did not belong there.

Everywhere we are tourists in the world, collegiate vandals trashing an ancient Lauderdale. We have grown large upon the earth, but we do not belong here. We do not know how to behave.

The immense beingness of a dark forest, the tens of millions of things—winged things, crawling things, hunting things, plants and moss and mold, soft hungry things in decomposing logs, ants, moths with huge spectral eyes, all in the intricate endless dance of life—these we do not know; we say chitinous exoskeleton and Gibb's free energy and adenosine triphosphate and Darwin, and believe we understand when we understand nothing, not whence nor whither now why nor how. In university I knew a white mouse, escaped from the biology people, that lived in the computer lab. Perhaps it thought it understood where it was because it could find the crumbs of potato chips left by students and the warm spot under the power supply. So with us. We can just about find the warm spots.

21 MEDDLING WHERE WE OUGHTN'T, YET AGAIN

Mexico, if left alone, would be a reasonably successful and stable country of the upper Third World. It isn't Haiti, isn't Bangla Desh, isn't a dying patient with multiple tubes in every orifice. If not strong-armed into chaos, it would be all right.

But the United States won't leave it alone. Washington is pushing it to wage Washington's "war on drugs." As usual, Washington has no idea what it is doing. Nor does it care. Should untoward consequences follow, it will be surprised, this being the characteristic condition of American foreign policy.

Untoward consequences are quite available. The narcotraficantes that Mexico is supposed to fight for Washington are a formidable armed force. They have unlimited money, which they use to buy heavy weapons. They have unlimited money, which they use to corrupt the government of a comparatively poor country. Mexico does not have the wherewithal to fight them. The army here is small and poorly armed. This is reasonable since Mexico has neither territorial ambitions nor enemies. Except, certainly in effect, the United States a an enemy.

The government is outgunned by the narcos. Further, the traffickers have the advantage of being dispersed and invisible. The situation is, or quickly could be, exactly that faced by the US in Vietnam, Iraq, and Afghanistan: narcos can appear from nowhere, blow up police stations, assassinate judges, or kill a dozen teenagers at a party. Then they disappear.

Thus they can destabilize the nation and hold the population hostage. This doesn't bother Americans, who barely know where Mexico is. It bothers Mexicans, who know their people are dying in an exported American war.

Bear in mind that anti-Americanism thrives here and throughout Latin America. Much of it is justified; some of it isn't. The US population, the most comprehensively ignorant of the advanced world, knows nothing of the reasons or of the countries. But the hostility is real. Shrugging it off could prove a mistake.

If Mexicans had to choose between the drug lords, who are

often seen as counter-culture heroes, and the US, seen as an enemy too dangerous to be openly called an enemy, many would go with their compatriots in the drug trade. A repertoire of narcocorridos, songs glorifying the narcos, exists. Los Tigres del Norte in Sinaloa have specialized in these.

Although Mexico doesn't have America's festering antagonisms—blacks hate whites hate browns hate men hate women hate Jews— there are groups, particularly in Chiapas, who are potential insurgents. If they should ally themselves with the narcos and go to the mountains, or set up cells in the cities, the result would be a long, bloody civil war: Afghanistan on the US border. This is not Freddian fantasy. Thoughtful Mexicans worry about it.

The Mexican army cannot handle an uprising of any magnitude. The Pentagon would then intervene to "help" Mexico. *Que dios nos ayude.*

he Pentagon is working toward intervention, whether it know that it is or not. There is something called the Merida Initiative, in which the US supplies money and advice to transform Mexican society to combat the narcos. The colonels in the Five-Sided Squirrel Cage really believe they can reform the Mexican judiciary and infuse the police with virtuous fervor for American ideals. I spoke to a field-grade American officer about this. He had taken a six-month intensive course in Spanish at the Defense Language Institute and spoke less Spanish than my daughter did after two weeks here. The money would be used to reform the Mexican government, he said, which would then make short work of the narcos. He explained this with the earnest mission-orientedness that officers display when they are about to do something senseless.

I didn't say, "Give me a freaking break," because I knew it would accomplish nothing. You don't "reform" countries you don't understand by solemn brainless enthusiasm. The money would vanish like water in dry sand. Mexico does not want to be remade in the image of the United States, for remarkably good reasons. The more the US meddles, the less legitimate the government that permits it will be. Not a good idea.

Why does the military regularly misestimate the nature of the Third World? Because soldiers live, and think, in a rigid, conformist, orderly world in which good (us) and evil (them) are starkly distinct, in which one gives orders and things happen, in which all are on the team and working toward a common goal. Officers are insular, self-righteous, ruthless (after all, they are fighting Evil) and clueless. The workings of the Third World are the polar opposite of orderliness of the military. The colonels are instantly lost in the complex relationships, informal arrangements, family loyalties and invisible politics of Latin America. And they do not understand that when they intervene, they are not the good guys.

This is why we hear again and again from some buzz-cut horse's ass with stars on his shoulders about how we are trying so hard to "help the Afghan people."

One might ask: Why are drugs Mexico's problem? Americans, huge numbers of them, want drugs. If they didn't want drugs, the narcos couldn't sell the stuff. But the American government doesn't want its citizens to have drugs. Fine. Let the government attack its own citizens. Leave others out of it.

Washington isn't going to rid the US of drugs any more than it rid the country of alcohol. Popular demand is far too great. The US crawls with crank labs, open-air crack markets, meth cookers, fields of marijuhweenie too large not to have been noticed by state authorities. California talks of legalizing grass in defiance of the Feds. All God's chillun loves drugs—good ol' boys, Ivy League students, their professors, high-school kids, middle-class suburbanies, congressman, musicians, and several Republicans. Mexico is going to change this? They must be smoking something good in DC.

A friend recently told me of being in a boat off Florida with several honeys in bikinis aboard. A Coast Guard cutter pulled alongside because the guys wanted to look at the babes. My buddy, being sociable, hollered, "What are you guys doing?"

"We're looking for drugs."

"Oh. We'll follow you."

So much for a populaiton united against trafficers.

22 WHY THE US CONSULATE, GUADALAJARA NEEDS TO IMPROVE ITS HIRING

Your government at work: Recently, having become legally blind as a result of early misadventures in the Marine Corps, I was notified by the Veterans Administration that my stepdaughter Natalia qualified for education benefits, but that she needed a social-security number. She should apply for said number at the nearest US consulate, in Guadalajara. All she needed was identification and proof, in this case the letter from the VA, that she needed the number.

I had an uneasy feeling about this. It should have been routine, but I had met two women from the Social Security section at the consulate. Both had been borderline rude and not at all helpful. I expected obstructionism, and got it. Since I have what are called anger-control problems when encountering deliberate uselessness, and suspected that some stuffy law forbade dismembering a federal bureaucrat, I wrote a letter to the Federal Benefits Unit, which ignored it. Finally, after an hour of trying, I managed to telephone one of the women.

I told her that the VA had granted Natalia eligibility for education benefits as a result of downstream consequences of my getting shot in Viet Nam ("defending your sweet ass" I would have said were I rude, which I emphatically am not, and anyway we weren't defending anything, but just killing Vietnamese.) She barely listened, asked to speak to Natalia (at eighteen understood to be an adult, I suppose), told her that she could not have a social-security number unless she were an American citizen, and then hung up before I could get the phone back. Natalia, though rocket smart and the best student in her high school, is still a teenager and has no idea how to handle hostile bureaucrats from another country.

I have various ideas, but all would get me a life sentence.

Having encountered this woman before, I was not surprised by her attitude. However, in response to an emailed question to the Social Security Administration, I had received the following:

"If your child lives outside the United States, we can assign the child a Social Security number if the child is: (1) a U.S. citizen or (2) a noncitizen lawfully admitted to the United States for permanent residence. Otherwise, we can assign the child a number only if a Social security number is required by law as a condition of receiving a federally-funded benefit."

Since the VA told me that she did need a social-security, the last sentence would seem to fit Natalia exactly. Three possibilities exist: (1) Either the Veterans Administration or the Social Security Administration doesn't know its own regulations and so gave me an incorrect answer. This seems to me unlikely. (2) The Social Security representative at the consulate has never read the Social Security regulations. (3) She knows the regs, but doesn't like either Mexicans, veterans, men, or some combination thereof, and intentionally wanted to harm Natalia. Take your pick. If any other explanation is available, she showed no interest in providing it, or even in being civil.

In any event, she brushed the kid off. Not good. If she didn't like me, fine. But for all she knew, she was denying Natalia a university education. (The VA benefits are not huge, and I'll get her through one way or another, but Miss Charm didn't know that. Or care.)

What earthly reason might there have been for her behavior? Easy. On a Kentucky-windage estimate, both of these Social-Security aces belong to that category of gringas who, disliking men to begin with, have lost their looks with the onset of middle age and become yet more disagreeable. They face many years more in dead-end mid-level jobs. They are angry. They take it out on anyone sufficiently defenseless. Natalia.

For reasons I cannot imagine, the word "motingator" comes to mind. This is a useful Southernism sometimes defined as "a change-of-life alligator with the hives."

Anyway, lots of expats are helpless against unfriendly 'crats. The consulate is almost impenetrable to us. Phone numbers are hard to find and tend to be eternally busy, out of service, or to empty into "for this press that" recordings that give no access to a human being and don't answer any but questions you aren't asking. For people who have not dealt with the federal government, being told "no" by An Official and hung up on is intimidating. To whom do you complain? The Secretary of State? The consul? Where do you find his number? A retired master sergeant likely regards a consul not as a human being who might actually want to help, but as a remote and awesome being, like Blackjack Pershing or Elvis.

Which brings us to another problem. Employees of the State Department are not evil, and not stupid, but they run to white wine and cheese, Holyoke and Princeton. They are slightly upscale and more comfortable with people like themselves than with enlisted veterans, who make up a fair part of the expat population. You don't see State's folk at El Gavilan, hooking down Herradura and remembering the good times in Chiang Mai when Murphy picked up this hooker with three thumbs, yeah, no shit, three.... Soldiers are blunt, say dirty words, and don't have much respect for office pogues. The styles are too different. Federal gringas typically make Mormon missionaries look like party animals. The chasm is unbridgeable.

Questions from vets ought to be handled by a vet, but where would you find one of those at State?

To an angry and frustrated gringa, of whom there are many hereabouts, veterans embody everything they detest. If a grunt who was at the Rock Pile or Khe San says "my stepdaughter," the aging gringa figures him for one of those dirty old men who marry pretty Mexicanas looking for submissive wives. (I haven't encountered these submissive Mexican women, but never mind.) They resent the wife for being young and pretty and perhaps happy, and, should there be an application for federal benefits, they suspect the step-daughter of being a wanna-be parasite.

The wine-and-cheese effect has consequences. During the lead-up to the fall of Saigon, I went to the embassy for some reason (being then the Southeast Asian stringer for Army Times). The NVA was rapidly coming south and the city obviously was going to fall. Thousands of American men were still in Saigon with Vietnamese wives, legal or not, and often with families. State was puzzled that these men hadn't flown out, not understanding that men do not leave their wives and children in toppling Asian cities. Of Vietnamese women, I heard one of the embassy gals say, "I don't see how anybody could marry one of them."

"Let's see," I thought. "The Viet women are smart, instinctively classy, feminine (consult your dictionary), don't bitch constantly, are beautiful, sexy, endlessly self-reliant, and tough without being masculine. Uh...what was the question, lady?"

If somebody smarter hadn't decided to allow men to take their families out, the NVA would have had thousands of hostages. Enlist, and serve your country. Miss Charm awaits you. CathA A church in Tepic, capital of Nayarit.

Whatever else it is, Mexico ain't boring. Not real Puritan either.

The taste of life differs. Towns have recently been overrun by automobiles, and Mexico begins to follow the American pattern of satellite "developments"—a curious word for sterile hamster plains of quietly unhappy sheep—dependent on cars. Today the rule remains: shops and restaurants that can be walked to, large stores on the plaza or close by and tienditas, small mom-and-pop joints every few blocks. Here you go for milk and dog food, tortillas and bolillos, which are bread not designed at corporate. Of a morning you can go to the plaza for espresso at the sidewalk coffee shop and supervise the beginning of the day. Italians in New York, now aged, would recognize their ancestral towns. It is not the American way. We value efficiency, money, return on investment, the bottom line.

Paradise it isn't, but nowhere is. Hunger is rare, but many live with little. While literacy is at ninety percent if the CIA may be believed—always a doubtful proposition—too many are too little schooled. This also changes: with the bad comes the good. Ambition in the driving desperate American sense is rare. Mexicans seldom work eighteen hours a day to make partner by the age of thirty. They tend to be content with a wife, children, and enough; so much for the entrepreneurial. But I for one feel at home here, which I do not in the devouring gray wastes of office blocks and concrete that so much of America has become.

23 IQ: AN APOSTATE'S VIEW

A few years ago I encountered on the web groups of people, usually very smart people, who called themselves Race Realists and IQists, and regarded IQ as a scientifically valid concept. Fine, I thought. Some people are clearly smarter than others, and so are some groups. You could measure height, so why not intelligence? On average, people with high IQs were obviously more intelligent than those with low IQs. One isn't supposed to talk about the intelligence of groups, of course, but that made it all the more interesting. I had read Arthur Jensen and the gang, and found many of their conclusions convincing.

But the more I listened to IQists, the less reliable the idea of IQ seemed.

There is a book called IQ and the Wealth of Nations, regarded as a sacred text by IQists. It purports to list the mean IQs of the world's countries and establish a relation between IQ and national income. It works, roughly, much of the time. At the top of the IQ list were Hong Kong (107) South Korea, Japan, Singapore, and Taiwan, with the US way down at 98 for American whites. So far, so good, I thought.

But…but….

Consider American blacks, regularly put at 85 by IQists, and Mexicans, at 87 in The Wealth, and India, at…81. Eighty-one? Ye gods and little catfish: those Indians must be really dim.

Are they? How do the numbers track with observation?

Not splendidly. Having trod this path before, I peered into Google's vasty deep for winners of the US national spelling bee. A lead paragraph from the The Times of India : "WASHINGTON: There was an air of inevitability as yet another precocious middle-schooler of Indian origin won the US National Spelling Bee championship for 2009 on Thursday night, extending a decade long run in which Indian-Americans kids have won the title seven times out of ten… Kavya, who had finished fourth last year, lived up to her billing as a hot favorite this year. Seemingly encyclopaedic in her knowledge of words, she wore down the final eleven, cracking words such as ergasia, escritoire, hydrargyrum, blancmange, baignoire, huisache, ecossaise, diacoele, bouquiniste, isagoge, and phoresy. Yeah, don't even try."

This is not compelling evidence for a genetic background of near-retardation. Indians are substantially less than one percent of the American population, yet they resoundingly drub our gurbling semiliterate gifts to a future which, so far as I know, hasn't asked for them. From this orthographic catastrophe (from an American point of view) one might draw many conclusions, none of them heartening for the US, but that Indians are dull-witted is not one of them.

(I'm not sure that these kids are regressing to the mean with any precipitation either. Maybe, having a low IQ, they have forgotten where the mean is, and are regressing upward, or even sideways. One never knows.)

The results of the spelling bee were not news to me. In my days as a science writer, I visited the web site of Bell Labs, a principal pillar of the technological superiority that the US then enjoyed. The staff lists were littered with Indians. (They were in fact top-heavy with Nguyens, Chins, Cohens, and Khans. Who was really doing America's research, I didn't wonder.) I also chanced on the faculty list of an engineering department in Florida, I forget which. It wasn't MIT but still a real school. The faculty read like the yearbook at Mumbai Senior High. That was then. Things are more so now.

All of this is anecdotal, but there seem to be an awful lot of anecdotes about Indians, and not about other groups with higher mean IQs. On a whim, I asked Google what it knew o , a highly brained colleague of mine many years ago at Federal Times. To my lack of surprise, Indy has become an internationally respected novelist. On and on.

It is gospel with IQists that IQ predicts achievement. Statistically this is certainly the way to bet, at least when IQs are measured within a culture, or in cultures with similar attitudes toward schooling. If we look at ten graduate students in chemistry with IQs of 170, and ten with IQs of 120, we can be pretty sure that the first group will excel the second. It doesn't seem to work so well across cultures.

Indians average four points below American blacks, six points below Mexicans, and seventeen points below American whites. Yet they win the spelling bees. They produce many of the best minds in Silicon Valley. (Search on "Indians" and "Silicon Valley." E.g., "Bay Area Indian Immigrants" represent America's most successful immigrant group. Collectively, they've created companies that account for $235 billion of market value.")

An obvious response, though not an answer, is that America gets the brightest of a nation of a billion people. No it doesn't. India is a country in development. (Unlike many developing country, it is actually developing.) I do not pretend to expertise on the country, but it is obvious that in a country still largely rural and very poor, cognitive stratification cannot have occurred to the extent that it has in Western countries. That is, the mechanisms to suck the best brains out of the entire country and school them are not as well developed as they are in the US, where anyone who can remember his name can go to some CSP or other. (College-shaped place.) In India, all sorts of little Ramanujans are probably helping their mothers make charcoal in remote villages.

Here I am guessing, but I will guess: The number of Indians who have access to a real education is way smaller than the corresponding number in the United States. (The CIA Factbook puts literacy at 61%.) America does not get the smartest of a nation of a billion souls. It gets some fraction of those smart and lucky enough to go to university.

I doubt that even the most desperate statistical legerdemain can plausibilate (I say it's a word) an Indian mean IQ of 81. There are just too, too many Indians who are too bright. If you like you can say that blacks perform poorly because they have been oppressed, that Latinos are sleeping in the somnolence-inducing grasp of Catholicism, that whites have turned shiftless, and that Indians are overcompensating or something equally nonsensical. As you like. But the IQs don't track achievement.

24 EVOLUTIONARY PSYCHOLOGY, SORT OF

People seem to need an overarching explanation of things—of origins, meaning, purpose, and destiny. Christianity provided these things for a long time but, at the close of the Enlightenment, was losing its luster among the educated. Too much in Christianity just didn't make sense in light of continuing discoveries. The sciences were more compelling, and a better fit for the changing mood of the times.

When the Origin of Species appeared in 1859, it offered a plausible and rational alternative to God Did It. Evidence in its favor existed. Selective breeding of animals greatly changed them. That this might have occurred by natural selection made sense.

But natural selection did not explain where life came from in the first place. The notion of abiogenesis—that life began by accident in remote primal seas—was tacked on to Darwin. Scientists passed sparks through flasks of chemicals hoped to represent the primal seas, and molecules of compounds usually found in living things were discovered afterward. This was exceedingly thin evidence, but it pointed in the desired direction, and was accepted.

Finally, in 1964, the 3K background radiation pervading the universe was discovered, and described as the result of a postulated Big Bang. We now had Genesis without God: the creation of the world, the creation of life, and its divergence into all creatures, including us. Instead of debating how many angels could dance on the head of a pin, we talked of the state of the world 10^{-44} seconds after the Big Bang.

To people thinking logically, as scientists not infrequently do, the three elements of this narrative were separable. The world could have come into being other than by the Big Bang, yet accidental abiogenesis might have occurred. Life might have arisen by means other than in the oceans by inadvertence, yet evolution by natural selection might still have occurred. In the minds of many, however, all three merged into a seamless creation story, and then acquired the emotional importance accruing to ideological dogma or religious faith.

In many respects it was a religion manqué. Faiths usually have standards of right and wrong, of morality, of Good and Evil, but evolutionism didn't, and couldn't, being in the philosophical sense purely material. The best it could do was to try to make moral behavior somehow conducive to the passing on of one's genes. It could not begin to explain consciousness, and so ignored it. The central question of religious concern, what happens when we die, evolutionism could not even ask, as doing so would imply the existence of realms beyond the material.

Though strictly speaking evolution doesn't imply progress toward anything, people want very much to believe that there is purpose or direction in life. Thus the ineradicable belief in the non-Christian popular mind that evolution is a straight-line advance from the primitive and inferior to the higher and better, with (who could have guessed it?) us at the pinnacle. Continuing motion toward perfection was sure to come.

Scientific inquiry is separated from ideological rigidity by a willingness to entertain questions and admit doubt. The giveaway of ideology is emotional hostility to skeptics. Evolutionists today have it in spades. Just as the church once reacted punitively to Galileo for abandoning the party line, so do ideological evolutionists to those who do not accept the dogma of evolutionary political correctness.

An example: In a column I once wrote regarding the alleged accidental formation of life, asked: "(1) Do we actually know, as distinct from hope, suspect, speculate, or pray, of what the primeval seas consisted? (2) Do we actually know what sort of sea or seas would be necessary to engender life in the time believed available? (3) Has the accidental creation of life been repeated in the laboratory? (4) Can it mathematically be shown possible without making highly questionable assumptions? And (5) If the answers to the foregoing are "no," would it not be reasonable to regard the idea of chance abiogenesis as pure speculation?"

The response was violent. I found myself accused of "trying to tear down science," of wanting "to undo the work of tens of thousands of scientists." I wouldn't have thought the tearing down of science within the destructive powers of this column, but perhaps I am playing with a loaded gun. I pictured smoking shards of laser physics, embryology, and organic chemistry lying in dismal mounds on a darkling plain.

The evolutionarily correct take apostasy seriously. Razib Khan, who largely runs the website Gene Expression (gnxp.com) flew into a rage and deleted all mention of me from his web site (to which I had never posted anything). I was, he said, arrogant and ignorant and just no damn good. What he actually said was, "Anyone engaging in a Fred Reed impersonation, that is, talking about shit they know nothing about shamelessly and without any humility in light of their ignorance, will now be deleted at my discretion."

I pondered this flood of unleashed humility and thought, "Huh? I asked questions. A question is an admission of ignorance. How is that arrogant?" And if my questions were stupid, why were so many of his readers, who are not at all stupid, impersonating me?

His reaction was less that of a scientist to questions than of an archbishop to heresy. Why the savagery? He or any other of my circling assailants could simply have answered my questions. For example, "Actually, Fred, residual pools of the ancient seas have been discovered, and you can find a quantitative analysis at the following link." Or "Craig Venter has in fact replicated the chance formation of life, but it didn't make the papers. Here's the link." (I made those up.)

I would have responded civilly, "Holy Catfish, Batman! I didn't know. Thanks." And that would have been that. But no one, not one soul, actually answered them. Why, I wonder?

If the answers to all four questions were "no," it wouldn't establish that the asserted abiogenesis didn't happen, but only that we didn't know whether it had happened. So why the blisterish sensitivity?

Because (or so I suspect) "no" answers would be conceding that the middle link of the Big Bang-abiogenesis-natural selection chain was pure speculation. It would be like asking a Christian to say, "Well, we don't really know that Jesus was the son of God, but he could have been."

Richard Feynman said that "science is the culture of doubt," Never happen.

25 THE PRICE OF FREEDOM: COULD I GET A QUANTITY DISCOUNT?

On February 17, at Dulles International Airport outside of Washington, DC, a young Nigerian terrorist named Farouk Abdul al Faisal attempted to board United Airlines flight 1497 to Stuttgart, Germany. He had eluded detection by the FBI, and was not on the Terrorist Watch List. He seemed to have succeeded in his aims.

Al Faisal had not counted on an alert TSA employee, as none had been encountered before. TSA agent Michael Trabinney noticed that Faruouk's cheeks were puffed out strangely. He pulled the young African aside for further screening and discovered in his mouth a condom filled with black powder and a detonator. Trabinney sounded the alarm and Farouk was arrested. The Department of Homeland Security immediately closed the airport for three days, saying that, since the terrorist was in custody and posed no further threat, extreme measures were necessary. Travel snarled around the world as flights were diverted or canceled.

Janet Napolitano, the chief of DHS, said in a press conference that the event "showed the lengths to which enemies of our freedoms will go. In order to keep Americans safe, the Department will initiate mouth exams on all boarding passengers. Henceforth no condoms will be allowed on board."

A contract for three billion dollars was issued to buy latex detectors, and an additional agent was added at each security gate in the nation, at a salary of sixty thousand dollars a year. They told barefoot passengers to "Say ah."

President Obama, according to some being worried about seeming soft on national security, announced that he would talk with his counterparts in other countries about requiring oral exams, and would fund research into automated ah-scanners. Manufacturers of dental equipment received development contracts totaling $1.2 billion.

The new measures went relatively smoothly, though there were isolated glitches. A woman with a broken jaw wired shut was pulled out of line, interrogated for hours, and arrested for refusing to answer questions except to say "Ummm, ummm." A TSA agent at Houston International, hired under federal affirmative-action guidelines, confiscated a latex glove, saying that it looked like a multiple-use condom and you never could be too careful with terrorists.

Following the implementation of the new measures, airline traffic fell five percent.

Then in early June a fifteen-year-old kid in Dubuque posted, to an Egyptian website, under the name of Sheik Wasabi, a disturbing story. While in Cairo, said "Sheik Wasabi," he had met a radical Islamic plastic surgeon who was fitting female martyrs with explosive breast–implants. The teenager then forgot about his post, having received a new X Box. However, some thirty people saw the post and called the FBI, which ignored them.

Finally Maxwell Bjorn, president of the instrument-manufacturer Artful Devices Inc., called Janet Napolitano directly. He had done the calculations, he said. A D-cup could unquestionably bring down an airliner. The only way to protect our democracy, he said, would be either to install automated palpators, or use x-rays. Fortunately for America his firm happened to have suitable designs, at $2.2 million each.

Napolitano chose x-rays, reasoning that while ugly women might prefer palpation, others would find it invasive.

The American Medical Association prepared a brief arguing that the radiation would raise cancer rates, particularly in frequent fliers. The surgeons in the membership scotched the brief, viewing it as being in restraint of trade.

Napolitano defended the new machines on national television, telling the country that, "cancer rates would go up slightly, but freedom isn't free. It has a price. Throughout the history of our great nation, patriots have given their lives to defend our way of life. We too must be willing to bear the burden." She then flew to an appointment in a private Citation.

Passenger traffic fell fifteen percent. Napolitano said that this was a good thing, as "it gives our enemies fewer targets. We must make it as difficult as possible to attack our freedoms."

For a while, terror seemed to have been defeated. Distant events changed the situation drastically.

In Afghanistan, the CIA ran drone strikes against Muslims from a remote and secret base in rural Helmand. Day after day the Predators took off to blow up villages that might or might not harbor a terrorist, thus protecting our freedoms. The base employed a young Afghan driver, Abdul al Hafetz. For reasons of security Abdul was always patted down carefully when he came on base, though he had worked for the Agency for over a year.

On the fourth of October, a month since his sister had been killed by a drone strike on her wedding day, Abdul drove up to the gate of the base. He was patted down. As always, nothing untoward was found. He walked into the main building and blew up in a shattering explosion that left thirteen drone operators dead.

None of the Americans in Afghanistan could think of a reason for this senseless act of carnage. The depth of Islamic hatred of our freedoms was simply incomprehensible.

Investigators wanted to know how he had smuggled the explosives into the compound. There was not enough left of Abdul to answer the question. The blast had been powerful. The volume of explosive necessary would have been far too great to have slipped past a careful pat-down. The possibility was considered that a drone-operator had mistaken the compound for a birthday celebration and attacked it. This didn't make sense, though, because the roof had clearly blown upward. The detonation had come from within.

The true explanation was chilling. In what was thought to be an al Qaeda safe house in Kabul, there was found a manual explaining the mystery. An extremist who hated our democracy could swallow a dozen balloons containing in aggregate over three kilograms of pentaerythryitol tetranitrate, or PETN. A detonator built into a watch would cause it to explode. In a sense, the new technique should have been expected. Drug smugglers had long used the same means to get drugs past customs.

Janet Napolitano rose to the occasion. She called a press conference and said, "these are difficult times and al Qaida's continuing assault on our way of life makes sacrifices necessary. Starting today, all passengers will have their stomachs pumped prior to boarding. This will include pilots and cabin crew. We cannot let our democracy be destroyed by extremists."

Twenty-seven airliners that had flown to Europe refused to come back, and overall air traffic dropped forty-six percent. Upon

Napolitano's pro-active announcement that automated rectal exams would be instituted to further protect our freedoms, traffic fell another ten percent, except in San Francisco.

Over the next two months, seven airlines declared bankruptcy and went into chapter eleven. Most foreign airlines announced that they would no longer fly to the United States. Boeing was ordered by TSA to retrofit automatic wrist-restraints on existing aircraft, and Artful Devices, Inc. won a twelve billion dollar contract for an integrated explosive-sniffer, puff-analyzer, millimeter-wave panty-viewer, shoe-x-rayer, stomach pump, CAT-scanner and nitrate-sniffing automated dildo. Our freedoms, at last, were safe.

26 AIR JOHN DILLINGER: AMERICAN AIRLINES: WORLD'S WORST AIRLINE

American Airlines is the only penitentiary I know that doesn't just sit there stolidly on the ground. No. It has to fly around and inflict itself on the innocent everywhere. It's every bit as dismal as Sing Sing, though, combining the elegance of a wrestler's armpit with the curiosity of having the thieves on the outside, at corporate, and the prison matrons on the inside. I'd rather fly in a Dempster Dumpster piloted by a drunk, since dumpsters usually leave on time and are not owned by pickpockets.

It's the world's worst airline. And I've flown Aeroflot during the days of the Soviet Union. American has the morals of a Wall Street gangster.

Thievery: We'll get to that in a moment. I used to be an American fragrant flyer, until one time they couldn't find a stewardess and held up my flight for several geologic epochs; on the second leg of the flight, they couldn't find the pilot. Honest to God. Just, you know, misplaced him. Maybe he slipped behind a sofa cushion or something. Maybe he was hung-over. Maybe he just didn't feel like flying that day. Maybe he knew the cabin crew, and just couldn't face it.

I sympathize.

The stews on that flight looked like retired police-women, but without the sensitivity and manners, except for one twerpy little semi-male parsnip with an attitude to match his teeth, which were bad. I considered pulling his head off, but decided that there might be some fool regulation against it.

So I told my travel agent, get me anything but this aerial disaster. Get me Air Equatorial Guinea. Get me Fat Robert's Catapult Service. I'll dangle under a goddam box kite. But not, not ever, American Airlines. I'd rather have smallpox. I'd rather have largepox, or anthrax. Anthrax is unpleasant, but at least you leave on time.

OK, I thought I was free of American. No. Its long sticky tentacles extend everywhere. A couple of weeks ago my buddy Joe Bageant flew down to Ajijic from Washington to finish a book. He wanted to bring me a box weighing maybe eight pounds, and a nice guitar for Violeta, maybe five pounds. These were excess baggage, meaning over two bags. Reaching the ticket counter, Joe discovered that American charges a hundred freaking bucks per extra item. At least, it's what they charged him. You see the technique: He either pays, throws away Vi's guitar, or misses his flight. He paid.

In addition to being licensed extortionists with the morals of a New York alley cat, they're stupid extortionists. Sure, they got two hundred rapidly devaluing green ones out of me. They also assured that neither Joe, his family, nor any of five friends of ours who have heard about this will ever fly again on their airborne intercity bus-line.

I mentioned this adventure to my travel agent and lo! She said American had been complaining to her that the agency wasn't selling many tickets on their embezzlement service. The reason, she told me, was that so many people refused to fly with such wretched pirates. Whoever runs this outfit must have a cookie sheet for a brain pan. Or an economic death wish.

While American is the worst airline I have encountered, its worseness is only a matter of degree, as in saying that Stalin was worse than Pol Pot. The airlines of the United States, which used to be pretty good, seem to have decided that customers are too much trouble, and should be discouraged: It's so much easier to fly an empty airplane. More accurately they have decided to rely on a captive national clientele of browbeaten bovines who don't have a choice. It's aviational suicide. At least I hope it is.

Think about this. Mexicana de Aviacion, a quite nice airline, allows you two checked bags, without charge. It also runs the drink cart down the aisle twice, with everything from a beer to whiskey and soda being complementary. The US lines charge five bucks a beer. Hey, I wish I could sell suds at thirty bucks a six-pack. I've seen villains on US lines charge three bucks for a large oatmeal cookie. Mexicana doesn't do that. And the stewardae are pleasant. You don't get the idea that they got their training at Leavenworth. And were fired for being excessively disagreeable.

Living in Mexico, I can usually avoid these aerial blackguards and road agents. Mexicana has direct flights to LA and San Francisco. European airlines fly to most places I want to go directly out of Mexico City. If I want to avoid the TSA Nazis on the way to Asia, I can fly Mexico City-Vancouver and then across the Pacific. This matters especially when I am traveling with my (Mexican) family, as there is no telling how much US immigrations will bully them. Power-intoxicated dregs in dead-end jobs are perfectly capable of putting them on the next plane back just to get even with life.

The only thing that keeps lousy airlines in existence is affirmative action. On their merits they would last as long as a restaurant with roaches swimming in the soup. Recently I flew with my eldest daughter from San Francisco to Katmandu. The first leg we took Singapore Airlines, which Macon's crafty daddy had made sure we got. She wigged out over the level of service and quality of food. You could almost get the impression that Singapore wanted to attract customers.

It is a scientific fact that you can cross the Pacific with a Chinese or Japanese airline, or Korean, and not want to guillotine the entire airline, its children and dogs and heirs and assigns to the fourth generation.

From Singapore to Kat we took Silk Air on a code share. Same thing.

The only reason these pirates can survive is, again, affirmative action. The law gives them a monopoly. You can't fly Chicago-San Francisco on All Nippon Airlines or JAL. If you could, the domestic lines would be out of business in three weeks. The only way they can clip customers for a hundred bucks per guitar is by being a federally mandated monopoly.

And the airlines become increasingly rapacious. Travelers have no way of protecting themselves. You can avoid a particular line that is worse than others, which is to say American, but you have to fly somehow. The Federal Aviation Agency follows the usual pattern of being controlled by the industry it is supposed to control, so who do you complain to? The feds now discourage carry-on baggage. Oh good, we can pay for even more checked bags.

Tell you what. There's a big alligator farm outside of Bangkok, where they grow all sizes to make wallets or something. When I'm dictator, I'm going to have a special fattening pen, and I'm going to throw the entire staff of American Airlines to those big green suckers. Except I'm not sure that even an alligator could stomach them.

27 SURPRISED BY DISASTER, BY FRED, SON OF TZU

In re Afghanistan, why, you might ask, is the world's hugest, expensivest, most begadgeted military unable to defeat a few thousand angry tribesmen armed with AKs and RPGs?

Easy: Character. The men running the war are mentally the wrong ones to do it.

Think about this for a moment. Suppose that your boss at the lab or law firm or newsroom demanded that, when he entered the room, you leapt spasmodically to your feet, stood rigidly erect with your feet at a forty-five degree angle like a congenitally deformed duck, and stared straight ahead until he gave you permission to relax. You would think, correctly, that he was crazy as a bedbug. If he then required reporters to stand in a square so he could inspect their belt buckles, you would either figure he was a gay blade or call for a struggle buggy and some big orderlies. This weird posturing is not normal, nor are those it appeals to.

Suppose you showed up for freshman orientation at Princeton and your professors bellowed at the tops of their voices, three inches from your face, "Your shoes ain't shined good, puke. Get down and give me fifty." (Pushups, that is, which in the military doesn't mean the better sort of bra.) You would decide that the loon had lost whatever mind he had ever had, and call Domino's for a cheese pizza, double Haldol.

Should you be so unwary as to suggest the foregoing in print, the response will usually be that militaries need discipline. True, and so do newspapers. However, there is a distinction between discipline and ritualized lunacy. At every publication for which I have worked, the editor was clearly and absolutely in charge. Yet I, seldom senior, could say, "Yeah, Wes, but if we do that, won't thus-and-so bad thing happen?" His decision was law, but he was happy to hear from subordinates, who might know something he didn't. Editors do not require vaguely sadomasochistic submissiveness.

This hoopla is not of use in combat. The Taliban seem to be doing rather well. Do you suppose their commanders check their beds to be sure that a quarter will bounce from their blankets?

Now, what kind of kid wants to go for robot training at West Point or boat school at Annapolis? Statistically these kids are bright, gregarious, "motivated" (a favorite military word), athletic, perhaps Eagle Scouts. Psychologically they want (need?) to live under a regime of rigid conformity and obedience that would appear as absurd as it is if we were not accustomed seeing it among soldiers. That is, they are autoselected not to think for themselves or question decisions from above. They are exactly what universities exist not to produce.

The service academies reinforce these unfortunate characteristics. Their schooling consists of four years of learning what to think, not how to think. There are hours of running in formation ("If I die on the Russian front...."), close-order drill, manual of arms ("Hen-spection...harms!"). Why? There is no military value in being able to shift your rifle from shoulder to shoulder crisply. Like the endless inspections of everything, all of this participation in the hive inculcates groupishness and a curious sense of safety in conformity.

The effects are remarkable and, from a standpoint of civilization, undesirable. Large authoritarian organizations make easier the compartmentalization of morality. A colonel typically will be a good neighbor, civic-minded, responsible, unlikely to steal your silverware or kick your dog. If the Pentagon tells him to bomb a city he has never heard of and has no reason to bomb, killing people who pose no threat to him, he will. He feels no individual responsibility for atrocious behavior ordered from above. "I vas only followink orders," the Nuremberg defense, is the bedrock of military ethics, if any.

Men trained in conformist obedience can work marvels. They just don't care whether the marvel is good or evil. If you need to handle some vast natural disaster, call on the military. They have the manpower, the aircraft, the medics, the co-operation to get things done now. They will stay on their feet for forty-eight hours without sleep. They take the "mission" (another favorite military word) seriously.

What they do not do particularly well is wage war. Why? Because they have in their minds a view of war that is partly that of offensive linemen—you close with the enemy and destroy him—and partly martial romanticism. They speak of duty, honor, country, bravery, fallen comrades, proving oneself. Military history is rife with silly pageantry, nobility of spirit, glorious charges, and impracticality. Having been trained to think rigidly, they do.

Before Agincourt, there were things the French might profitably have learned about long bows, but didn't bother because chivalry didn't concern itself with peasants. It was the glory of the thing, not whether they were committing suicide. English generals killed 20,000 young Brits in one day at the Somme; they hadn't compared the ideas in their heads with then-current military reality (such as that infantry charges over long distances against massed machine guns, artillery, and barbed wire are not especially productive, unless you manufacture embalming fluid.) Authoritarian group-think, love of ritual, romanticism, inattention: not a happy brew.

Further, military service encourages an often-catastrophic sense of masculine potency. Running in formation with fifty other men ("lef-rye-lef-rye-lef-rye-layeff....") or watching a fighter cat-shot from a carrier deck—the thrill is gonadal, appealing to something deep in the male psyche, a challenge flung at life. It is wonderful, but not a sound basis for judgement.

A consequence is a tendency for militaries of the First World to gravely overestimate themselves, and thus underestimate their enemies. This is why they usually expect wars to be far shorter and cheaper than they turn out to be. As recent examples, the French did not expect those slanty-eyed little zipperheads (les jaunes) to win in Viet Nam, nor did the Pentagon have any idea they the US could possibly lose 60,000 dead and the war in that country, Iraq would be a cakewalk, and those louse-infested towel-heads in Afghanistan had no hope against American swoosh-kerpows. The US military in particular has a compulsory can-do attitude, with slogans like "The difficult we can do today, the impossible takes a bit longer." This substitution of morale for comprehension is regularly disastrous.

Having no idea what they are getting into is almost doctrine among professional officers. A major does not become a colonel by saying, "General, the French didn't do all that well at Dien Bien Phu. Maybe we ought to, you know, do something else. We could invade Vanuatu."

America's problem is not that its generals prepare for the last war, but that they don't prepare for it, and then fight it again the same way.

28 TSA: GOING IN A BAD DIRECTION WITHOUT WANTING TO

After hearing account after account from friends and acquaintances of rude and sometimes abusive behavior by federal officials in Immigrations, TSA, and others, I spoke by telephone to a fellow at TSA in Washington. He was agreeable and helpful, which is not a response one always gets in the capital. Anyway, I subsequently wrote him a letter, reproduced below, which addresses matters that in the past have been of interest to readers.

Dear Mr. ,

After our conversation of last week (and I appreciated your taking the time) I thought carefully about the problem of "TSA"— which, as I mentioned, has become a catch-all world for everything people don't like about governmental intrusion on traveling. It is true that in airports the emigrations officers are much more obnoxious than the genuine TSA personnel.

I discussed the matter with a group of friends who, like me, are roughly in their mid-sixties—that is, who remember the United States as it was years ago. We agreed that we are seeing an anger in the United States, chiefly directed at government, that is new to us. There was widespread anger during the war in Vietnam, but it was directed at the war, not the government in general. Today we have something different.

There is a sense that the government now is not only hostile to the public, which it never was before, but out of control. The degree of intrusiveness has grown from almost none to almost unrestrained—or so people feel.

A few examples:

It is widely assumed by sane and educated people that NSA monitors all email; whether this is true I am not sure, but it is believed. Habeas corpus seems to have gone away. The Fourth Amendment no longer seems to exist, "random" searches on the street being legal. Finances are tracked. You can't buy a commuter train ticket without a governmental ID, information from which goes into a computer (my experience on MARC).

Police are more militarized and more aggressive. The financial crisis is seen, with ample evidence, as the result of corruption and lack of federal regulation. A million people are said to be on the no-fly list. Metal detectors proliferate. Toothpaste and deodorants are confiscated at airports. The country is seen to be in serious decline while the government spends a trillion a year on the Pentagon and wars of mysterious purpose. Children are forced to take Ritalin. The bureaucracy is unresponsive: It takes a year even to get records from the VA, any dealing with IRS can turn into a years-long nightmare even if it is only a routine matter, and the paperwork is so complex that you can't do anything without a specialized lawyer. I could go on for pages.

This is the context in which "TSA" (in the sense mentioned above) operates. I do not suggest that much that TSA does is illegal. Anything is legal that Congress says is legal, except in the unlikely event that the Supreme Court disagrees. Rather I question whether much of "security" actually accomplishes what it is supposed to accomplish, and whether the benefits outweigh the harm done.

Consider the inspection of all photos in a passenger's camera, which recently happened to me. It is grossly intrusive and potentially humiliating. Depending on circumstances, the traveler may have nude pictures of his wife, or pictures of himself engaging in sex with a Thai transvestite. Neither is illegal, and neither is the government's business.

Do these searches in any sense inhibit the dissemination of child pornography? Yes—for about a week. Once the pedophiles learn of the searches—and people who smuggle extremely illegal photos make a point of being aware of such things—the measure becomes worthless. The malefactor puts the memory card with the porn in his back pocket, and leaves a card of innocent photos in the camera.

Of course "TSA" could go through the traveler's pockets and do a detailed search of his luggage for a tiny chip secreted in a pair of dirty socks. TSA personnel do not have tight connections. A friend recently showed me a memory chip, four gig I think it was, no larger than a pencil eraser. Will "TSA" begin doing random body-cavity searches? Does minor and ineffective inconvenience to the pedophile offset massive inconvenience and indignity to the innocent?

So much of "security" is so obviously pointless that one wonders why it exists. If you randomly search one in fifty passengers boarding Amtrak at rush hour, you do not detect the terrorist ninety-eight percent of the time. In the case of a suicide bomber, the detection leads to an immediate explosion and, unless you conduct the inspection robotically in a blast-proof room, several dead.

To the public, at any rate to the many people with whom I have discussed the matter, the air of federal fear seems almost demented. I have had an (actual) TSA woman solemnly examine a pair of tweezers to determine whether they were blunt-nosed (acceptable) or pointed (posing a threat of hijacking). Do we really believe that a team of Al Qaeda terrorists are going to leap up brandishing tweezers? Equally absurd is that a woman cannot enter the US consulate in Guadalajara with her lipstick. Yes, I know it could contain a cyanide dart or a hidden vial of Tabun. So could anything.

How much security is enough? Any amount of intrusion whatever can be justified on grounds of slight or imaginary benefits. Those strip-scanners that famously reduce travelers to near-nudity are loathed by women; have they actually accomplished any desirable end, except for the manufacturer? People in the federal security business tend to believe that surveillance is for the safety of the public, then to believe that more surveillance will produce more safety, and finally to fall into the rationale that "if you are doing nothing wrong, you have nothing to fear from inspections etc." Police in general tend naturally to believe this. Always, always, it leads to abuses that render the public fearful of the police. For this reason the Fourth Amendment was propounded.

In my eight years as a police reporter for the Washington Times, the police needed probable cause to conduct a search, this being defined as "an articulable reason to believe that a specific person was committing a specific crime." (Sometimes they lied when they wanted probable cause, but the requirement nonetheless provided a degree of protection for the public.) Walking through Penn Station in Baltimore does not meet the definition of probable cause, yet the PA system constantly announces that people are subject to random search.

The knowledge that one may be searched at any time is intimidating, and being searched, humiliating. Yes, it is legal. A judge can always be found who will find constitutional almost anything. Yet the ability to say "no" to causeless searches was a thing that distinguished America from the Soviet Union. It no longer does.

Finally, there is the tendency for industry to see federal programs as money spigots. (Having long covered the Pentagon, I know the game well.) A company comes up with a better x-ray scanner at $170 thousand per each, times 2500 or however many airport security gates. That's money. There are also the contracts for training TSA personnel, for maintenance, and for upgrades. A race ensues to come up with an even better scanner, or nitrate sniffer, or blast-proof trash cans for Metro, which can then be sold to the government.

So it isn't just the rudeness and bullying of Immigrations people, or the confiscation of toothpaste and shampoo and bottled water. It is the sense that the government, if not quite an enemy perhaps, is not friendly, and is endless trouble. For a large and, I thank, growing number of people, the most fervent wish is that the government leave them the hell alone.

Sincerely,
Fred Reed

29 FRED ADMITS JOURNALISTIC DISHONESTY ABOUT MEXICO

I have a confession to make to my readers. I have been lying about Mexico. Yes. I am a poor sinner and meant no harm, but the devil got into me, and I have done wrong. I have said that Mexico is a pleasant country of agreeable people, and harmless. I have said that children here run and play in the fountains and enjoy the blessed life of the happy young. No, no! It wasn't true. They die of hunger in the streets. Nay, Haiti must seem a paradise by comparison.

Oh, if I could repent and redeem myself! I know now I have lured many innocent Americans, virgins (well, that may be stretching it), children, people of ripe years and helpless, into this hellhole of disease and corruption, where they have been robbed and killed and left to moulder in unmarked graves, like Ambrose Bierce. I laughed at Americans who asked me whether Mexico had paved roads. Oh, the shame of it! The truth is that Mexico does not. There are no paved roads in Mexico.

How I repent my lies. But it is too late.

What changed my life, and brought me to truth and the hope of salvation was the horrid death of my friend Richard and his sweet family. We found his mortal remains in the burning rubble of his home in Jocotepec, a village on the north shore of Lake Chapala. Beside his half-eaten body we found his diary of his family's last days. I reproduce parts of it here with other accurate and damning verities about this abominable country.

Sign indicating a nude beach. These signs are common, showing that there is no morality in Mexico.

"July 2. We have been hearing gunfire in the hills but figure it is just narcos settling accounts. It has happened before."

"July 6. Explosions in the hills last night. Probably RPGs."

Any American living here, if honest, will tell you that rocket fire is common. Especially during fiestas. Veterans of Viet Nam say that at times the detonations are as intense as anything they experienced in Asia.

"July 9. My daughter Chuleta arrived late at school today. A rabid coyote was in the street outside the house. She came back right away, having found that her class had been kidnapped again, except those at home with swine flu. The teachers say that if the children are released they will have to make the days up."

And to think that I once made fun of Americans who believed disease to be everywhere in Mexico. How many of them have I killed with my fabrications?

"July 17. We stay in the house. Chuleta is sick with cholera. Dr. Perez came from the government clinic and sacrificed a chicken, but she got no better. He said it was a difficult case and would require a specialist who would chant and burn pig entrails."

Food has become scarce in Mexico, a failed state. The reason of course is that the narcos have taken over all the farms to plant hemp, coca, poppies, and marijuana. A certain amount of corn is grown in clandestine fields in the mountains, but aircraft from the government spray these crops with herbicides.

Starvation is rife in the cities. The authorities do not even collect the bodies.

"July 19. Chuleta died today. We were going to have a funeral but the wild dogs ate her."

Indicates nude beach for mutants. A country that encourages harlotry and promiscuity among the genetically differently-abled is clearly reprehensible.

"July 21. I am alone. Even the government is attacking us. The helicopter of the Mexican air force dropped a load of cheap plaster bulls on the house. One hit my wife on the head. I was able to bury her decently because the sewage overflow from the water treatment plant has drowned the wild dogs."

We who live in this inferno have learned not to trust the government. For years we heard from the peasants of nightmarish creatures that came from volcanic vents and devastated whole populations. We didn't believe it. President Calderon himself assured us that it wasn't true. Strange creatures? What nonsense. But then....

These things, whatever they are, prowl Guadalajara, eating pedestrians. The government, as always concerned about tourism, keeps very quiet about it.

"July 23. We are doomed. This will be my last entry. The sewage has reached the front gate and feral possums have come from the hills to feed on corpses. If anyone finds this, tell my daughters in Spokane goodbye. For God's sake stay away from Mexico.

The possums are coming...."

30 I SHOULDN'T READ THE NEWS. I REALLY SHOULDN'T.

I love it. The following is an account of Admiral Mike Mullen, chairman of the Joint Chiefs of Staff, talking to Albert Jazeera:

"When asked why the United States was not in FATA despite having the knowledge that Al Qaeda was present there, he [Admiral Mullen] said, 'Because FATA is in Pakistan and Pakistan is a sovereign country and we don't go into sovereign countries.'"

Hahn? The hell we don't. What was this buoyant cannibal thinking? The US loves to go into sovereign countries. It hardly does anything else. I suppose Iraq wasn't sovereign. It isn't now, but it was. How about Panama, Laos, Cambodia,? We gave Pakistan, until recently sovereign, the choice of inviting us to kill its people with drones, or else be bombed into the Stone Age. Recently we have bombed Somalia, technically sovereign.

When the Pentagon's alpha-floater says something so transparently nonsensical, so patently false, one wonders: Is he merely lying, or does he somehow actually believe this stuff? I mean, drugs are supposed to be discouraged by the Navy.

Next, more comic-book moral leadership, this time from Ralph Peters, the pay-per-view Clausewitz for Fox News. Walphie, a retired colonel, is hugely in favor of the war against Islam. Grrrrr. Fierce he is. He is a retired "intelligence" officer, and therefore all-wise in things military. And he is Upset. Good.

Before exploring his upsettance, we might note that Walph is of the school of martial ferocity holding that other people should go get killed. Not Walph. He is what in a forgotten war in Asia we called a REMF. That's Rear-Echelon Motherfucker. It refers to paper-pushers who sit safely way behind the lines while men in the military fight. Walph spent his career largely in Europe, a real hardship post . I mean, sometimes your martini might not be properly chilled. A veritable Tamerlane of the cocktail circuit, Walph.

But don't underestimate him. The blood lust of a podium

doughnut is a thing to reckon with, I reckon. Kings faint. Empires quail.

Another point worth considering is that "intelligence officer" doesn't mean "an intelligent officer." Except during WWII, the intel analysts have had a dismal record. Just off the top of my head, Naval Intelligence didn't know where the Japanese fleet was in 1941, oops. The Korean War caught the spooks flatfooted, as did the entry of the Chinese into the war. The intel weenies didn't predict that the Viets would fight, though the French experience wasn't secret. There was the comic-opera Son Tay raid, in which the military choppered into Hanoi to rescue American POWs, only to find that the spooks hadn't noticed the prisoners had been moved. The CIA didn't predict that the Cubans would fail to turn against Castro in the Bay of Pigs. They were surprised when the Berlin Wall went up, and when it came down, and again when the USSR, its chief object of study, went tits up. There was the clownish business of the Glomar Explorer. The Air Force bombed the Chinese Embassy in Belgrade because the weenies didn't know where it was (try the phone book, maybe?). They didn't warn that the Arabs might fight in Iraq, perhaps never having heard of Israel. They didn't predict 9/11, and can't find bin Laden.

I'm impressed, Walph. You're an intelligence officer.

Now, why is Peters all wrought up? It seems that an American private by name of Bowe Bergdahl got captured by the Taliban in Afghanistan, or got tired of killing Afghans and deserted, or something. Bergdahl then showed up all over the internet drinking tea with his captors in a video in which he pleaded for America to bring its troops home. Peters waxed wroth over this "disloyalty," and opined that it would be a good thing if the Taliban killed the kid to save the cost of a trial.

There is something unseemly in this over-promoted clerk, for whom a war wound would mean a paper cut, savaging a young man in the hands of the Taliban. If Bergdahl was captured against his will, and the Taliban are as bad as the Walphies tell us, he faces torture if he doesn't cooperate. How manly of Walph to urge that Bergdahl be peeled alive and have his joints crushed. Typical officer.

After the death of my father, a veteran of the Pacific in WWII, I found a published letter he had written to the Washington Post during Korea. Dad, who spent his life as a weapons-development mathematician, was no peacenik. He said that captured American troops should be told to confess to anything whatever rather than be tortured.

You are a hell of a man, Walph. You really are.

But suppose that Bergdahl got tired of killing people he had no reason to kill, and escaped to the Taliban. Why would this be disloyalty to the United States? Where is the benefit of the war to America? The Pentagon is killing GI after GI after GI for no reason. It is also killing Afghans for no reason. Loyalty to America would seem to consist in refusing to do it.

There are countervailing retired colonels. Try Ltc. Karen Kwiatowski, (she has an archive at lewrockwell.com). She suspects that Peters is worried because the Bergdahl affair may indicate that the troops are getting fed up and preparing to bail by one route or another. True? I don't know. Yet it has to be the prevailing nightmare in the Five-Sided Death Box. This sure happened in our Asian foray into the dissemination of democracy. Fraggings were the most conspicuous form of disagreement, but there were enough unreported mutinies and refusals to fight.

Then I find this: "A U.S. military spokeswoman in Afghanistan, Lt. Cmdr. Christine Sidenstricker, said the Taliban was [sic] using their captive for propaganda. 'They are exploiting the soldier in violation of international law,' she said. U.S. military spokesman Colonel Greg Julian added, "We condemn the use of this video and the public humiliation of prisoners."

Most harrumphish, Christine is. This brings me back to the question of Admiral Mullen's assertion of the obviously untrue. Humiliation of prisoners? Does this twit Christine Whatever compartmentalize her mind to the point that she isn't aware of Guantanamo? As for international law, I have the impression that torture of prisoners transgresses it. Torture is American national policy. Anyway, who was humiliated, the prisoner or the Pentagon? Christine will of course say whatever she is told to say, that being the function of flacks, flacks being the low-rent Goerings that they are. I need a drink.

31 CALVIN, LOLA BELTRAN, AND MAHALIA JACKSON. WE DIDN'T REALLY NEED CALVIN

I have concocted a theory that does wonders to explain American politics: We are ruled by history's most boring people. This is a seminal political idea, up there with Plato's invention of Stalinism in The Republic.

I refer of course to those thunderously bland people, the white middle-class Protestants, or Hagvacas (House and garden variety Caucasians). Just typing the words makes my fingers want to sleep. In all things that distinguish mankind from a loaf of store-bought bread, Hagvaca score zero. Unless it involves transistors or regulations. These they can do.

Consider music, the soul of a society. Caucaso-prots of the middle class barely have any. From early on blacks have been the main force driving American music, starting with whatever Ledbelly and his contemporaries did, through blues, first in those silent, hot, humid fields in Mississippi where time dripped slow as Karo syrup on cracked china, and later in a thousand hopping gin mills in places in Chicago where whites didn't go. Gospel, which Elvis understood but Yankees can't, and then jazz, and rock, to today's hiphop and rap—all have more black roots than an inattentive bottle blonde. French Catholics in the swamps of Louisiana invented Cajun while side-stepping alligators in black water lumpy with cypress knees, and blacks improved it into Zydeco. Presley, a poor white from Mississippi, managed to turn black music into something whites would listen to. The South has always been more musically fecund than other regions, being poor, idiosyncratic, and not giving a damn. Rockabilly was the music of poor whites, as were C&W and bluegrass. Jews have been thick on the ground in show music and what passes for classical, or almost (Gershwin, Copland, Bernstein), and in, well, just about everything.

Middle-class albinobaptists have been…a catastrophe. Boring. Horribly boring. They remain so.

In fact they are so bad that other groups have had to condescend to them. Blacks for example have usually regarded Hagvacas as disguised elevators, and written music for them that they wouldn't inflict on living people.

Yes, there are exceptions. And yes, I understand that Prots can do some things well. With a lot of Jewish help, they have put golf carts on Mars, which is an historic feat up there with anything up there. Why they thought anyone on Mars wanted to play golf is another matter. I guess they are better at engineering than market research, but the technology was lovely. They can do organization, and therefore government. Note that the entire continent was one country by 1865, though parts didn't want to be; Europe is still a collection of tiny geographical curiosities. Albinoprots are good at industry, and therefore at industrial war. But that's pretty much it.

Permit me an example, with which I am intimately familiar, since I grew up in it: The small-town Southern lower middle class. These folk are often described as "the salt of the earth," and in a sense they are, though maybe "starch of the earth" could catch them better. But god they are boring. They explain much about the United States.

OK, some jackleg sociology: The great fear of the lower middle class is that of falling back into the actual low class, from which most of them have scrambled like crabs from a bucket. The desire to distinguish themselves from those below drives their whole being, and makes them exciting as drywall. This is Middle America—though with increased prosperity America has become a lower middle-class country with an upper middle-class income, which is why it dominates.

These people live in nice but boring houses, never shacks but never anything unusual. They drive boring cars, Chevies or Fords, but new and carefully washed and waxed. No old Merc' up on blocks for them, and no Maserati. It's not that a Maserati costs too much, though it does, but that it is...unusual. They wear good clothes from Sears, carefully cleaned. Respectability, respectability, respectability, but no imagination, and a zero boogey factor. No style either. They produce Republican women with helmet hair, who constitute the Bermuda Triangle of style. A Puerto Rican girl in jeans and a really colorful sweater comes much closer.

Small-town Hagvacas have great respect for education, but no interest in it. (This is why the schools have deteriorated; the

Chinese, Jews, or Koreans would never have let it happen.) They were the prey of the encyclopedia salesman. A set of the Britannica in the living room, or even the Great Books (never read) showed that they were lettered people, and they prided themselves on looking things up occasionally. Very common were what I think of as Museum Rooms, usually the living room: unpleasantly clean, nicely but tediously furnished, and never used. It was to impress the bridge club.

They were scrupulously honest, worked hard, and made good neighbors. They prized civic responsibility, good manners, and good grammar, because the lower class didn't.

But they didn't dance, never read anything wilder than Reader's Digest Condensed Books, didn't care for music, and generally made Mormon missionaries look like party animals.

Decent, stiff, productive, and colorless, traits they passed on to their somewhat richer cousins in the suburbs today, they are the country's dominant class. At the very least they think they ought to be. Isn't it their country? Didn't a bunch of Hagvacas in Virginia start it?

It's not just music they stultify, but architecture. A Protestant church is a square brick box with a squatty pointed tower on one end. In any Mexican town, you find distinctive churches, often gorgeous, alive with color. Latins. They dance, have great sprawling town-wide fiestas, live in houses that don't all look like each other. Catholics have class. Not too good on organization, though.

All of this horrifies serious Hagvacas. Those…people…they're all brown and those gaudy awful churches and music with those horrible horns and there's no orderliness (there sure isn't) and….

It's all because Calvin didn't dance.

In a rare case of Lamarkian evolution, boringness has become embedded in the genes like a tick in a dog's ear. One does not readily imagine Hillary twirling through a fast Texas two-step, quick-quick sloow-sloow, skirt flying, in some converted barn outside Austin in '72.

It's not fixable. A friend of mine said of blacks, "They burn at a higher emotional temperature than we do." Latins too, in spades (so to speak). Middle-class Prots? They are wild as potted plants. There isn't enough cocaine to change them.

A bit of guy wisdom used to be to get a Republican to run your bank, but date Democratic girls. Yep. Today America looks like Sweden ruling over Rio during Carnival. Same principle, somehow. You'll excuse me. I have a date with Padre Kino and Lola Beltran, channeled through good speakers.

32 BAEZ, COYNE, AND REED: ALL THE ANSWERS YOU'LL EVER NEED

Last night Vi and I watched for the first time a documentary, (*Carry It On*) shot by my friend Jim Coyne, on Joan Baez and the movement against a war no one any longer remembers, far away, on another planet. It was lovely filmwork. Jim is a genius. I may have to stop having friends. I feel inferior to all of them. It gets depressing.

Of no interest to anyone but me, perhaps, it completely changed my understanding of Baez, whom I had regarded for forty years as just another pretty voice. No. Smart, tough, principled in a world that isn't. I hereby apologize.

In that war—I forget what planet it was on—the freaks and professors and mothers and the simply decent finally managed stop the carnage, though only after the Pentagon had killed 60,000 American kids and a million or so Vietnamese, not to mention devastating Laos and bringing Pol Pot to power. God I'm proud. We're such a force for democracy.

When the GIs left Asia in '73, the commie peaceniks thought they had won. And they had, for ten minutes. The grip of the military on the country loosened briefly.

Unfortunately the soldiers learned. Not how to win wars, which they do poorly if at all, but how to keep a war going. Winning a war isn't all it's cracked up to be. The promotions and contracts stop. When you are paid to do something, it is in your interest not to finish doing it.

The Pentagon's first lesson learned was to avoid conscription, as the conscripted and their families will take to the streets. By using an army of volunteer suckers about whom nobody of importance cares, the military severs its wars from most of the country, which loses interest. The brass are then free to do as they choose.

The second lesson learned was that while defeating the enemy is not necessary, and perhaps not desirable, controlling the press is everything. And they did it.

So forty or so years after all the love-ins, the marches, the righteous dope (all of which may seem silly, but in my view preferable to watching a Cambodian mother screaming over the opened bleeding guts of her child) the Pentagon is at it again. Once more the jets howl over remote primitive countries, countries that did nothing to the US and couldn't have, and promotions flow, and contracts, and generals demand more troops and more money to stop communism. Excuse me, terrorism. Soon, the Chinese, a better threat, coming to a theater near you. With the passing of years, one demon fades into another. Switching enemies is much easier now, what with search-and-replace.

But it's all about democracy and freedom and patriotism and Saving America from…from something. The hoopla changes little, and how well it works. Patriotic friends sometimes say to me of the military ardent things like, "When your country says go, you go!" I seldom point out that no one in their families is in the slightest danger of having to go, nor that "the country" is recruiting hard and they aren't urging their children to enlist; nor do I ask, "What is your attitude toward having your daughter drafted onto the streets of Baghdad for five tours, perhaps coming back drooling and gurbling for life after having her brains scrambled by a roadside bomb?" Patriotism is important to patriots. They are full of it, and I'm about a quart low. I shut up. I don't want to lose friends.

Yet…I think I must be a communist. It seems to me that when your country says "go," you should ask, "Why?" Do you have a reason to kill whoever you are being sent to kill? Then go. Otherwise, don't. If I told you to go to Ottawa and kill Canadians, you would think me mad, and think it correctly. Why then should you obediently kill them because a politician in Washington tells you to do it? I do not understand.

And of course "your country" doesn't tell you anything at all. Countries are abstractions. Men tell you to go, and for their own purposes: Dick Cheney or George Bush, Nixon or Nitze, or the men who run the petroleum industry, or people in the Israeli lobby, or men in the military companies who want contracts, or officers who want to give war a try.

Why are these people "my country"? And why isn't Joan Baez my country instead of David Petraeus? I will choose who is my country, thank you. Ledbelly, Benny Goodman, Carl Perkins and

Miss Emily Anne will come before Lemay, McNamara, Lyndon Johnson, and Obama. Long before.

Soldiers talk much of honor. I do not understand how military service can possibly be thought honorable. If the Wehrmacht were landing in North Carolina, yes, but I do not believe that it is. Where is the honor in bombing from the air lightly armed peasants who can't fight back? It is cowardly, yes, and obscene, but do not talk of honor. Murder for hire is murder for hire.

We now have men who sit at screens, drinking coffee and firing missiles from remote robotic aircraft at people on the ground whom they cannot identify. Brave men, they. I could burst into a kindergarten and kill the children with a ball bat. The one is as honorable as the other.

Recently I saw on television a black sergeant in Afghanistan, probably chosen by his commander for photogenicity, standing in front of a tank or mobile gun, I forget which. He said something scripted like "This is a such-and-such unit, the most powerful fighting force in the world." This sort of ritual cockiness is carefully ingrained. Near my barracks in Parris Island was a sign, "The most dangerous thing in the world is a Marine rifleman." If it had said "an ambitious colonel" it would have come closer to truth.

But one may wonder (unless one already knows) how good the Pentagon's military really is. A pissed-off peasant with an RPG would seem on the evidence more effective than the pricey zoom-kapows arrayed against him.

I cannot endorse the politics of the Taliban. If one of them told me that my daughter couldn't go to school, one of us would leave the room on a stretcher. Yet as fighting men, are they not magnificent? They have only rifles, explosives, RPGs, and balls. Their enemies have unlimited air support, helicopters, armor, artillery, sophisticated communications, night-vision gear, good food and excellent medical care. The Taliban take heavy casualties, their enemies almost none. The ragheads do not even have PX privileges. Yet they have not been defeated. A fight on even terms would last perhaps five minutes.

This, for a trillion dollars.

What the hell. Plus ca change, plus ca doesn't. Next year in Beijing. Tell you what, though. I never liked Kum Ba Yah, and "We Shall Overcome" is probably the sappiest song every written.

But those people had nothing to be ashamed of.

On a pleasanter note: I have decided to become a famous song-writer and make millions. The following is a beginning, copyright Fred Reed, all rights reserved. Major recording studios can send large checks.

33 UP AND COMING: A SONG FOR OUR TIMES

Way up North, 'round a mile from Niagara
Pfizer built a plant, makin' Viagra
The old-folks home was a mile to the West
Some call it cursed, though I'd say blessed
Amazingly
About a year later disaster struck
The main flow pipe got hit by a truck
That love stuff got where it shouldn't oughter
It all leaked into the drinkin' water
Lots of it
Chorus
Viagraaaaaaaa!
Bringing resurrection to a pinnacle of perfection
In Paducah, Chatanooga, DC, and Mian'
A laudable inflation that grows the population
And a king-hell motherlode of spam
Granpa took a drink from outta the spout
The look on his face said, "Granny look out."
A devilish glint came into his eye
Granny took a look and said "My oh my."
It's what she said
Grandpa leaped to his feet and he said,
"I'm not tired but I'm goin' to bed.
You still strike me as a purty gal
But I've had a little trouble getting vertical.
Until now"
Granny hollered "Pa, now don't you fret
There's a dance left in the old girl yet.
I don't see how but somethin's givin'
Us a hell of a rush toward better livin'
Through chemistry"
The seismic lab down at Memphis State
Said, "There's trouble up North, we think it's a quake."
A reporter for the Post reported back
"Yeah there's a tremor but it ain't exack

-Ly an earthquake."
Lawyers like roaches thought they smelled some loot
They wanted to have a class-action suit
Pfizer had to do a lot of explaining
But Granny and Grandpa weren't complaining
But things got stranger
Springtime rains washed it into the ocean
Where it got spread around by the waves in motion
The Navy reported that to its surprise
The old Titanic had started to rise!
Eagerly
When the stuff reached bottom the seabed rose
Pushed to the surface by volcanoes
Scientists said upon reflection
They had never seen such a massive erection
Geologically speaking, of course
Viagra fumes leaked into outer space
From lava that was flying all over the place
Such was the power of the drug to excite
That the sun came up in the middle of the night!
What we've learned from these events is
Everything you do has consequences
If chemical bliss is what you seek
You gotta make sure the pipes don't leak
You gotta make sure
You gotta make sure
You gotta make sure the pipes don't leeeeeeeeeeak....

34 ISLAMO-FASCISM, JUDEO-FASCISM, BAPTO-FASCISM, AND
WHY WE NEED MORE BARS

The wheels are squeaking on the tumbrel methinks. At a recent conclave held by AIPAC, unease arose, reasonably enough, over eroding American support for Israel. What apparently did not arise was any indication of understanding of why support is eroding.

In Haaretz I find the following account of a speech by Howard Kohr, the executive director of AIPAC: "'These voices [not hostile to Islam] are laying the predicate for an abandonment [by the US of Israel]...The stakes in that battle are nothing less than the survival of Israel, linked inexorably to the relationship between Israel and the United States. In this battle we are the firewall, the last rampart.'"

This sort of shrieking-dental-drill end-of-worldism is of course the boiler plate of alarmed extremists, and extremists are congenitally alarmed. Eeek, we must stop the (blacks, Muslims, commies, Mexicans, Jews, secular humanists) before they destroy (Western Civilization, America, Israel or, you know, something Really Important.)

Haaretz goes on to speak of AIPAC's loosening hold on America, of what I call Israel fatigue, which seems to be growing. Not long ago, criticism of AIPAC was a firing offense at newspapers. Today, less so, probably because the internet has outflanked the print media.

However, it seems to me that AIPAC is not the firewall defending Israel that it believes itself to be, but rather the carpenter putting the first nails in Israel's coffin. Permit me a few thoughts:

First, Jews are in no danger in the US. It is to AIPAC's benefit to pretend otherwise. Howwsomever, America is not an anti-Semitic country. Yes, you can find websites like Loonfront.com and Stormbird.org. (I made those up. I think.) It remains that Jews, once outsiders, are now insiders. They are deeply integrated into the country, intermarriage is high, and few care. The only potential source of anti-Jewish hostility is the belief that Jews have pushed the US into some international catastrophe, as for example war with Iran. Otherwise, few Americans seem particularly interested in Jews.

Second, few Americans, as best I can tell, object to the existence of Israel. What huge numbers of people object to is Israel's constant savage bombardment of Beirut, butchery in Gaza, and colonization of the West Bank.

Third, AIPAC, by its ownership of Congress, enables the current unprincipled (and, I am inclined to add, un-Jewish) government of Israel to continue these policies that, yes, very much undermine American public support for Israel.

Is this really a favor to Israelis?

Ponder the dilemma that Israel presents to me, to Americans who are not Jewish.

I loathe America's militarism, the carnage it wreaks in its wars against Iraq, Afghanistan, Somalia, Pakistan, and earlier in Southeast Asia. Why am I supposed to approve of identical behavior by Israel? Am I to have one morality for Israel and another for my own country and the rest of the world? Am I to believe that gratuitously bombing Baghdad and Hanoi is wrong, but gratuitously wrecking Beirut is right?

Although I am a Southerner, and like being one, I detested the apartheid practiced in the South. I was there. Don't tell me 'bout dem happy niggahs plunking dat ol banjo undah dee big oak tree. It was ugly. Jews, I note, didn't like it either, and in fact led the movement for civil rights.

If I didn't like brutal repression (which it was) engaged in by my own people, why am I supposed to like it when engaged in by Israelis? And why do Jews, who didn't approve of it in the South, support it in Israel? Why don't they tell Israel to stop it? They could.

Repressive custody of others does not make nice people. My family (the Venables) for two centuries lived in Prince Edward County, Virginia. In the early Fifties, as desegregation gained ground, we were the resistance, the Power Structure, the AIPAC of the region. Those with an idea of history may remember that Prince Edward shut down the public schools to avoid contact with blacks. The reasons given were many, some better than others, but ultimately the system was just wrong.

I spent a fair amount of time listening to my parents and

relatives drinking bourbon in stately living rooms in Farmville, the county seat, and talking race. I know how their heads work. I know the grinding hatred, the contempt that dripped from every sentence, the herdishness as they confirmed each other's snarling.

They sounded exactly like American Zionists speaking of Arabs. There was the same insistence on racial inferiority, on the filthiness of blacks or Arabs, their historical uselessness, their incapacity to fit into a civilized world, their sexual appetites. There is nothing Jewish in this. It is the normal moral sewerization that results from the relation of masters to slaves. Prison guards have it. South Africans had it. The only good Indian is a dead Indian. The underclass are always vermin, and the masters always become moral monsters. The Nazis, early Likudists, had identical notions of Jews.

I find myself wanting to say to AIPAC: What are you clowns thinking? How do you see the end game? You support a goose-stepping government in colonizing the West Bank to the point that it is irreversible. Then what? Your choices are extermination of your Arabs, ethnic cleansing on a horrific scale, or South Africanization. And how well did that work?

Because Jews have a well-earned reputation for being intelligent, one might make the mistake of expecting them necessarily to behave intelligently. No. Brains only provide the means to be more elaborately and ornately stupid. The smart merely make more complex mistakes. Historically, horrendous misjudgements have usually been the children of good minds. When you mix acuity with fanaticism, you get an ungodly stew almost certain to end in disaster. This may be worth thinking about.

Intelligence does allow the fabrication of high-sounding motives. Thugs simply hit people on the head. It is a straightforward and honest undertaking. The smart come up with grand justifications. Americans had Manifest Destiny and now have Spreading Democracy. Israel says its settlements have the right of "natural growth" or, in German, lebensraum. All these amount to "I want it. Give it to me or I'll kill you."

It is curious how many people believe that Jews are copies of Ariel Sharon, marching in robotic lockstep behind Likud. It just isn't so. From Ha'aretz: "...but alternative Jewish voices are rising

114

who are less concerned with being accused of 'self-hatred' or treachery. They see it as their duty to damn what is wrong and not simply support Israeli government policies. A thinking, more enlightened Judaism is emerging, a necessity in the face of apartheid realities. The cause is human rights, not Zionist exclusion."

If they want a fellow-traveler, count me in.

35 MOWING THE SWARD OF DAMOCLES. I HAVE NO IDEA WHAT I MEANT BY THAT

I've been reading the news again. It's great fun, like watching an EEG trace as it...slowly...flat-lines. Reading a newspaper increasingly reminds me of watching a leper to see which finger falls off next. You can make bets.

In the news I find more on torture. I'm so proud. Home of the brave, land of the free, though we may pull your fingernails out. What nobody talks about is where we get our torturers. I mean, is it a rating, like Radioman First Class? Do recruiters offer it? What civilian applications do they see when an eager young Torquemada leaves the military? Local police?

The question of recruiting is fascinating. How much would you have to be paid to crush knees with a sledge hammer? Where do they find these guys? The boss at Langley presumably doesn't just walk through the office saying, "Hey, we need someone TDY for Guantanamo to crush genitals. Sally, you up for it? Bill? You get overseas pay and it looks good on your resume."

Or does he? The military didn't have any trouble getting those girl soldiers at Abu Ghraib into it. Ooooh! King-ky!

Sadism is sexual. People don't do it who don't like it. We're not talking fun and games among suburban S&M hobbyists who like to spank each other. Don't even think about what goes on in Saudi prisons in league with the American military. Do our twisted patriots spend a few hours breaking some poor kid's mind and then rush into an adjoining room to masturbate? Do they swap techniques?

Next, I see that some guy named Ahmadinnerjacket claims he has been elected Prez of Iran again. It seems that he is being threatened by the Prime Minister of Israel, who for some time I believed to be named Bibi Nut-and-Yahoo. This struck me as unusually candid. Why don't I care? Sounds like a personal problem. If they nuked each other, the planet would be so much quieter.

Meanwhile North Korea threatens South Korea with nuclear war, and the US pledges noisily to defend the South at all costs.

Why? The South has lots more population and industry than does the North. If South Korea wants to defend itself, it can. If it doesn't want to, I don't care. I'm not Seoul's mother.

When you enlist in the military you pledge to defend the Constitution. Is it in Korea? I didn't pay much attention in high-school civics.

Next, I see that the US has killed thirteen more civilians with drone strikes in Afghanistan. Lovely. What fun. I picture some wet-lipped CIA psychopath goobering at his screen in search of someone to blow up. It's a cinch they don't know who they are aiming at. The CIA has never been very good at intelligence, but it doesn't matter. It's the spirit of the thing. Besides, Afghans breed like flies. If you splatter one kid with a really neat drone, got buttons, got knobs, they can beget another.

Next, California is broke. Good. They deserve it. It's not as if bankruptcy were an act of God, like getting hit on the head by a giant meteor. It was deliberate stupidity. Spend more than you make, and you end up on the street. I'm supposed to feel sorry for that? I've known roundworms with better sense. As I understand it, the Democrats refuse to cut spending and the Republicans refuse to raise taxes. See? A lobotomy in two-part harmony. Sounds like the whole country.

Next, I see that Precedent O'Bama wants to take on the pharmaceutical companies to lower the price of prescriptions. The subhead alleged that important congressmen have "ties to the industry," as if this were somehow not right or normal.

OK, a brief excursion into cosmic truth. First, socialism. Hard-line conservatives with little grasp of economics refer to anything they don't like—Hillary, national health care, regulation of anything if it might cost them money—as "socialist." It's a utility pejorative, devoid of meaning, as "racist" and "elitist" are for political south-paws. Socialism is of course a system in which the government owns the means of production. Check your dictionary.

Ah! But in America, the means of production own the government. Inverted socialism it is. Here is a far better thing. If you are a means of production, anyway.

Example: Bausch & Lomb makes ophthalmic salt water, useful in treating corneal edema, under the trade name "Muro." In the Yankee Capital, it costs $23 for 1.8 ounces; in Winchester, Va.,

$19; in Farmacia Guadalajara, about $6. The identical product. The generic here, Hipoton, comes in at about $3.

You could call it price-fixing, but I prefer to think of it as governmental regulation of prices. It is perfectly legal, because Big Pharma owns the government.

I believe that Econ textbooks say that price controls haven't worked from Diocletian on. Wrong. They work splendidly. Ask Bausch & Lomb. If you could make over twenty-two bucks on a dime's worth of salt water, wouldn't you be in favor of governmental interference in the economy?

Let me explain medicine briefly. It's an unholy scam. Here in Mexico my wife occasionally gets ear infections. At any pharmacy, we pick up Amoxicillin, 250mg three times a day for ten days. Six bucks.

Recently we were staying in Maryland with friends, and she got an ear ache. Amoxicillin is by prescription only in the US, which means that doctors have a monopoly on ear aches. It was Friday evening. It was either agony until Monday or go to one of those mall-based walk-in clinics, which wanted $150 for the appointment and prescribed $78 in medicines.

It's a scam, pure and simple. Above the level of county government, the US is as corrupt as Mexico could ever be, and it's mostly legal. Yes, I know all the who-struck-John from doctors about engendering resistant bugs. Funny. Any pharmacist in Thailand will tell you the same thing a US doctor will— Amoxicillin, take all ten days' worth, etc. Scam.

Finally, I find that Northrop has "unveiled" an unmanned fighter, the X-47 I think. ("Unveiled" is a curious word, suggesting a blushing virgin.) Again, it's inverse socialism. America has no military enemies and the country is going broke, but the means of production own the government, and so we'll get the thing at some huge cost. Northrop is picking the pocket of the corpse as it begins to decompose. Reminds me of Wall Street. Government by looters.

Aaagh!

36 THE WHOLE WORLD SUCKS, AND EVERYBODY THINKS IT'S GRAVITY

I'm going to take poison. Every time I read the headlines, I want to take poison. Always they are a concentrated tale of avarice, wretched judgment, murderousness, and lugubrious taste. I'm thinking potassium cyanide. To sleep, perchance to dream....

Headlines: "Chrysler Heads Back to Bankruptcy Court Friday"; "Crash Diet: GM Getting in Shape for Chapter Eleven"' "Economy Sinks at a 5.7 Percent Rate in 1Q."

We're a Second World country and working on Third, I tell you. We probably won't be able to make our own cars before long. The economy is croaking. So what we need to do is have a lot of expensive foreign wars. Anybody can see it. You can't run your own country? Then kill a bunch of thirteenth-century peasants. That'll fix it.

I think I may have to take over the economy. Yes, I hear you asking, "Fred, what arrogance, even by your vertiginous standards. You aren't an economist. What makes you think you know anything about economics?"

To which I reply, "What makes you think economists know anything about economics? Who got us into this mess, me or economists? I have never bought anything on credit in my life, and I have zero debt. Would you rather have me running things, or economists?"

Headline: "North Korea Tests Missiles." Oh good. North Korea has the Bomb and, now, missiles of short range. Short is how long the range is to Seoul and the American bases in South Korea. Bad juju, says my astute military mind. And so Hillary Clinton, former First Housewife turned Millie Metternich and expert on all things foreign, wants sanctions against North Korea. This makes perfect sense. They've got nuclear weapons, so let's piss them off. Sanctions will have no effect on their Bomb, but may make them desperate enough to use it. What could be a better idea?

Remember when George W. Huffenpuff was never going to let the malignant Northerners have the Bomb? No, indeed. He was going to pyong their yang if they even thought about it. That worked, didn't it? Now President Blackbush is making threatening noises at Korea as if he could do anything about it. He's going to make those heathen behave, and put the cost on the national credit card with the Bank of China.

Headline: "Army Chief: US Can Fight N. Korea if Necessary." Yes. General George Casey, Army chief of staff, says we're ready. In the accompanying photo he has the daft look of a Moonie Boy Scout. I have thought that officers must be issued some form of psychological disturbance when they sign up. Anyway, the US economy is rattling its death rattle, industry either leaves the country or goes tits sunward, America is now the world's greatest debtor nation, and this dazed silver-haired bull dog wants another war. Why? What's wrong with the wars we've got?

Headline: "Israel Dismisses US Demand on Settlements." I guess that doesn't leave much doubt about who controls Washington. Israel, being utterly dependent on the United States for its existence, is the one country that Washington should be able to dictate to. If the US were an independent country, and told the Knesset to wear tutus and toe shoes, in ten minutes they'd be grunting their way through Swan Lake. I don't know, though. Given how the US manages its own foreign policy, I can see why the Israelis might not be enthusiastic about American suggestions.

Headline: "Senator Lautenberg: US Won't Be Upset if Israel Strikes Iran." Well, Senator Lautenberg, presumably an Arab, won't be upset. But with which Americans has he consulted? Me? I guess I missed his call.

Real answer: He has consulted with Congress, 535 commoditized temple monkeys pawing through the ruins of America in search of bribes. The bicameral whorehouse on Capitol Hill works like a vending machine. You put coins in the slot, select your law, and the desired legislation slides out.

Thing is, Israel can't attack Iran without an American OK, which Iran knows, so that puts us at war with Iran, and our Iraqi colony shares a long border with Iran, while Israel doesn't. Something to think about. Should we ever take up thinking.

Headline: "Study: Israeli Attack on Iran Unlikely to Work." If I were an Israeli, I'd worry about that too. Right now, Iran and Israel are making unpleasant noises at each other, but no more. What if Israel, that least Jewish of countries, attacks but doesn't kill Iran's nuclear program? Bombing is an act of war. It would give Iran every moral and legal right to bomb back with anything it had, or might make soon. Kerblooey.

Both America and Israel are accustomed to attacking countries that can't hit back. There is such a thing as getting too comfortable.

Headline: "White House: Solomayor Says She Chose Word Poorly." She is Blackbush's choice for the Supreme Mausoleum. Court, I meant. Apparently what she said was that a "wise Latina woman" would reach better decisions than "a white male." Oh. Then why have a Supreme Court at all? We could just replace it with a wise Latina woman. I wonder who she has in mind.

My thought was, oh god, more smug misandry. More man-bashing from an angry brown female who doesn't know how her car works. I'm happy with Latinos on the Court, or –as, or women or blacks or Jews. But not another wielder of mortal boredom, blathering about white males.

See why cyanide appeals?

Headline: "Pakistani Army Retakes Largest Town in Swat Valley."

Once more we see the iron claws of the Pentagon digging at the eyeballs of backward countries. Have we no shame? (No.) We want the gas of the Caspian Basin so we invade Afghanistan, yelling and honking about democracy and terror. Next we start murdering Pakistanis from the air with really fun drones, and now we force the Pakis to kill their own people. This is the Southeast Asian paradigm. We killed a million Vietnamese for no particular reason, savaged Laos, brought Pol Pot to power, and then went home to swim at Malibu. Iran, however, is a rogue country.

New headline, just popped up: "Gates: Nuclear Armed North Korea Not Acceptable." What the hell does that mean? They are nuclear-armed. You either nuke them, invade them, or accept them. Which? Anything any country does is acceptable unless you are prepared and able not to accept it. Fizzing and blowing serves only to advertise impotence.

Headline: "Swine Flu in Ecuador." I guess that explains why it isn't in Mexico: It's somewhere else. For weeks Mexico has been standing on its head to repel the dread epidemic. Schools closed, bars closed, public events were canceled, the government handed out little masks. No flu. I'm thinking of importing a case and charging people to look at it. It would be a bigger draw than a three-headed goat. We have yet to see a case of flu.

I can't stand it. I'm off to Farmacia Guadalajara for something deadly. There are limits.

37 BRIEF NOTES FROM THOSE WHO ARE ABOUT TO DIE

OK, yesterday on final into Guadalajara, at the height of the flu epidemic, indeed pandemic, predicted to be even more cleansing than the killer flu of 1918, perhaps the beginning of the long-expected plague that would eliminate mankind from the earth, no doubt to the earth's relief, I was ready for the worst. I had read the papers, after all. I was sure there would be piles of festering corpses in the streets, such as one would expect after a Burundian election. I had read Defoe's account of the bubonic plague in London, and knew that men with wheelbarrows would be collecting the dead. Especially with today's littering laws.

Except that, when I had called Violeta every night during the two weeks I was in the US, she always said "What flu?" Ain't got no flu heah. The schools were shut down, bars closed, everybody hiding from the flu, but they couldn't find any flu to hide from. My friend Ken, in another town near Guad, reported an equal epidemic of perfect health. It was media flu, he suspected.

I knew better. I had read of the lightning spread, the hundreds of dead, the frightening appearance of cases in New Zealand, comparisons to the Black Death of 1348. Ohmygodohmygodohmygod. The only logical explanation was that the Mexican government was quietly disposing of thousands—nay, tens of thousands—of dead so as not to alarm the tourist trade.

We deplaned. An official of some sort was handing out those funny little masks to anyone who wanted one, which practically no one did. Coming out of customs, everybody had to stand briefly in front of an infrared camera that made you appear green on a big screen if you didn't have a fever, which nobody seemed to. No corpses. I guess they removed them really fast. No coughs. Come on, I thought. You've advertised the flu. Now produce it.

Violeta and Natalia picked me up, apparently not dead, and we headed south to Jocotepec. The streets were semi-deserted, traffic light. Maybe, I thought, a plague was a good thing. I mean, you could find parking. Mexico seemed to be taking the disease seriously, doing all the responsible things that one does with a plague. All it needed was a plague. Can you order plagues online, I wondered, being a practical sort.

That evening we went with friends to the Tortuga Sedienta in Ajijic for hamburgers and wine. (I'm not sure you are supposed to drink wine with hamburgers. The question consumes me.) One of said friends was a Mexican doctor, shock-trauma variety I believe, who had worked all over the world. In two hours of conversation, she never mentioned the careening extinction, the eminent PCS to the sky, the Permanent Change of Station that loomed over us like a bad divorce settlement. I guess it just didn't make an impression on her. Or anyone else.

This morning I leaped like a startled jackrabbit to La Puta Dora and checked the Yahoo headlines, which didn't mention the plague at all. This was ominous. I figured all the journalists must be dead. A news story I had read put the mortality from the Monster Flu at ten percent, so the reporters must have gotten it several times each to all be dead. So surviving it didn't confer immunity. Bad, very bad.

What's the deal? Sure, tomorrow the virus may erupt with renewed virulence and carry off whole populations. I suppose it's more likely than an asteroid strike. Maybe. The Yahoo headlines say that someone in Illinois or somewhere is suspected of killing his third wife. All right, perhaps this is of greater import than a disease that is going to depopulate the earth. You have to respect the editor's news judgement. (Murdering your wife is a family matter and nobody else's business. How about a little respect for privacy?) But if this flu business isn't just a media frenzy staged by bored news weasels, why aren't we hearing more about it? How come I can't find it, and I'm supposed to be in the middle of it? Habeas corpus, I say.

38 MESSIN' WHERE WE SHOULDN'T OUGHTA: A USER'S GUIDE TO THOROUGHLY STUPID FOREIGN POLICY

I strain for words to describe adequately Washington's policy toward Latin America. Candidates come to mind: Imbecilic, moronic, catatonic, Pollyannaish, blind, incurious. No, these are poor creatures and frail, not equal to the task. Retarded? Anencephalic? Those too lack descriptive power. The EEG has flat-lined. The patient is dead.

I recently found the following from McClatchey news service:

WASHINGTON — As the Pentagon eyes a bigger role in Mexico's drug war, the military's efforts to open the door to a new relationship with its southern neighbor …."

Book me a ticket to Mars. The Pentagon is eyeing something, a sure recipe for disaster. Previously it has eyed Vietnam, Laos, Cambodia, Somalia, Iraq, Afghanistan, Pakistan, and made a horrendous mess of each. Now the Five-Sided Sand Box is eyeing Mexico. Oh good. Let's get involved in another third-world catastrophe by meddling in what we don't understand.

Continues McClatchey: "During a trip designed to expand U.S. Mexican-military relations, Adm. Michael Mullen, the highest-ranking U.S. military officer, visited the graves of American troops who died during the Mexican-American war just as Gates did during his first visit in August."

How stupid can you get? (The question is rhetorical. Pentagonal stupidity does not converge, but increases without limit.) To improve relations with the Mexican army, we rub its nose in having defeated them. "Haha, Pedro, you got a few of our guys, but we kicked your hindparts good, didn't we?" The unspoken subtext to any Mexican being, "And we can do it again."

Let me explain something. To Mexicans, the US is not a friendly nation. The reasons are countless, some valid and some not, but Mexicans do not see America as benign. They fear the US military, which they regard as out of control, invading country after country in pursuit of oil.

Mexico has oil. America lost control of it in 1938 when Lazaro

Cardenas nationalized it. Mexicans believe, in dead seriousness, that the US would love a pretext for invading to get it back. A pretext such as coming in to help Mexico fight drugs, and just not leaving. Iraq comes instantly to their minds.

And so the good admiral and the SecDef come to pay homage to the American soldiers who conquered Mexico. What diplomatic genius.

While they are at it, why not lay a wreath in Hiroshima to the brave American airmen who died over Japan? Or maybe erect a statue to Sherman in Atlanta? What if the Mexican army chief went to New York to commemorate the courageous freedom fighters who took down the towers?

No. No, no, no. Keep the gringo soldiers out of Mexico. To Mexicans, the US military means only one thing: unshirted aggression. The dates 1846-1848 might convey something to one American in a hundred. Mexicans know that in those years they lost half their country to what U.S. Grant called an utterly unjustified invasion. They remember.

You don't have to agree with Grant's assessment (though I don't see how it can be intelligently disputed). Mexican behavior is determined by what Mexicans think, not what we think they ought to think.

Peoples remember invasions for a very long time. It is not smart to step on a country's national corns. Even today a lot of Southerners would march on Washington under arms if they thought they had a chance of winning.

It is not just that Mullen and Gates did what they did, but that they had no idea what they were doing. I mean…look, Mexico is not the Dry Tortugas. It is a country of 110 million people sharing a very long border with the US. What happens here has consequences for the United States. It might make sense to treat the place with a modicum of thought, to have some grasp of how Latins think. I don't mean a firm grasp, or real understanding. I am not an extremist. But…maybe just a clue.

From Guadalajara, our policy towards the continent below seems determined by bumbling children, by domestic politics, by truculent and heavily armed Boy Scouts. Is Hillary Clinton the Secretary of State for her long experience abroad, her command of languages? Or because her appointment healed a schism in the

Democratic Party and soothed the Israeli lobby? No one in power seems even to know that there is anything to know about South America. I suspect I could count on the fingers of an amputee's hand the number of high US officials who speak Spanish. It is ridiculous.

In the past it perhaps didn't matter much whether Washington knew anything about Caracas, La Paz, or Brasilia. Latin Americans were all the same—serape, tequila, exaggerated sombrero, sleeping under a cactus, burro waiting. I am still asked by Americans, "In Mexico, do they, you know, have paved roads?" Unbright. Very unbright.

Today wiser policy is in order, but seems unlikely to be forthcoming. In particular, a ratpack of colonels in arrested development are the worst possible people to handle relations with Latin countries. Colonels live in a clean-edged, simple mental universe in which orders are followed, everyone is a good guy or a bad guy, and you can trust those thought to be on your side. They believe in American values, in military values, and believe that everyone really wants to be like them, like us. Nothing to it: You bomb the bad guys into submission, teach the people to be honest and emocratic as America isn't and never was and, bingo, a docile Reader's Digest version of Switzerland pops into existence. Good luck.

Latin America doesn't work that way. It is complex, often profoundly corrupt, at times chaotic, and inclined to view the rule of law as an interesting idea perhaps worthy of examination at a later date. Power flows through channels written nowhere. Latins intensely resent American intrusiveness. Most would prefer their own narcos to US soldiery. The world below the Rio Bravo is not suitable for military fiddling.

In today's complicated world, with the Asian giants rising and seeking raw materials, maybe we should pay more attention. Maybe sending the Marines isn't the answer to every problem. Since World War II, the Pentagon has displayed a nearly solid record of failure in fighting either drugs or peasants with AKs. We do not need to blunder into new and better Afghanistans. We seem to want to, though, and it will bring more leftists to power. In the last election here, a truly nutball leftist (AMLO—Andres Manuel Lopez Obrador) came within a few chads of being president of

Mexico. Hugo Chavez thrives on American hostility. We treat Cuba as an enemy and, sure enough, it acts like one. None of this is in the American national interest, boys and girls. It's just brainless.

39 THE ROAD TO RUAD

The practical question regarding Israel's recent invasion of Gaza is not "Who is right?" but "Can Israel last?"

As I write, Israel is using a military designed to fight hostile countries to fight a hostile population. In the modern world, this has seldom worked. To defeat a country you destroy its military and capture its territory. But Gaza has little military to destroy, no tanks or aircraft, and Israel already owns its territory. The IDF can invade but, afterward, the population will still be there, and still be hostile. Stabbing jello doesn't buy you much.

Israel remains a small state in a region that intensely doesn't want it. The rights and wrongs change nothing. Again and again, Israel lashes out, lashes out, against enemies that can be defeated but never decisively. And so the bombs fall on Gaza, on Syria, on Beirut, perhaps on Iran. Each war guarantees the next: 1948, 1956, 1967, 1973, 1982, 2006, 2009, world without end.

Israel today is not the country once dreamed, in which Heidelberg professors escaped from Europe would work the soil with their hands on kibbutzim and play chess and the violin at night. It looks more like what the professors fled. Brutal conflicts breed brutal people. Atrocities engender counter- atrocities, extremists come to the fore, and military solutions seem the only solutions.

Where is this going? How long can it continue? Another fifty years? A hundred? Say I, either the country finds peace with its neighbors or it goes the way of the Crusader Kingdom. We can stipulate that the Israelis are the world's best people, or the worst. It doesn't matter. You can die in the right as easily as in the wrong.

The Israelis appear to be trapping themselves in their own policies. They continue their annexation of the West Bank. The settlements are now so numerous and so populous that dismantling them is probably politically impossible for any Israeli government, which rules out a two-state solution. To control a large hostile population, you need harsh methods, which keep the population hostile. Arabs outbreed the Israelis, so that a proportionately declining number of Israelis rule a slowly rising tide of Arabs. Think: South Africa. How is this going to work? For how long?

Israel also has a large internal minority of Arabs. These also outbreed the Jews. If this continues and the internal Arabs can vote, Israel will one day become an Islamic state. Sooner or later, the question will be: Democratic, or Jewish?

America killed its indigenous population, the Spanish married theirs, but Israel can do neither. Now what?

Since Israelis do not yearn to get in touch with their inner Muslim, the choices will be disenfranchisement or ethnic cleansing. Disenfranchisement would, again, leave a diminishing proportion of Jews ruling more and more Muslims. Think: Alabama in 1930.

Disenfranchisement apparently is starting. Israel just banned its Arab parties from voting in the upcoming elections, and then the courts unbanned them.

Ethnic cleansing? Rounding up a large minority and expelling it would require horrendous brutality. This is the least moral but perhaps most practical solution. It is barely possible that Congress would balk but, I suspect, not until it was too late to matter. If Israel nuked Chicago, Congress would approve.

The long-term indicators point downward. Israel's military position is not as good as one might think. It has, or had when I last covered such things, a splendid air force, a good militia army, nuclear weapons, and inferior enemies. None of these is particularly useful against angry populations.

It seems probable that Islamic countries will eventually have nuclear weapons. The danger is not that a Muslim country would spontaneously launch them against Israel, as this would constitute national suicide. But you don't have to use nuclear weapons for them to be effective.

Today, the Bomb is Israel's trump card. If, say, Syria attacked and (improbably) began to win, its cities would turn to green glass, and Damascus knows it. Thus Israel is in exactly zero danger of conventional defeat. But if Arab countries had nuclear weapons, the trump card would lose its value. You have to be very careful about bombing countries that can vaporize your cities.

Further, Israel depends entirely on a foreign country, namely America, for its survival. The US provides the weaponry, the financial aid, the vetoes in the UN, and the last-resort military support that comes when Israel is in trouble (1973, for example).

Without this support, Israel could not last. Small countries without oil cannot support massive militaries.

If I were an Israeli, I would be uneasy about this. American support depends crucially, if not entirely, on the Israeli lobbies. Should these falter, so will Israel. It is not that the US seethes with repressed anti-Semitism awaiting its chance. It doesn't. But Americans don't much care about the outside world, know little of history and less of geography. Congress is loyal only to itself.

Today one reads of the recent overwhelming vote in Congress in support of Israel, but the number is highly artificial. The rub is that today is today, but there is always tomorrow. Congress supports whoever pays it or intimidates it, and today the Lobby can exact a heavy price for opposition. If the winds blow another way, Congress will sway in another direction. What might constitute a sufficient wind? I don't know. I note that Israel has no oil, its enemies do, and world demand is growing fast. Think: Taiwan.

Further, I doubt that public support for Israel is nearly as strong as we are told it is. Among conservatives, no small group, there is considerable mild hostility to Jews and a far stronger dislike of Israel. I'm not sure how serious the antagonism is. To be annoyed is one thing, but to want to see the country fall with the nearly assured hideous results is another. But people seldom think that far. Many, if they could, would shrug and say, "Whatever. It's their problem." A national shrug would end Israel.

Methinks a faint smell of doom hangs over Tel Aviv. American power appears to be on the decline, the outcome of its Islamic wars in doubt, its control over its Muslim client states uncertain. Nothing Israel is likely to do looks workable in the long run. The demographics are terrible, regional Arab hostility assured, the military balance only able to deteriorate, the whole enterprise hanging by a lobby. I remember thinking about the Soviet Union, "This can't last." I couldn't see how it could stop lasting either. It did stop. Unless something changes, and I don't have any bright ideas, I don't see a happy ending.

40 THE PRICE OF HONOR: I'D RATHER PLAY MARBLES

I read that America must find an "exit strategy" from Iraq that will bring "peace with honor." My God. Honor? I'd rather have infected hemorrhoids. These at least are not a mental aberration. Well, depending on where your head is.

Honor means nothing more than prickly infantile vanity dressed up, usually, in desperate class-consciousness. Of all the symptoms of a weak ego, honor is the most embarrassing, and the most harmful. In a right-minded society it would be made a capital offense. (In women honor usually means chastity, also a bad idea but not nearly as pernicious.)

I do not mean to rail against the virtues, manly or otherwise. A few of them seem to have merit. Courage is doubtless admirable, at least when not engaged in by criminals or ambitious soldiers. Loyalty to friends in the face of adversity is to be commended. Common decency has its allure and occasional practitioners. Honesty? I think it worth trying, though with care until we ascertain its effects. But honor? It is a sure indication of a bad character.

Consider its usual display throughout history. A duke or baron, or some such befeathered artifact of excessive inbreeding, encounters another, a count perhaps, or more likely a no-count, who is in a bad mood. This latter says, "Yomama, Monsieur. Your granny wears combat boots."

Whereupon the duke, instead of saying, "Oh buzz off, Lancaster, before I York a knot on your head"—this would be sensible and therefore inadmissible in affairs of honor—takes off his glove and throws it on the ground. This benefits dry cleaners, though a man with one glove looks eccentric. Anyway, this constitutes a Challenge, more to common sense than anything else.

And so the Duke and the Count meet on the Field of Honor, in the manner of small boys settling a dispute on the playground after school, but with more gauds and glitter. A duke disposes of greater resources than does a third-grader, though this may be the only distinction. After fulsome precedent ceremony, they fight with swords, suggesting grave inner dimness, until one pokes the other, who thereafter waits for peritonitis to set in. The survivor stalks off with the ostentatious pride of a swamp bird in mating season, his honor satisfied.

Smarter people would settle quarrels by playing marbles, I think.

Now, credit where credit is due. Most often, the code duello approach to honor served to rid society of men it would be better off without. A country can prosper without dukes, while a strike by the plumbers would be disastrous.

But sometimes the effects of aggrieved vanity were actually deleterious. In 1832, Evariste Galois, a preternaturally talented French mathematician, died in a duel at age twenty, fortunately having invented the theory of groups beforehand. His was an extraordinarily unuseful foray into the practice of honor. What might he have done had he insisted on marbles? Honor has a high price.

Military men are particularly susceptible to notions of honor, and should be indoctrinated against it in their formative years. They employ it largely as a veil covering their actual business, which has generally consisted in killing, raping, burning, and pillaging, in putting cities to the sword, massacring the unwilling conscripted peasants of the opposing army, and generating widows, orphans, and prisoners for the slave trade.

None of this would seem particularly honorable if examined carefully, so it carefully isn't. The soldierly focus is on teary-eyed memories of fallen comrades, on the bravery of the cavalry at Balaclava or of the leather-jacketed bomber crews who burned a hundred thousand civilians to death per night, and such like.

The infantilism undergirding honor can be seen in the game of chicken. This curious parallel to aristocratic bloodletting was played decades ago by brooding teenagers with ducktail haircuts and a pack of Camels rolled into the shoulders of their tee-shirts. One adolescent duelist-in-waiting would insult another in some mortal manner. "Yer a yellow-belly Yankee," perhaps, or "You're a four-eyed sissy." The other, experiencing a hormone surge frequently confused with a call of honor, accepts the challenge to play chicken. They're going to settle it man to man, though emotionally they belong in diapers.

So they meet in their cars at night on a deserted stretch of road, each with friends as witnesses and supporters (exactly like nominally adult duelists with their pistols and seconds: there is no difference). The witnesses get out and the antagonists, facing each other from behind the wheels of their cars at a distance of perhaps a mile, race furiously at each other like rutting mountain sheep. The idea is that whoever swerves to avoid a collision is a coward, and thus besmirched. Of course they then both survive, and can continue trying to tap the cheerleaders.

Here is the very essence of honor, an engorged, all-consuming vanity, a willingness to die for one's ego. Marbles, I insist. Much better.

This irrational behavior finds a place in international affairs. In fact, it comes close to being international affairs. One sees it often in the unwillingness of countries (read: psychological short men in charge of countries) to back down when nothing important is at stake, or to cut their losses when hobbyist wars go awry.

As noted, today our thunder-thump patriots say that we must find an honorable exit strategy from Iraq. This means that if we can't steal the oil, we can at least pretend we won the war gloriously. Again, honor is ego: We aren't going to swerve. Better that we bankrupt the country, fill the hospital wards with paraplegic and blind teenagers, kill who-cares-how-many Iraqis, than blink. Mine is longer than yours. It is, it is, it is.

Honor is a protective device for people whose self-esteem needs protection. Picture some archduck in England—actually "archduck" was a typo, but I think it better conveys the sense. Anyway, this gorgeous trinket of chivalry, which is itself a loathsome hotbed of honor, probably has twelve toes from more intermarriage than a holler in West Virginia, and a thistle-down intelligence, and the self-reliance of a queen ant. He is a monument to non-hybrid unvigor.

How does he protect his etiolated parsnip-like self-esteem from some village kid named, oh, say, Newton, who would regard him as the intellectual equivalent of a turnip? Easy. He invokes his honor. Defensive vanity. "A mere commoner. Pish." Elevated nose, depressed intelligence.

None of this is necessary. Perhaps the greatest military thinkers in history are Fredwitz and James P. Coyne, in that order. Dr.

Coyne's proposed exit strategy is simple: "OK, on the plane. Now." Should this seem unfathomable by its complexity, it could be reduced to four words. But no. What general, what president who has said "Mission accomplished," is going to admit that it didn't work so well? We must leave with honor. Not necessarily with all our body parts, or all the soldiers we came with, but with honor.

41 FRED IN THE CARIBBEAN

This Fred, he obviously ain't got the sense God give a crabapple. With writers, it doesn't matter.

The world is indeed too much with us, late and soon. We have too many contracts and iPods and too little time or calm for looking about. One readily forgets this amid blatting buses and blowing exhaust and sprinting for the subway, amid bills and commercials and forms to fill. Yet still there are things other than elections and recessions, maybe things even more important, certainly things that have been around longer than we have or will be.

Some years back I was on a scuba trip to the Caribbean with Capital Divers, my then dive club out of Washington. I forget just where we were. We made these trips annually for several years and they blur together. The club usually chartered one of those 125-foot or so specialized dive boats and spent most of our time underwater. Dive, burgers, beer, sleep, dive. Bright sun, blue water, explosion of bubbles as you stepped off the dive deck and finned at ten feet to the anchor line. Cool water leaking into wetsuits and running down your spine. More bursts of bubbles with a diver magically materializing from within.

One day we swam along a deep wall at 120 feet, maybe fifteen of us, the sea dropping below us to blue-black night and the wall colorless in the crepuscular dimness of depth. It was deeper than a basic instructor would recommend, but Cap Divers was a bit of a cowboy outfit, and everyone was experienced. Curling misshapen growths of deep water projected from the rock like tangled ropes and distorted cups in some nightmarish basement. The only sounds were the slow sssssssss-wubbawubba of breath and exhaust and the locationless clicking of arthropods.

A curious relaxation comes over you at such times, a sense of not mattering at all to the sea, of the world as an older and bigger place than Washington or even New York, of detachment from fizzing little wars of columnists and from pols and polls. Call it a salubrious triviality. If I could bottle the feeling, drug markets would wither overnight.

In a hundred thousand years, if we do not manage to poison the seas, the deep walls will not have changed. That is a long time, longer even than the life span of the most august of brokerage houses. Permanent we are not, and will not be noticed in the long span of time. A soothing thought, that.

Those droning nature shows on television say that the ocean is hostile to man. I think it is not, though it is a bad place to make mistakes. The ocean is a huge, huge world that doesn't care about us, isn't interested, has other things to do. You see documentaries that try to make sharks sound dreadful. In fact they do not seem to regard as food a weird humpbacked creature with one big eye and emitting bubbles. In murky water they will sometimes make a run at a diver and then veer off when they see what it is they were attacking. Few creatures underwater are hostile to people. Yes, odd things swim or flap or drift by, but usually pay no attention. They have their agendas, and we have ours.

You can wonder what God or Darwin had in mind. Whatever goes on at corporate, it is well above our pay grade.

I forget who I was buddied up with, but she stopped and hung, fascinated, with her mask over a big barrel sponge. A small diver could crawl into some of these things. She motioned me over. In the glow of dive lights I saw a bright red arrow crab sheltering. At that depth a dive light makes everything it touches burst into color as if you were throwing paint at it. Color gets filtered out rapidly as you descend, leaving only a wan lifeless blue. It turns the growth on walls to ugly and dark grays and browns.

The beastie was built like an aspirin tablet with great long jointed legs, a daddy longlegs of the ocean. It stalked slowly about, puzzled by our lights I suppose. I wondered what it thought it was doing, or we were doing. Seeing these odd confections at home is not like seeing them on television, with some tedious voice-major reading fourth-grade platitudes about mysteries he doesn't begin to understand. He doesn't even know that they are mysteries. Maybe we spend too much time in the suburbs.

The sea is a dead world, though living. In a forest you can imagine communing with the deer or squirrels or having a pet bird sit on your shoulder. The land is our world. The sea isn't. Fish swim slowly by, eyes cold and devoid of thought, of anything we would grasp. Few things can be as dull and empty, as stupid, as the eyes of fish, though news anchors come close. For untold millions of years they—the fish— have done this, and will. I do not think that even a renegotiation of NAFTA can change it.

Below a hundred feet you don't have much time before your computer squeaks warnings about going into decompression tables. With single tanks we didn't have air enough for deco stops and anyway it is tedious spending half an hour hanging of a down-line. We were starting to drift our way upward when they came by, three of them: Big dark rays, flying in formation. Their wingspan may have been four feet. It is hard to tell with the magnifying effect of water. People describe rays as oceanic bats, as flying bathmats, but these don't catch the smooth rippling flexing flap of soft chilly flesh. A marine biologist would class them as elasmobranches, in-laws of sharks, the clinical jargon giving an impression of infinite understanding. The marine biologist would be wrong. Rays are…God knows what, but nothing Greco-latinate.

We had all seen rays before, but this was prettier, a privilege, and we knew it. I cannot explain how anything so ugly as a ray can be so lovely, but they manage it. I have heard them called devil fish by people of the surface, but they are as ominous as potatoes. They passed us, graceful, fast, as if going somewhere with a purpose in mind. And disappeared. We chased them a bit, knowing the futility but doing it anyway. A garden slug might as profitably chase a whippet. I felt like a mouse in a computer room: Something was going on, but it wasn't my business.

We stared—programmers, GS-14s, journalists, graduate students, all the detritus of Washington—and resumed our ascent. Our computers were becoming importunate. Underwater, one does not ignore computers.

42 WHAT HAVE THE BASTARDS DONE TO MY COUNTRY?

Oh god. It's getting worse. Everything. I knew it would. Death and taxes are long shots by comparison.

So I'm in Washington, a federal enclave, as someone said, surrounded on all four sides by reality. This was supposed to be a medical trip to have vital internal organs pawed, sliced, and injected with strange fluids. Kidneys, carburetor, remaining brain, that sort of thing. But this is Washington. Horrors everywhere.

Hillary. I don't hate Hillary. She's smart, tough, sane, been around, corrupt, and personally repellent as a fanged garden slug. By today's standards, that's a bargain.

But why the hell is she Secretary of State? How many years has she spent abroad? What languages does she speak? What does she know about the street in Karachi, Cairo, Guadalajara? She probably thinks Mumbai is what you eat with a RC Cola.

See, what's happened is that we are ruled by an incestuous bridge club clucking to itself in what amounts to a thermos bottle. Hillary is SecState because Precedent O'Bama wants to heal rifts within the Democratic Party. It would make more sense to poison the lot, but never mind. Everything is about domestic politics. And these dismal retreads promote each other in circles. Hillary goes from governor's wife to First Basilisk to senator to SecState. Oh help.

Same with Cuba. The good of the country doesn't matter. We gotta keep the rubes gurgling with delight. That's all that counts. The US continues to make itself loathed in Latin America, in substantial part because of that stupid embargo. Why? Because a noisy rabble of pseudo-Cuban losers in Miami votes Republican. But of course it doesn't matter what the rest of the world thinks. All those funny little countries around the world really don't have anything we need, except our economy, and China will give us visas to visit our industry. Perhaps.

And then there's this business of having a black president. It seemed like a good idea. We've had white ones forever and it hasn't worked, so a black one made sense. We have now established that a black president is exactly like a white one. Next time, maybe a Melanesian or Lao. I hoped O'Bama would stand in the Rose Garden and holler, "You blue-eyed muhfuhs done got it all wrong, and I'm gonna unscrew things." No. Smart guy, decent guy, guy you could heist a brew with and tell dirty stories, but it's business as usual. Same tired hacks.

I think I know why. Inexperience. Ponder his relation to the Five-Sided Wind Tunnel on the Potomac. I spent thirty years covering the military and I know all the Pentagon's songs. O'Bama doesn't. He missed Vietnam, wasn't in the military, hasn't had much to do with generals or soldiers. It's not his fault and it isn't a character defect, but there it is.

So in walks Power Point Petraeus, back from bombing weddings in Afghanistan. Power Point is impressive. I've never met him, but I've met plenty of identical units. Erect posture, firm handshake, carefully deferential enough but you can just tell he's strong and reliable. And he can sling the lingo ("Ohhhh, I love it when you talk that way.") with the stern honesty of an overgrown Boy Scout and the guile of a serpent, and he's patriotic to the gills and he's got charts.

And O'Bama doesn't know better. So Afghan brides will continue to need Kevlar dresses.

Meanwhile, things get loonier on the street. I went to Johns Hopkins in Baltimore from DC by train and, so help me, they're doing the same garish security theater on trains that they do at hairports. Cops and German Shepherds everywhere. To buy a freaking commuter-rail ticket, you need a photo ID, and they type heaven knows what into a computer.

Okay, suppose I show up at the Obedience Training window with my suitcase full of Semtex, buy my ticket with my own ID or any ID with a balding ugly mutt on it—they barely look at it—and blow the 9:07 MARC to metallic sawdust. After the fact they assemble my shards, check the computer, and determine that It Must Have Been Fred. This miraculously brings the dead back to life. Bet you didn't know I had such powers.

None of it makes sense, except as Pavlovian conditioning. Every few minutes a tedious recording plays in stations saying to call some number if you see suspicious behavior. Blah blah blah. No one pays the least attention. No one writes the number down.

Has anyone ever called it?

"Uh, I want to report suspicious behavior."

Voice, annoyed at having the Redskins game interrupted: "Yeah, what?"

"Well, there's like, this guy, he has a funny looking raincoat and he keeps, you know, looking around, and I think his left hand is twitching."

"Uh...yeah. Tell him to stop twitching."

"What if he, you know, blows up or something?"

"What am I, your mother?"

I don't get it. Something is happening to this country. It still has a lot going for it—friendly people, great diners, good blues, country bands, widespread availability of illegal drugs. But the government is out of control. Everything is illegal and watched. It's getting so you can't shoot cats from a car window with a twelve-gauge any more. Who wants to live in that kind of world? We'll probably be overrun by cats, drown in them.

Today I went to the Hill to see the new Visitors Center. As usual, cops everywhere, squad cars parked on sidewalks, steel stop'em-cars plates rising from streets. People don't seem frightened, but the government is, or pretends to be.

The Visitors Center turns out to be underground at the Capitol. It is said to have cost $621 million temporarily deflated green ones and has the mental fingerprints of Albert Speer all over it: It's huge, drab, squarish, monumental without even being imposing, with the élan of a K-Street office building.

I don't get it. This is the country that produced Peggy Lee and Tampa Red and the 'fitty-sedden Chevy, the country that spits techno-whizz golf carts onto Mars just like it was even possible, that brought the hamburger to gorgeous bejuiced perfection and invented most of the modern world. It's the home of sand-lot baseball and Little Peggy March and BB guns and Tasty Freeze. It is, in a phrase, one fine place.

How did it sink to being a proto-Soviet surveillance state that builds vast awful Visitor Centers in the style of a Hitlerian mausoleum? You can't go to the john without a photo ID anymore. Something ain't right.

43 ZOOMING AND BOOMING FOR THE SHEER HELL OF IT

OK, today I'm going to tell you everything you need to know about air power. You will never need to read anything else. These revelations will provide blinding insight into our current wars. Here we go. Hold on.

The key: Air power is really good for things it is really good for, but works lousily for things it doesn't work well for. (If "lousily" wasn't a word, it is now.)

The foregoing is genius incarnate, and would revolutionize military thinking if the Air Force understood it, which it doesn't. As is usual with our late-simian species, the fly-guys' motivations are instinctual and emotional, with reason a pretext slathered on afterwards and accountability a no-show.

Now, it is chic among Military Reformers and other fern-bar Clausewitzes to say wisely that air power is impotent and useless and accomplishes nothing. This is not true. In its own kind of war, it works splendidly. Often it is the only thing that could. Anyone who thinks that airplanes are pointless gewgaws should talk, say, to Japanese survivors of the Coral Sea and Midway, or of Yamato's death run.

See, what airplanes are good at is blowing up expensive, visible, identifiable things, to include other airplanes. An aircraft carrier in the open Pacific fits the bill nicely. You can't hide aircraft carriers very well. They don't look like anything else. Even a Marine pilot would never mistake one for an olive orchard, or the cathedral at Chartres, or the Gobi Desert. They just don't look the same. With enough bombing runs, an airplane can hit a carrier, which reduces the number of enemies instead of increasing it.

What air power isn't good at is fighting guerrillas and insurgents, especially in populated areas. Why? Lots of reasons. First, pilots have no idea what they are bombing. They are flying at three hundred miles an hour over countries, often obscured by trees, in which everybody looks exactly like everybody else. So they guess, or bomb where the intelligence children tell them are terrorists. (That was almost a sentence.)

Now, the word "intelligence" sounds much better than "bureaucratized clandestine confusion," which is more accurate. The intelligence agencies have enshrouded themselves in an aura of inexorable usually fatal infallibility. ("My name is Bond...Fred Bond.") This is good PR. It is little else.

These are the same intelligence agencies, remember, that didn't know where the Japanese fleet was in 1941 despite rumblings of war, agencies that were taken by surprise by the North Korean attack in 1950, and then by the Chinese entry into that war, that didn't anticipate the behavior of the Vietnamese in that war, despite Bernard Fall's books and the highly documented experience of the French. When the military made a well-executed raid into Hanoi to free American prisoners at Son Tay, the intel people hadn't noticed that the prisoners had been moved. They were surprised when the Berlin Wall went up, and when it came down. They failed to foresee the collapse of the Soviet Union. (Their reason for existence was to know about the Soviet Union.) They missed on 9/11. Earlier, when the Air Force bombed the Chinese embassy in Belgrade, it was because the spooks didn't know where the embassy was that day. (Granted, embassies are hard to locate. They roll about on wheels, creep down alleys at night, and wear dark-colored clothing, that sort of thing.) The intel weenies also didn't foresee the behavior of either Iraqis or Afghans, despite great archives of historical evidence (unless you think the US knew about these upcoming messes and invaded anyway). And so on.

These are the geniuses picking targets. You see the problem.

Now, we read a lot of PR about "surgical strikes" and "precision weapons." Think carefully about this. Intel says a terrorist leader of indescribable potency is in a house in a flimsily constructed suburb. The Air Force then makes a surgical strike with a five-hundred-pound bomb, taking out half a block. Pretty surgical, that. Perhaps it was the right block—it is possible—but still kills seventy-five people. The male relatives of the dead then join the insurgency. Ray-rah air power. The Air Force can't afford to understand this, as then it would have to find a day job.

So why does the Air Force engage in counterproductive tactics with totally inappropriate airplanes? Because it's the only kind of airplanes it has. Why? Because fast, screaming, roaring, flashy zoom-buggies with lots of screens and switches and rockets are fun. Never, ever underestimate fun as a driver of military policy. A hot fighter is the world's pizzazziest, priciest, swooshiest video game, an air-borne dirt bike with all the fixin's. Really. You may think I'm trying to be snotty and clever. Think again. (All right, I'm trying to be snotty and clever, but what I'm saying is still true.)

Do you think I spent thirty years covering the military because I wanted to butcher puzzled third-world illiterates tending goats? No. It was fun. Low-level pop-and-drops in an F-16 out of Shaw AFB, F-15 air-to-air against Guard A-7s over Holloman, bomb runs at four hundred feet over hazy Wyoming badlands like the doorway to hell in a B-52—god, what a freaking trip, far better than growing up. Snazzy mask and helmet, five-g turns with your face flowing back behind your ears, world going inverted, burners kicking in…Hoo-ah!

It's not called a joy stick for nothing.

And jet jocks get paid to do this. Whether it serves a practical purpose doesn't matter. Not with rides like those. If you think these things don't matter, you are out of your mind.

However, the glory days are coming to a close. Fighter guys are now in the position of cavalry in 1914, addicted to the Noble Horse but, in an age of machine guns, wire entanglements, and massed artillery, as viable as slide rules in Santa Clara. The reason is the armed drone, the Predator being a good example. These things now have the range, optronics, data links, and so on to carry serious missiles to hit the wrong targets and piss off entire populations as well as real horses—fighter planes, I meant to say—can. They are lots cheaper than piloted whiz-gizmos, and a bloodless unaccountable CIA geek in Colorado or wherever can fly them. Same stupid effect, but none of the fun. Call it anti-chivalry. Death by nerds without souls.

In a century we've gone from Baron von Richthofen to a dinosaur eyeing a thin crust of ice forming on his swamp and thinking, "This can't be good."

See? Now you understand air power.

44 WINTERING: AN INCOHERENT INTERLUDE WITH THE ELITE

AJIJIC, MEXICO—On the north shore of Lake Chapala, in the depths of a Mexican winter. It is cold, hellishly cold. Sometimes a tee-shirt isn't enough. We may have to eat the neighbors if the temperature drops ninety degrees. It could be the Donner party all over.

When life hangs on a thread—I sense that this column isn't going to be obsessively organized. This could be the result of residual pharmaceuticals from decades back. Or Padre Kino red, or some shift in the earth's magnetic field. I don't know. Details can wait. You have to deal with whatever state of consciousness you find yourself in.

Anyway, when life hangs on a thread, you can't afford mistakes. In mid-afternoon we went to Tom's Bar, which is never a mistake—me, my quietly wise-ass stepdaughter Natalia, and my wife Violeta who sings Aida while driving. If you are going to freeze to death, do it in good company, I say. The girls are splendid co-conspirators in any plot. Tom's is the center of hemispheric intellectual, cultural, and social life. It is where everyone goes who is anybody.

More correctly, everyone who isn't anybody, but this is a much better crowd. I mean, who would you rather talk to, Alaskan bush pilots and Navy fighter jocks, guys from the oil rigs and fishing fleets, disreputable writers peddling lies and distortion to unprincipled editors—or some bubble-brained socialite in one of those wretched Georgetown cocktail herds?

Tom's was bleak, though. Instead of NASCAR or the NFL playoffs, all the televisions had some guy being enthroned as president of the US. It was awful. I can stand singing commercials for toilet paper. I once watched a half hour of Oprah and recovered, though with psychic scars. But twelve hours of embarrassing imperial pomp, chattered about by boringly dressed dullardesses with the intelligence of catfish? A freaking coronation with everything except inbred hemophiliac nobles?

In a sane world, a president would sign in online. User ID,

password, bingo, he's president, spare me the media circus. Why involve the rest of us? When I get a new job, I don't need a $150-million parade that blocks the streets everywhere. It's a sign of a defective character.

In fact we could probably do a president in software, and save the upkeep on that funny-looking double-wide on Pennsylvania Avenue. Server space is cheap these days. Little processing power would be needed to simulate the average president. An abacus would probably do it.

Anyway, Tom's. The place is a monument to the familiar and comfortable. It's like a worn leather bomber jacket you've had for years. There's nothing really special about the jacket. You could get a fancier one at a store in Houston for gay cowboys for a thousand rapidly rotting green dollars. But you like the jacket because you're used to it. It works—stops the wind, mosquitoes can't bite through it. You like the Air Force patch, "Ad Astra per Scrotum" on the shoulder. That's Tom's. Good music running to blues and rock, fine chili and wings, bartenders you know. No lobbyists.

Anyway, I claim comfortable familiarity is in short supply in too many places. I knew all manner of restaurants and bars around Washington, but none of them was mine. At Tom's you feel like you are going into your own living room. That's how it should be. That's how it is in English pubs and a lot of corner joints in Chicago. No bartender in these places ever says, "Hi! I'm Luis, and I am so happy that you chose to patronize Tom's, and I'm going to be your wait-person today, and you just call me if you need anything, ooooh!" This is important as it probably saves me from a murder charge.

On the lobotomy box the babble-blondes kept nattering on like concussed parrots about how wonderful it was that we had a black president. Oh God, I thought, spare me. I mean, so what? So he's black. Lots of guys are black. It's a pretty common thing, really. He isn't a freak, an unexplained natural phenomenon, just some guy who probably couldn't find a better job so he took what he could get. I mean, if we had elected, say, a giant fronded barnacle from a geothermal vent, then, sure, I'd want to hear about it. For at least five minutes. Or maybe if we chose a hitherto-unknown tube worm. Though I grant we came pretty close last time. What's the big deal about a black guy?

I figured a black president couldn't possibly be worse than the white ones. This O'Bama guy hadn't done anything terrible yet. Good as any, better'n some. OK, I figured, we've done that. Now can we watch NASCAR? I like looking at really fast Japanese cars.

Tom's in fact belongs to Tom. You've heard of Caesar's in Las Vegas? It's a fraud. Caesar isn't even on the board. He died even before the Beatles started singing, but they don't tell you that. Tom is an actual person (photo entered in evidence). Good guy, checkered past, really nice Mexican wife, three swell kids, dog till somebody poisoned her.

Dogs. (I told you this wasn't going to be coherent,) Tom's policy is that if you have a civilized dog and it wants to curl up under the table while you fertilize your dendritic pathways with elixir of grape, that's fine. I like this. I grew up with dogs and preferred them to most people. They never drive while talking on cell phones or say "Have a nice day!" like gurgling metrosexual smiley-faces. There's a Weimeraner the size of a small burro that occasionally wanders into Tom's. Perfectly good dog.

Once I looked up and a horse had its head in the door. Its owner had ridden to Tom's and parked, and I guess the horse wondered what was inside. So it stuck its head in to see. It's what I would have done.

Some of the local gringas get their skivvies in a knot over, ewwwww, dogs. These feral drabs, who may really have come from a geothermal vent, probably having been asked to leave, seem to think it their mission to remake Mexico in the image of the US. This is the principle of American foreign policy writ small. You know how well that works.

In a notorious case one of these militant frumps began hollering "Get that dog out!" The reasonable response, which I was not there to make, was that if she didn't like Tom's, she needed to find another bar, and better yet, another country. Actually the reasonable response would have been to hit her on the head with a table.

In any event she demanded her tip back from the bartender, and went storming out. Given a choice of dogs, I would have preferred the Weimeraner. He is a mannerly beast.

45 ASLEEP AT THE WHEEL: THE US BECOMES WHAT IT WASN'T

The Pentagon, methinks, is out of control. We no longer have a military in service to the state, but a state in service to the military. Few notice (I suspect) because of two ingrained habits of mind.

First, we think of the President as just that, the President, the country's civilian governor who, oh yeah, is technically the Commander-in-Chief. "Technically," because he isn't really in the military and doesn't strut about in a uniform with ribbons and feathers. He seems more a CEO than a general.

Second, we tend to think of the military as a federal department under civilian control. The Pentagon carries out policy, we believe, but doesn't make it.

Would it were so. The military today is hardly under civilian control. Note that Congress long ago gave up its power to declare war. This is crucial. Politically it is far safer to acquiesce in a war than to declare one.

In practical terms, the checks and balances in the Constitution no longer restrain the Commander-in-Chief, and thus not the soldiery. (The Supreme Court has become a mausoleum. It might be replaced by a wax museum without anyone's noticing.) The Pentagon is now the private army of any president who chooses so to use it.

Our foreign policy has been militarized. This is not just a matter of countless alliances and bases abroad. A few days ago, the military attacked Syria. This, an act of war, was a result not of national but of military policy. So far as I know, the attack was neither ordered nor authorized by Congress. The soldiers do as they please, and we find out about it later. This is not civilian control.

Such occurrences are inevitable when the military controls policy. Soldiers are truculent by nature, think quickly of military solutions, and need enemies to justify both their existence and their budget. Among recent consequences: attacking Syria, occupying Iraq and Afghanistan, bombing Pakistan, bombing Somalia, threatening Iran, threatening North Korea, encouraging Israel to bomb Beirut, arming Georgia, and aggressively expanding NATO to encircle Russia.

Ominously, we now accept that the behavior of the armed forces is none of our business. Note the years of expectancy as we waited to see whether the Commander-in-Chief, a de facto six-star general, would attack Iran.

I suspect that few realize how militarized the United States itself has become. The transformation has been inconspicuous. The Pentagon avoids undue attention. Quietly it has expanded its reach.

Abolishing the draft was an important step, since it severed any connection between the upper levels of society and the armed forces. The educated don't much care what the army does as long as they don't have to help do it.

The economy also has been militarized. Although the United States has no national enemies, it spends phenomenally on a martial empire whose only purpose is to be a martial empire. Add up the "defense" budget (it was last used for defense in 1945), the war bills, black programs, Veterans Administration's budget, on and on, and you reach a trillion dollars a year. A country in decline cannot long waste so much money. Perhaps as important, the military cannot spend so much without gaining great if unnoticed political power. In particular, the production of hugely pricey weapons has been woven into the economy to such an extent that it cannot be brought under control. Cancel the F22, the JSF, and suchlike, and the economies of politically powerful states go into recession. None dare do it. Close big bases? Whole towns would shut down.

The country has no need of such a military, and especially not of the formidably costly weapons. Having no plausible enemy of any sophistication, the Pentagon exercises itself by attacking primitive nations in the Third World, and usually losing. For this you do not need an F22. You could lose as well with slingshots.

The spectacle of an alleged superpower struggling to beat yet another collection of ragtag guerrillas may seem darkly comical, but winning or losing isn't the point; the endless wars keep the contracts flowing, the promotions coming, and fuel demands for a larger army.

We would do well to bear in mind the dangers of excessive military influence in national life. Professional soldiers have little in common with the rest of the country. We like to think of them as Our Boys in Uniform, the brave and the true and the patriotic, defenders of democracy, and so on. It isn't so. The officer corps is authoritarian to the roots of its soul, has little use for democracy, and prides itself on blind obedience. Soldiers do not readily distinguish between dissent and treason. Further, they regard civil society as an unworkable anarchy of weaklings who lack the will to fight.

The gap between military and civilian consciousness is huge. The ideal officer goes to a service academy where, in late and impressionable adolescence, he learns to walk in squares, always obey, and regard the polish of his belt buckle with insane concern. Thereafter the only answer he knows is "Yessir." To a civilian, the conformism, the lack of independence and, yes, the pride in the lack are incomprehensible. Then, for thirty years, the soldier spends most of his time with similar people and comes to believe that it is not just a reasonable but the best way to live. Like cops, soldiers tend to socialize among themselves because they fit awkwardly into civil society. Watch a colonel at a civilian cocktail party. He isn't sure whether he is "Sir" or "Bob."

And soldiers seek war. They will say they don't, of course. Can you imagine Tiger Woods spending thirty years practicing his golf swing without wanting to get into a tournament?

The military mindset is not American, not consonant with the ideals the country stands for and to some extent achieves. Most imperfectly, yet genuinely, America has cherished dissent and eccentricity and freedom. Yes, I know about the intolerance of small towns and I grew up in the South. But compare America at its worst to any military dictatorship.

Which is where we seem to be heading. Today the Pentagon—again, Mr. Bush is the Pentagon—openly seeks domestic power. For example, (this from Salon) Army combat troops will now be 'assigned on a permanent basis to engage in numerous domestic functions—including, as the article put it, "to help with civil unrest and crowd control."' That is, the Pentagon will be able to crush dissent. One expects this from Guatemala, which we seem bent on becoming.

Recall further that the Pentagon has been calling for the power to conduct domestic surveillance of the general population, as for example in its program of Total Information Awareness. The NSA, CIA, the Commander in Chief are all military or paramilitary, and Homeland Security is very much in the vein of military dictatorships everywhere. The new rights of the FBI to spy on everything from library records to habits of travel fit the pattern well. The FBI is not military but its behavior is authorized by the Commander-in-Chief. The lines are blurring.

We are going to pay for this.

46 BRAIN ROT, APHASIA, AND GOD KNOWS WHAT

Damn. The longer I live in Mexico, the more I realize that I know less about it than people who don't. Apparently it is a far simpler country than the one I live in, being summed up by pat assertions, neat statistics, and confident descriptions often bearing little resemblance to anything I see. Curious: Almost everyone who comes down here responds, "This isn't what I expected." To understand Mexico, it seems important to do so from somewhere else. Things are so much clearer that way.

I am part of an internet list of people who take a very dark view of Mexico, in many ways justified, but in many ways not. In particular, members of the list, like most of America, cannot conceive that there might be any intelligent life at all in Mexico. A couple of my (slightly edited) postings:

"We [my wife and I] dropped the car off at the Toyota dealership and to pass the time we walked to Plaza del Sol, a majorly upscale shopping center in the suburbs of Guad. In it is one of the Gonvill chain of bookstores hereabouts. There are many.

Wandering around, I noticed a book called Fundamentals of Circuit Analysis—shrink-wrapped, but I'd guess about 600 pages of circuit analysis. Next to it was Elements of Electronic Design or something very close to that title, and many other such. A substantial pile of Differential and Integral Calculus was at eye level, both the height and pile suggesting that the store expected them to sell. Countless high school books—Biology I and II, etc at length—were there for kids going to private schools. (They feature purines and pyrimidines, the genetic code, and suchlike primitivism. Thanks to ex-president Vicente Fox, public school students get their books free.)

I saw shelf sections labeled Physiology, Anatomy, Biostatistics, Surgery, etc. Wandering by the computer section, I saw many titles such as "Data Structures and Algorithms in Java," and Network Design, as well as inevitables such as C++ and Visual Studio. The store not being specifically technical, literature outnumbered tech stuff.

Most of the lit you would find in a Border's was there: Dusty Evsky, Twain, Kafka, all that, plus odd titles like Dracula in Acapulco. Authors were well-covered. For example, I counted 12 books by Mario Benedetti who, like a lot of South American authors, gringos have never heard of. There were Elements of Esthetics, biographies of Mozart etc, books of paintings of the Ashcan School and such, books of all the usual philosophers. All of this was in Spanish. It was not a store for pale bwanas. There were plenty of people looking at the books. I was the only gringo.

Now, Mexico [according to the computer list on which I posted this] has a mean IQ of 85. That at any rate we are told. So do American blacks. Does this compute? Show me a bookstore in America primarily patronized by blacks with these titles. This doesn't make sense, boys and girls. IQ is supposed to predict outcomes. It appears not to.

I note that yesterday my family went to the local dental office, consisting of Hector Haro (he's on the web) and three dentists, all female, trained at U. Guad. (Haro did postgrad in prosthdontics at U Md.) He has another seven or so girl dentists working for him in Guadalajara. Modern equipment, absolutely competent as far as I can tell, speak English (how many US students speak a language learned without leaving the US, or at all?).

I read Steve Sailer on Mexico and expect to wake up in the morning and find illiterate doctors curing people by sacrificing chickens. It ain't so. Somebody's wrong. Either American blacks could do these things if they weren't culturally disadvantaged, or the IQ business needs a bit of work under warranty. Take your pick.

'Nother posting: "Peter, I couldn't agree more. Permit me an eyeball rather than a numerical analysis [of Mexico's mediocre economic performance]: Academic fervor in Mexico is almost unknown. Years ago I walked home through poor sections of Taipei, and kids were at orange-crate desks in the alleys to avoid some of the heat, studying. Mexicans, kids and adults, regard studying as distasteful and regularly accuse those who study of being snots, stuck-up, thinking themselves superior, etc. It is an exact parallel of "You tryin'a be white."

Apart from my wife and stepdaughter, who genuinely are bookish, I have never seen a Mexican voluntarily read a book, or seen a book in a Mexican home. This applies to highly bright Mexicans, of whom there are a fair few. However, I live in a small, largely agricultural town. I'm not sure things would be a whole lot different in Waldorf, Maryland. The anti-intellectualism is a subset of valemadrismo, a word derived from "me vale madre," meaning "I don't give a shit."

It might be described as comprehensive half-assedness. It is a stew of lack of ambition, irresponsibility (as in not showing up on time, or at all, and not calling), of short time-horizons (they don't look ten years ahead), a preference for corruption over work, a focus on just getting by, a lack of interest in organized behavior (ignoring traffic laws, for example). No push, no drive, no plan. Whether all of this is a consequence of low intelligence might be discussed. But without reference to IQ, it is an adequate explanation. Incidentally, my wife agrees.

The astute reader might object that the two letters contradict each other. Perhaps, but they are accurate. A great many things in Mexico are contradictory, and many things gringos believe about the country are wrong. For example, many Americans believe that people here breed like oysters. Not so. The birth rate is wa-a-a-ay down. The stats show this. So does the eyeball. I know several women from families with ten or twelve siblings. They have two kids and want no more.

Many Americans believe that the Catholic Church bears responsibility for high fertility. No: Mexico is still Catholic and yet far less fertile, and it ain't rhythm, friends and neighbors. The radio station of U. Guadalajara regularly urges the young to use condoms.

Mexico is thought to be a macho country in which women are badly mistreated. It certainly was. Watch Mexican movies from the thirties if you want to see the problem. Even a generation back girls weren't allowed to go far in school because their function was to abrir las patas, open their legs, and nothing more.

But you have to keep your eye on these things. Today my stepdaughter's prepa (part of the feeder system for U. Guad) is half girl, the university is loaded with girls, and I encounter lots of female lawyers, dentists, what have you. None of this is universal and among the poor, who are many, and in rural regions changes come much more slowly. But 1930 it isn't.

Mexico is said, horribly correctly, to have a very low average level of education. It's just a fact. From my bedroom window in the morning, I can see kids riding bareback into the mountains to care for goats. They don't go to school.. This isn't governmental policy, but it's how things are.

However, this bleakness is hardly universal. It might be surprising to look at the tenth-grade physics text of my stepdaughter, in the free Prepa in my small town. (fisica General, by Hector Perez Montiel.) A few outtakes:

p. 5 "Faraday enunciated the following principle: electromagnetic induction is the phenomenon that causes the production of an induced electric current by the variation of the magnetic flux due to relative movement of a conductor in a magnetic field

p. 76. (below; scanner busted, but you get the idea) "With the displacement of a motion as a function of time, we form the graph to the right and calculate the instantaneous velocity after six seconds. To calculate the instantaneous velocity at any moment, we draw a tangent to the curve at the point considered; taking two points on the tangent we determine the slope, which is to say, the instantaneous velocity." That, amigos, is differential calculus in vigorous embryo, and tolerable for the tenth grade. My translation is close to literal and a bit awkward in English, but it isn't in Spanish.

p. 63 "The vector product of two vectors, also called the cross product, gives as a result another vector which is always perpendicular to the plane formed by the multiplied vectors. By definition, the magnitude of the product vector is equal to the product of the magnitude of one by the perpendicular component of the other with respect to the first: $|a.b|$ = ab sin theta....." (Word doesn't do vector notation well.) Now, a college book would give the cross product in determinant form, [(i,j,k); (A(1), A(2), A(3); B(1), B(2), B(3)]. Maybe American high-school tests do this. The foregoing isn't altogether shameful, I wot.

p. 301, which I'm too lazy to re-scan, begins "Another interesting application of Bernouilli's Theorem...." It may be most Americans can handle all of this. I promise that Natalia can.

Further along, incidentally, I find explanations of Heisenberg Indetermimacy, the Pauli Exclusion Principle, and (simple) problems involving Plancks's Constant.

How badly does the above compare with an American high school in a small town? Maybe better, maybe worse, but we're not talking Haiti. But, hey, everybody knows more about this country than I do.

47 IS MCCAIN ABEL? ELECTING A HEAD CASE

I frankly don't believe John McCain's medical records, or at any rate the portions released to the <u>New York Times</u>. The man was held in solitary for years, tortured until bones fractured, until he confessed to war crimes, until he tried to hang himself.

That he broke can't be held against him: Almost anyone would have. (In my view GIs should be told to confess to anything whatever right from the start.) But the assertion that he came through unscathed, warm and humorous and psychically sound, just isn't plausible. It doesn't happen that way.

Now, PTSD. A lot of people, including vets, don't believe that PTSD exists. I didn't. One reason is that they tend to think of it as something verging on the psychotic, as for example seeing nonexistent snipers in the hedgerows of suburban Philadelphia. The other common notion is that those who have it dive under tables at the sound of a backfire. Vets tend to think, "I don't know anybody like that. I certainly don't see snipers in the rafters. This whole PTSD business sounds like a crock."

So it does. But it isn't.

And of course many people, chiefly men, regard with suspicion anything that smells of psychobabble, anything touchy-feely. To them PTSD sounds like Can't-Get-a-Date Personality Disorder—something for Oprah to talk about to bored housewives. So they dismiss it.

Let me de-babble the discussion and state a simple fact: A lot of guys come back from wars really, truly messed up in the head, and it doesn't go away. They aren't going to talk to you about it. They figure it's none of your goddamned business. If you push, they will tell you so, angrily.

If you weren't in those forsaken paddies, they think, if you didn't go through what they did, you're off their radar screens. They'll talk to you about football, the weather, and whatever happened in the newspaper yesterday. Just don't even try to talk about Viet Nam. Or whatever war it was. They don't want to think about it, and talking about it to weenies feels like being naked in a train station.

There are a lot of these brain-burnt guys out there. They don't want your pity. They don't pity themselves. They just don't want to expose that part of themselves to you. They put a wall around themselves. You can't see it. It's there.

Often they seem like fairly normal guys with three divorces who drink too much and their children say, "It was like he was somewhere else." Perfectly normal guys who have had seventeen jobs because their bosses are always useless bastards. Perfectly normal guys who live out in the desert and do serious scuba or hang glide because they just don't give a fuck.

Not all. Some manage to hold it together and become things thought to be respectable, such as senators or writers or defense attorneys. A subsurface lode of hostility can be useful in a trial lawyer. Anger is energizing. It can fuel a career.

With PTSD, or whatever you want to call it, the anger is the giveaway. These vets carry a load of subterranean fury that you don't want to look at. As they would say, I shit you not one pound. I know a lot of these guys. A buddy of mine—two tours in bad places, killed a whole lot of people up close-- now has no tolerance for frustration,. He's ready to spread your teeth over a wide radius if you even seem to think about getting in his face. Admirable? No. But don't make the experiment.

Sounds like McCain. His explosiveness is notorious.

Another guy I know, writer, freelanced all his life because he couldn't get along with people in offices. A writer can package this as sturdy independence, as being a colorful maverick. The fellow is approximately sane, or at least apparently sane. Get three drinks in him, bring up the war, and his voice starts shaking and it's time to change the subject right now.

A fair few PTSD guys become writers: It's solitary, you don't have to put up with bosses, and you don't have to be stable.

How do these vets get this way? Not by anything you want to hear about, anything that you will see on the nightly news. The RPG hits your tank, the cherry juice cooks off, and three of your buddies burn to death screaming because they couldn't get out fast enough. You lose a leg and half your face to a mortar round. You just see things: A Chicom 122 cuts a cyclo driver in half and you watch him trying to crawl with his guts hanging out. He doesn't crawl long. You get shot down over Hanoi and spend years being tortured. The military is a fun place. You have all sorts of unusual experiences.

It messes your head up. I promise.

I said anger—yes, but anger at what? At whom? Here I'm on soft ground because vets don't talk much about this stuff among themselves. At least those I know don't. But, to the extent that I am competent to judge, they aren't mad at those who shot them, or shot at them. "The VC were only doing their job." They hate those who sent them to a pointless war, who exposed them in thousands to Agent Orange, knowing that it was poisonous and carcinogenic, at those posing fat-ass pols who sent them to die for nothing while they ate prime rib in DC.

Or they just hate. Psychologically the verb can be intransitive. They don't know what they hate, but don't get in the way of it.

Not all respond this way. Some choose to intensify their patriotism—it avoids admitting that you have been suckered—and direct their hatred at the hippies, the liberals, the press, all of whom they figure lost the war. But the anger is still there. Most of the time, you don't notice it. They turn off, often seem emotionally cold. But that explosive venom remains. We're not talking about a fiery Irish temper. We're talking half crazy.

Those who seek help, typically from the VA, end up on Thissa-dol and Thatta-dol, on antidepressants and calmants and even antipsychotics. They sorta help. Sorta isn't good enough with men who control carrier battle groups.

From the New York Times story, "Mr. McCain also learned to control his temper and not to become angry over insignificant things, the doctors said." I don't believe it. It doesn't fit accounts of people who know him. It isn't how heads work.

McCain is well known for his violent and irrational temper. A friend of mine, Ken Smith, was flack for Governor Mecham of Arizona during a meeting with McCain. The governor somehow irritated McCain. Says Ken, "McCain was leaning forward with a clinched fist. I reached out my left arm, as politely and as non-threatening as I could, and I pushed McCain back. What I remember is how taut and hard his body was, not from working out and lifting weights, but rather from anger and adrenalin. I made an excuse to leave and get them apart."

For what he went through in Vietnamese jails he deserves sympathy and admiration. It isn't qualification for the presidency.

48 FRED THROWS SOMBRERO IN RING: THE ONLY THING WE HAVE TO BE AFRED OF IS FRED HISSELF

I see that I shall have to come out of retirement and become President. It is the only hope for the country and the world. That I am willing to undergo the humiliation of the office is a measure of the depth of my sense of duty. Though perhaps I will do it under an assumed name.

First things first. I will need a stirring bumper sticker, this being the key to high office. What? I'm considering "Fred! Piss Poor but Look at the Rest." Or "A Fred in Every Pot," or perhaps "Better Fred than Dead"? Or "Tippecanoe and Frederick Too." The possibilities are endless. In any event, election is a mere detail. Given the competition, the country will flock to my standard. Or wish it had.

Next I'll need some promises. How about :When in office, I will do the following wholesome things:

Education. Put a bounty on members of the teachers unions. The season will start with a week for bow hunters and black powder and then be open to all. No bag limit. Think stuffed heads over the mantle. "Ah, yes, Miss Grundy. I knew her well."

That accomplished, I will require a score of 1200 on the old SATs, before the dumbing-down, for teaching positions. I will then raise salaries until such people take the job. The schools today are in the hands of people too dim to know what schooling is, and resentful of people who have it or might want it. They remind me of vegetarian butchers: The whole concept doesn't work.

Then I will have everyone in the Department of Education strangled (possible electoral slogan: "Strangulation in the Common Interest"). Local governments will run their schools as they damned well please. Ha. Ha ha!

The military: I will support a constitutional amendment requiring that Congress declare all wars. (I know, but it doesn't work.) This would have spared us Korea, Vietnam, Iraq, and perhaps Afghanistan. The first urge of Congress is reelection, and the second, the avoidance of responsibility. They will never spawn a war they have to admit to.

Further (an old favorite of mine), I will require that the mothers of the graduating class at Harvard be strapped to the glacis plates of any tanks sent to foreign wars. Joan Baez will be my Chairman of the JCS. She's a decent woman, sane, and has a nice voice. I bet the incumbent can't sing at all.

Under my guidance, the military will assume a new mission of defending the United States rather than being a presidential hobby. I know: This is radical, but radical times require radical solutions.

I will put the defense contractors under Apple Computer. They will then beaver away making groovy if unnecessary gadgets to sell to bored teenagers. This will at least do no harm, and perhaps allow the US to compete with Japan in consumer electronics. Though I doubt it.

Energy. I will issue a cyanide pill to all Americans. When vines begin growing through the fan belts of the SUVs, because there is no gas, they will pop the pill. This will reduce the consumption of energy, and for that matter drop the population to a reasonable level—say, twenty people.

Suicide really is the only practical solution. Democracies have the foresight of retarded rabbits and never notice the inescapable, such as that the world's demand for oil grows and the supply doesn't. Anyone who points this out is called a commie, anti-market, un-American, a green, and accused of links to the Sierra Club.

Pills on the way.

Social policy. I will end affirmative action, zap. It does nothing but inspire division and resentment. Well, it also prevents its beneficiaries from doing anything to better themselves, since they don't have to. Like all federal do-goodery, it is a magnet for grifters, crooked lobbies, charlatans, shysters, and bus-station rabble. If you need affirmative action, you aren't good enough; if you if you are good enough, you don't need it; and if you take it anyway, you are a freeloader.

Foreign policy. I will end the embargo of Cuba. It's stupid, gives the US a terrible rep in Latin America, accomplishes nothing of use, and makes life hard for eleven million perfectly good Cubans. If the professional pseudo-Cubans in Miami object, I'll have the frauds freeze-dried and air-dropped on some starving country in Africa. (Possible slogan: "Every cloud has a protein lining.") Cannibalism gets a bum rap.

I will tell the Israelis to get back inside the 1967 borders, be a Jewish state, and shut up—especially the latter—or they will never see another American dollar or F16. I will then give the Palestinians exorbitant aid to build a country unless they attack Israel again, at which point I'll spray anthrax on the whole place. This probably won't work, but it has a better chance than anything else.

I pledge to end the lamebrain policy of looking for a war with Russia. The US has now put NATO, an anti-Russian military alliance, in the Baltics, on the Russian border; in Poland, on the Russian border, and is trying to bring Georgia, on the Russian border, into NATO. The US and NATO have large combat forces in Afghanistan, on the Russian border, and want to colonize it. Not smart. Think Canada, Mexico, and Cuba in the Warsaw Pact.

There are three levels of military stupidity: stupid, really and truly stupid, and war with Russia. Right now we're going for the brass ring.

I will bring the GIs home from Korea. If South Korea wants to defend itself, it easily can. If it doesn't, I don't care.

Further, (I'm really getting into this) I will bring the GIs home from Europe. There's nobody there we need to fight. As for Bosnia and suchlike geographic trash, last time I looked they were in Europe. Europe can worry about them. The US is not Europe's mother.

Purple-haired dyke feminists: These venomous lynxes have done enough harm that I shall have to be firm. All public doorways will have a spectrophotometer to detect purpleness at hair level. When this happens, a laser will light up and, sssssssPOP! her head will explode. The entire membership of NOW will be sent to Bangladesh to work in a jute factory. Since most of them look like fire plugs with leprosy, on their return they will be required to wear burqas.

The economy. I am against compulsory redistribution of wealth. This usually means taking money from those who earn it, and giving it to the federal government. If federal employees want to eat, they can plant corn. Or eat their cyanide pills. I will encourage the latter as simpler.

Finally, patriotism will become a capital offense. It serves chiefly as a mechanism allowing rogues and pathological short men to send our puzzled teenagers to kill someone else's. Iraq can kill its own damn teenagers if it likes. I understand the urge, having had teenagers, but it isn't my job.

How can I lose? The Age of Fred dawns.

49 REFLECTIONS ON AN OPERA BOUFFE ELECTION

Just dragged my scrawny carcass in from Washington, the heart of darkness, with the usual sense—usual now—of having visited an asylum. I figure Salvador Dali designed the government. Or maybe Ionesco or someone deeply twisted with a sick sense of humor.

In the airports, the same obedience training—take off your shoes, belt, watch, fillings, prostate, so we can to learn to respect the authority of low-IQ federalized renta-cops with the psyches of school-yard bullies. God save us from the congenitally unimportant. From PA systems came the same pointless security-babble having nothing to do with security, in the same over elocuted I-wanna-lick-the-microphone female voices. Well, it's not quite pointless. We must condition the rubes, give them an inspiriting sense of danger so they will do as they are told. It's awful. I'm going to apply for a change of phylum.

It got worse. I discovered that America is about to have an election. Why? Every time they do that, no good comes of it. You'd think they'd learn.

As usual, the election is a popularity contest run for dimwits. And to elect a dimwit, which is worse. We've got this woman Palin, an angry Betty Crocker, absolutely unqualified for the presidency in case McCain goes tits up. She's ignorant of foreign affairs, at best moderately bright, a whackjob Christian, and a "pit bull." This is said admiringly.

Oh good. An aggressive ignorant dull-witted pit bull. How is that better than a passive ignorant torpid pit bull?

Oh god, McCain. A senescent replica of Bush who says he wants to stay in Iraq a hundred years. Actually, the idea has its appeal. Why doesn't he go there and get a start? A perfect match for Palin, another pugnacious dunce, bottom of his class in boat school—the Naval Academy, I mean. He says he plans to "confront Russia." Now there's a plan. It seems that American policy is to make enemies of everyone who has oil or nuclear weapons. Or doesn't.

Meanwhile the Pentagon prepares for war with China. Is it something in the water?

Next we have Obama, whose only qualification is that he's maybe a tad less bellicose than the rest of these Oprah Neanderthals. His veep, Biden, is a grey nonentity, a cipher with no characteristics. Well, that's better than the other three. I mean, he's as close to no candidate as we can come.

What are we doing? The country has gone nuts. If a giant squirrel began collecting us and storing us for winter, I'd understand. Three hundred million people, and these factory rejects are the best we can do?

Actually, I do understand it, barely. The undergirding of American politics is the seldom-stated but always audible cry of "You ain't no gooder'n me!" We have government by inferiority complex. The last thing the great burger-chomping, reality-show-watching mental vacuum out there wants is anyone who might make reglar folks feel inferior. The cloth of the country is woven of resentment. The public wants a regular guy, comfortingly stupid, who watches NASCAR and in broken English as if recently concussed. Few would select a cardiac surgeon from a bus station, but it's how we do presidents.

You probably can get elected holding a chain saw and a severed head, but not if you know words of three syllables.

It's getting scary. The more angry and miserable things get at home, the more people want to smack hell out of someone. It doesn't matter who. The American attitude toward the world is, "Not only can I lick anybody in this bar, but I can lick all of you at once." Before I said that, I'd want to be real sure who was in the bar.

At least two of these gong-show dregs, Palin and Bush, blame their personality disorders on God. Yes. They think God wants them to blow hell out of more or less everybody. We're talking wars of religion, boys and girls. Christian loons in the US, Jewish loons in Israel, and Muslim loons widely distributed, all wanting to blow people up because God told them. I want a signed affidavit from God. Or a drink. Whatever happened to grownups?

I babble, but it's hard to think straight when contemplating nuclear-armed kindergarteners. In Washington, I saw about ten friends, many of them biochemists, lawyers, programmers, freelance screwballs, what have you. Sitting at the Zoo Bar one night (so called because it's across Connecticut Avenue from the zoo, not because of its clientele) a dismal epiphany struck me, kersplat, like a sock full of hog kidneys:

I don't know anybody who isn't better qualified to be president than anyone who is or is about to be.

Of the ten friends I mentioned, the baseline IQ is close to 140 and goes up, often lots up. All of them are well read and many have spent a lot of time overseas. All speak and write good English and, some of them, foreign languages. They aren't geniuses, just upper-middle-brow. But they are way better than the rabble running for the White House.

I don't get it. For president, I want somebody lots brighter than I am, who knows history, who speaks a few languages, maybe spent time in the military without being an officer and therefore a warped buzz-cut Boy Scout. They exist. I have friends who knew where South Ossetia was twenty years ago, and why, who know the military and military history and what works and what doesn't and why. I'm not like that. Not smart enough. But they are. Yet we get candidates who could probably run a small-town hardware store. Reglar folks, though.

Democracy is a bad idea, I tell you. Granted, we've never really tried it. From Jefferson to our current bumbling mutant, the trick has been to let people think they have power without really trusting them with it. For a long time we had rule by a high-WASP elite that actually had some sense of noblesse oblige, tempered by sufficient corruption to keep them in gravy. The Roosevelts for example. You can disagree with their policies, but they weren't penny-ante pickpocket proles with learning disabilities.

Today we get grasping zeros who would embarrass a trailer park in Arkansas. Ah, but they are of the people, and don't make anyone feel inadequate. In everything that counts, which means involving money, we have rule by corporations, through legalized corruption far more lucrative than Latin America could dream of.

I have a theory that countries deserve what they get, at least when it's internally generated. Belgium didn't deserve to be overrun by Germany, but Belgium didn't elect Hitler. It's going to be a funny eight years.

50 SHWEI-GWO SYAU-JYE: A VIEW FROM THE BRIDGE

It was 1975, just after the fall of Saigon, and I was in Taipei, studying Chinese and waiting for the next war, which didn't come. I abode downtown in the winding labyrinth of backstreets inhabited mostly by workers since I was pretty broke. My roommates were a Chinese teenager, Dingwo, who wanted to be a rock star, and Sakai, a diminutive Japanese mathematician with penis envy, and Ron, a Peace Corps guy back from India who astounded hotel guards by speaking to them in good Punjabi.

Chinese back alleys are wonderful places, or were anyway before Starbucks. They reek of spices and good cooking and kids sat outside to avoid the heat and studied at orange-crate desks. The Chinese study. We will one day think this important. We ate in tin-roofed restaurants with trays of little baby squid like grey vitamin pills and things less identifiable.

Near the apartment was a sort of concrete overpass with the space beneath it walled off to provide a low-rent place for food stalls. It was hot and steamy inside because of long rows of women frying this and steaming that. We ate sheets of fried squid, youyu, and then go to the fruit-juice stall.

I forget her name. We just called her Schwei-gwo Syau-jye, Fruit Girl. She was about twenty-five, roughly my age at the time and spent all day behind a white-tiled counter, selling fruit juice. Her mother was dead, her father eighty-something, and she had to take care of him. Schwei-gwo was slim and pretty, a common condition among Chinese, but tired.

I'd order a complicated juice concoction and sit there for an hour, practicing Chinese. Unless you want to read it, it is an easy language. She was usually in jeans and sweatshirt, and was trying to learn English. Have I said that the Chinese study? Somehow she remained cheerful despite brutal hours and not much of a life, which made me sad but that's how Asia was. Between customers she would flip through her dictionary and a copy of Newsweek.

In the East you meet many people like Schwei-gwo Syau-jye, intelligent and decent, who deserve better than they will ever have.

It can get to you. She had a little white powder-puff dog that ate rice to keep her company. At night she walked home through the dark streets, a little nervous but feeling less alone with her dog. Crime was low because the government didn't tolerate it, but still....

Nights were different for Ron and me. Sometimes we went to Wan Wha, where you found the snake-butchers, and rough looking men came to the worker's brothels. (Preposterously, Wan Wha means "Ten Thousand Glories." It was pretty much a slum.) The butchers had cobras and the occasional y-bai shuh, which means one hundred paces because that's how far they think you would get if bitten. They slit the beasts from head to tail, massaged the blood into a glass, and sold it to workers. "Dwei shen-ti, hen hau," good for the body. I always figured watermelon juice was a better idea. But I ramble.

The next war didn't come, and I left Taiwan. Marriage came, much water under various bridges, and my daughter Macon, Blonde Poof as we called her, made her appearance. I was working for a paper in Washington. The Taiwanese PR operation offered me and my wife a junket to Taipei, which we took, carting along Blonde Poof. I forget how old she was but she sat up successfully the first time in Taiwan.

We were staying in the Grand Hotel, Madame Chiang's gorgeous pile on a hill overlooking the city. We went downtown to my old haunts, Poof included, and found Gwo-yu R-bau, my old school. Was my teacher, Jang Lau-Shr still about, and would they tell her I'd like to see her? They would.

She showed up and we were both astonished that I could still carry on a conversation. It was odd after so many years. The neighborhoood wasn't much, just low stores selling ordinary things, but there is a flavor to Asia that seeps into you and you never really leave. My wife, who had never been to that part of the world, said half-seriously, "Now, why are we going to go back?" Yes.

Then, on the off-chance, we went to the bridge.

There, in the same stall, hardly looking older, was Schwei-gwo Syau-jye. Nothing had changed. She was delighted to see us and we ordered the old concoctions. Same steamy heat, same smells. I don't know whether the dog-puff was the same or new. Her father was still alive and she was still working herself to death to care for him.

For a bit she played with Blonde Poof. The Chinese regarded a golden-haired child as almost a tourist attraction. They are a pretty people, the Chinese, but not a blond people.

No, she still wasn't married. She didn't have time to do much because she had to keep the stall open. We talked of fond memories of no importance and my wife and I left, vowing to write. I would have if I hadn't managed to lose the address. We never saw Schwei-gwo Syau-jye again.

Maybe she is still under the bridge, squeezing melons. Possibly things somehow got better for her. Taiwan has prospered mightily since those days. Maybe she got a job in an office. But I doubt it.

Forgive the horrible Romanization. Too many systems scrambled in my head

51 OF MOOSE AND PIT BULLS

I wonder whether the United States hadn't ought to re-ponder the place of the military in society and in the world. There is not the slightest chance that this will happen, but wondering has not yet been forbidden. It appears to me that bureaucratic clotting set in years back, and is now having its effect in spheres martial. A robust economy can afford frivolities that one in decline cannot. And that is where America is.

The US military is the military of World War II, but with better technology. The Navy still consists of carriers surrounded by ships intended to protect the carriers. The heart of the army is still armored and infantry divisions with artillery and close-air support. The Air Force too. All are designed to fight enemies like themselves. However, there are no enemies like themselves, and WWII forces do not well fight the enemies they do have, such as ragtag dispersed guerrillas, because they are not intended to fight them.

Why a World War II military? Because of institutional inertia, because men delight in fast, powerful things that make loud and stirring noises, because the ships and tanks and submarines are magnificent. Relinquishing them is too painful to contemplate. Instead of changing its forces to suit present needs, the Pentagon keeps them as they are and tries to use them where they do not work well.

WWII militaries are intended to destroy expensive point targets and to conquer crucial territory. For example, they try to destroy the enemy's aircraft and conquer his cities. This America does very well indeed. The difficulty is that dispersed guerrillas do not have any expensive point targets, crucial territory, or cities. The Pentagon is using baseball bats to fight mosquitoes. The absurdity of using a B1 intercontinental bomber for close air support is manifest. But you've got the plane, the pilots don't want to miss the war, and so you find something for them to bomb.

A current American weakness is that it has a small army. Controlling large countries full of dispersed enemies requires large armies. America's is a small army because it is an All Volunteer army. Not many young men want to be soldiers. The Pentagon likes the All-Vol for two reasons. First, volunteer soldiers are much better than unwilling short-term conscriptees. Second, the public doesn't care if volunteers get killed. After all, they volunteered. They come from blue-collar families. These regard the death of a son as a noble sacrifice rather than a human sacrifice for large commercial firms. And they have little political influence anyway.

This matters. The Pentagon has learned that it cannot sustain a war in the face of united public opposition. If students in college were drafted, hell would follow. The key is not to disturb the public, which the military recognizes as more of a danger than the enemy actually being fought.

The true enemy, always, is the press. Should reporters turn against a war, they would rouse that great sleeping Public Monster, and then the military would face a war on two fronts. Fortunately the press consists of a few large corporations and holding companies owned by people of the same social class, who are not opposed to the current wars.

Since World War II, political power has become increasingly concentrated in the presidency, the concentration having become very rapid in recent years. Most crucially, the Congress has relinquished its power to decide whether the country goes to war. Thus wars are no longer determined by the national interest but by presidential whim. These whims can be directed by the desires of the president's friends, by powerful groups with agendas, by writers at intellectual magazines. Quite often these know nothing of war. And the military by enshrining obedience avoids responsibility.

The US is phenomenally if discreetly militarized. The country is neither a democracy, nor a government of laws, nor of men, but an oligarchy of lobbies that press for whatever is of benefit to themselves, though not necessarily to the country. The underlying principle is that honey attracts flies. The federal government collects vast sums in taxes and the lobbies come to get it.

In the military racket, the money is in big-ticket weaponry. The carriers, Aegis boats, subs, fighters, tanks, B1s, B2s, and satellites sell for billions. These sums attract a vast aerospace industry that would collapse without sales to the military. The Pentagon is a captive market, and often a haven for firms that couldn't compete in the commercial marketplace.

Much of this money goes for pricey gear that is both unknown to the public and of little use for the wars the country fights (but probably shouldn't). To hide a program from the public, you don't have to make it secret, which would only draw attention. Just don't talk about it. The press, which is owned by big business and manned by reporters of preternatural technical puzzlement, will say little. For examples, search on JSF, F22, V22, ABL, and ABM.

As always, the key is to avoid waking the public. Thus the military avoids attention. But add up overt and hidden military expenditure: the "defense" budget, appropriations for the wars, the black programs, the Veterans Administration, the national laboratories, TSA, and so on. The sum is backbreaking for a nation in decline, but the public knows neither that it is backbreaking nor that the country is in decline.

To countries competing with the US, as for example Japan, the American military budget is a godsend, the equivalent of a golf handicap on a rival, because it represents money the US cannot spend to become more competitive. Fortunately for Asia, American military expenditure cannot readily be cut back. Too many jobs, military towns, and corporate profits depend on it. Consequently China builds infrastructure while the US builds fighter planes. The only plausible brake will be conflict with Social Security and Medicare, cuts in which will wake the Public Monster.

The illusion of omnipotence dies hard. The American military has been dominant for so long that neither it nor Americans can grasp that there are limits to its power. America now tries militarily to encircle Russia, Iran, and China, which increasingly looks like an aging pit bull trying to encircle a herd of moose. The Pentagon is planning for a war with China and talks of "Full Spectrum Dominance." The current government in Washington wants to attack Iran and Pakistan, threatens Syria and Venezuela, and seems bent on igniting another Cold War with Russia (if one ignites cold wars). The Army is to be expanded.

Meanwhile China builds infrastructure.

52 OTHER TIMES AND WAYS

When I ponder our curiously unbalanced civilization, able to put golf carts on Mars but unable to equal the verse of muddy Elizabethan London, I wonder why we are as we are. In all things technological the United States is magnificent, the Athens of solid-state physics. Yet the great orchestras die unlistened to, we have no Shakespeare or Dante nor notion why we might want them, and religious expression grows mute, or crabbed and hostile. Why?

I think the answer is that our surroundings determine not just what we think, but what we can think. We live in cities urban but not urbane, among screaming sirens, in air grayed by exhaust and wracked by the blattings of buses. The complaint is not invalid for being trite. I cannot imagine a Whitman composing in a shopping mall.

The rush and complexity of everything take their toll. As a people we might well be called The Unrelaxed. And, therefore, the Uncontemplative.

Other lives are possible, or were possible. Years ago I passed a summer in Hampden-Sydney, my small college on a huge wooded campus in then-rural Virginia. The students were blessedly gone.

Along the Via Sacra, as the only road on campus was called, under blue skies going on forever and forever there was silence, absolute silence, unless you count the twittering of birds and the keening of bugs in ancient oaks. These may be sounds, but they are not noise. They are not even music, but something before, older, earlier, better. Vivaldi was a great man, but here he was out of his league. The professors' homes, old often and dignified without pretension, watched from yards shaded by old, old trees. And it was quiet and warm and you were with your thoughts.

It was terribly unmodern. At night the stars shone in the black infinite and there was no noise. No noise. There a Thoreau could have written or Corot painted. I do not think this possible in clangorous suburban ugliness.

Following the Via Sacra you came to Black Bottom, where the road ended in woods and there was a pond with a swan in it. The place was not the stuff of photographic magazines, just the quiet, bug-loud second growth of Virginia. In a lengthening life I have seen nothing more peaceful. To the left a trail of red clay, speckled with mica, wound through the pines down and down to Slippery Rock. Here deep in the woods a small stream plashed through the red banks and slid over a flat rock covered with moss. Few knew of it. My father, before there was electricity, came here to slide into the pool below. As did I.

On many afternoons I read there, or did nothing, or watched the water striders skating on the surface, their feet in little depressions in the water. Being then a student of physics and chemistry, I knew somewhat of surface tension and surfactants and the preferences of hydrogen bonds, but I also knew I was looking at something beyond my comprehension. It was not a scientific observation. Scientists take things apart but, except for the greats, do not notice the whole. The greats are few on the ground.

Such places change one's inner world. At Slippery Rock I thought things I could not in Arlington, Virginia, just outside of Washington, with its sirens and traffic and quietly angry people connected to iPods. Wilson Boulevard, where I lived, was by no means horrible. I liked its restaurants and bars and sushi joints. The people weren't evil. But it was terribly unquiet.

I am not religious, at least in the sense of believing that I have the answers, but I am religious in the sense of knowing the questions. I know that there are things we can't know, things even more important than making partner before the age of thirty. Doubtless most of us know this. Yet the tenor of life is not easily escaped. We try. People rush to Europe in search of the old, the quiet, and the pretty. Peddlers of real estate understand the urge, and hawk tranquil rural life while building the malls that will make it impossible. And so hurry comes to Arcadia. People then think of escape to the next small town. We spend a remarkable amount of time fleeing ourselves. Maybe instead we should build a place we like.

We cannot, because the nature of things is determined remotely, at corporate. We have little choice in where we live, not because we cannot move but because everywhere becomes the same. A Southern town with old houses and grey-green Spanish moss hanging in beards from trees gives way to malls and Ruby Tuesdays. The town center may be retained, with parking for tour buses, so that people from elsewhere can have a Southern Experience. A town turned into a freak show is no longer precisely a town.

So little remains of the local. Time was when two-lane highways wound through misty valleys in the Smokies with little towns scrunched onto the slopes of a wrinkled land and mom-and-pop restaurants, no two alike. Barstow was a desert town of desert people, and New Orleans was a city, not a theme park.

Now, no. Things are both uniform and ugly. Corporates everywhere have learned to stamp out stores, houses, developments, cheap because identical, because of the wonders of mass production, and who can tell them no? You can't stop progress, boosters say, though I can't see that we have had any.

And of course people want, or think they want, the noise and sprawl and franchisees. Construction does briefly provide jobs, Wal-Mart does sell power saws at low prices, and the food at Ruby Tuesday's is good. The young like noise, and surely a store selling thirty brands of running shoes for people who don't run cannot be a bad thing. It is only later that the boredom and emptiness set in for kids who have only the malls, never the woods. Hamsters have exercise wheels. We buy things.

Few precisely like what we have, I suppose, but how does one escape it? Perhaps they don't sense exactly what it is they want to escape, and anyway there is nowhere else to go. In noise-ridden cities smelling of exhaust, crowded, where the stars languish obscured by smoke, the rivers run semi-poisonous and much of the populace can barely read, how can anyone think beyond the stock market and the next empty copulation? The Milnes and Donnes and Marlowes don't exist because they can't, and we don't want them because we can't want them.

53 A SOUTHERN APPROACH

All night it rained in Jocotepec, my small town in Mexico. Rain isn't unusual, but this was different. It was heavy. It didn't stop. Come morning, my wife and I looked out the window and saw inches of brown water sluicing down the sloping street from the mountain.

About nine o'clock that morning the speakers on the church tower began: "Necesitamos personas, ropa, comida. Personas, ropa...." We need people, clothes, food. Something had happened.

The towns of our region—Chapala, Ajijic, San Juan Cosala, Jocotepec—lie along the north shore of Lake Chapala, squeezed into a narrow strip between the mountains, or high hills anyway, and the lake. You can walk from the shore to the upslope in about five minutes. The hills, which have little vegetation, are dotted with roundish boulders stuck in raw earth. The vegetation that once held the earth in place has been eaten by goats, which graze in the hills. When enough rain washes away the soil, the rocks begin to roll. This had happened.

A moving mass of boulders—first small rocks, then those of basketball size, then some as large as Volkswagens—had ploughed through San Juan Cosala. A commonly quoted figure, entirely plausible, is that two hundred houses were destroyed. Nobody was killed I think, but houses were crushed or filled to the ceilings with mud. It was a massive disaster in a small way. Katrina's baby sister, call it.

We didn't know how bad it was.

At about eleven Violeta and I went to the square to offer our services and to buy food to contribute. By that time a food-distribution center in the church was accepting donations and sending them to the scene in the trucks of volunteers. The clothing collection-point was busy. The town gym had been turned into temporary housing for the shelterless. When your house has eight-foot ceilings and six feet of mud inside, a gym looks pretty good. At a desk in the gym volunteers lined up, waiting to be assigned jobs.

The only road along the lake was blocked by police to avoid

interference with rescue teams, whose trucks came and went. Late that afternoon Vi and I managed to get to San Juan. Things were horrendous. Walls of mud and rock had rolled down the vertical streets and across the main road, leaving hills of debris. We saw a pickup truck squashed like an accordion.

Heavy equipment was arriving from wherever Jalisco, our state, keeps such things. What in the military would be called tank transporters, huge flatbed trucks, roared down the lakeside road. We saw bulldozers, front-end loaders, all sorts of big earthmovers painted yellow. Their scoops made them look like nightmare scorpions. A few were already working to clear the rubble and others appeared at intervals. Heavy white dump trucks labeled "Department of Public Works" waited to be filled. Mexico is corrupt and does not run quite like a well-oiled Rolex, yet the government does a much better job than Americans would ever credit. And sometimes better than Americans do.

The response had been fast and vigorous, and participation almost universal. Doctors had come from neighboring towns, though miraculously they were not much needed. A businessman in Chapala had donated a large truck full of five-gallon garrafones of bottled water. Nobody required them to do these things. They just did.

Next day the streets were lined with men with shovels and the big cats worked with much clunking of metal against rock and growling of diesels. We talked to a man whose house had been on a sloping street. It no longer was, or at any rate was no longer a house. He said he had heard an odd rattling outside, looked out, and saw a river of water and rocks like softballs racing downhill. A couple of bigger rocks came by. He figured that out, and his family went through a downslope window and ran hard. No injuries. No house, either.

People we talked to did not seem to regard themselves as victims. Rather they had a disaster on their hands. There is a difference. We saw nobody sitting about, waiting for someone to take care of them. They were not overjoyed, but neither did they seem beaten down or passive.

The place was a mess. It needed cleaning up. They set about cleaning it up.

The upper part of San Juan is the Racquet Club, a posh gringo retirement community. Vi and I and Natalia, my stepdaughter, climbed through streets awash in boulders that hadn't been there before and found pricey houses wrecked. Not good, but not as bad as it could have been. Gringos have money, and some of them probably had insurance. Mexicans in San Juan have neither. They had much to complain about, but didn't, being too busy trying to dig out.

We walked farther up the hill, finding more streets entirely clogged with mud, rocks, detritus. Around reasonably intact houses kids looked at the surrounding destruction, more interested than dismayed. On the side of the mountain we could see what seemed to be the path taken by the boulders in their downhill run. Finally we had enough and went back.

A month or so later San Juan seemed back to normal, though I'm not sure where those went whose homes were unsalvageable. Kids ran perilously close to the edge of the road as usual and stores were open. I thought about the pole-axed helplessness of New Orleans, the bureaucratized uselessness of FEMA, and wondered where the Third World lay.

So far as I know, nothing of the disaster appeared in the US media, apart from a reported one-sentence mention in a world wrap-up on Fox News. The town asked for no outside help beyond the state level, and got none. There was no looting, no incompetent federal agencies to gum things up. The town was devastated and so, with far fewer resources than the United States could bring to bear, they undevastated it as best they could, which was pretty well, and went about their business.

That's how a small Mexican town handled its Katrina.

54 LA FUENTE, SLOW AFTERNOON

So I was sitting with Tom the Robot and Jonesy in La Fuente, an old and cavernous beer bar hard by the cathedral in Guadalajara, and swapping lies. Except they weren't lies, because some people can't lie to equal the truth. Otherwise I guess they would. Thing is, lying is a limited form. Life isn't.

La Fuente is dark and inelegant. It covers about a roaring acre of locals hooting and hollering and you pay for beers as you get them.

The Robot was talking about social interaction. Like Jonesy, he has what writers call a checkered past, but chaotic is more like it— ground Marine in Nam, paramedic in New York, curious jobs in remote parts of Alaska. He once played a bottle-nosed dolphin in a movie, hovering two feet below the Gulf of Mexico in scuba gear and waggling a plastic dolphin's head above the water.

The Robot is crazy. He is also a dangerous brawler and has anger-control problems. Actually, he doesn't see a problem. He's perfectly happy smacking the hell out of people who need it.

Anyway, social interaction. He comes out of a bar in Guad late one night, three sheets to the wind, and probably the blankets and pillow cases too, and these young bad-asses come up with a knife and request his wallet. When that happens, the smart thing is just to give it to them. So the Robot reaches for his wallet and nails the sumbitch with a drop-shouldered sucker-punch, hard, and the jerk goes down leaving teeth on the concrete, and the others decamp.

"Bloody chicklets," said the Robot, referring to the teeth. "I was stupid. I coulda got killed." He has anger-control problems. And his wallet.

He wasn't bragging, just telling beer stories.

Jonesy is a retired bush pilot out of Alaska with a soft Southern accent like Karo syrup dripping on busted china and he'd talk about flying way up north with ice on the wings and in a fog in places that made nowhere look like somewhere. Maybe he was in a high-wing Cessna, but I forget.

"What happens if you can't find a place to land?" asked the Robot, who knew the answer.

"Shucks, you can land anywhere," said Jonesy. "Nothing to it.

What you want to do is find a airfield before you do it."

I guess you could drink beer with a tax accountant. But I wouldn't want to try it.

The waiter came by on a resupply run with more Corona and I mentioned coming out of Angola on a story for Soldier of Fortune in a DC-3, flying ten feet over the trees to keep SAM-7s from getting a lock. This was this when Cuban soldiers, whom I rather like, were supporting the evil commie government in Luanda. I didn't care. The world is complex. I didn't need to solve all its problems, or take sides.

Anyway, among a certain kind of riffraff and rabble, such as us, the DC-3 is a legend. It first flew about 1936, and still does, age seventy-five and re-engined, and it was the platform for Puff the Magic Dragon, a gunship popular in Asia. More popular with one side than the other, I guess. With Gatlings firing tracers it looked like it had ray guns.

But that's neither here nor there. La Fuente was getting noisier as people came in for an after-work brew. There was nothing hostile about it, just good times and bad acoustics.

Mexico changes fast. You see women in lots of bars. You've heard a lot about machismo, but it's on life-support, at least in the cities. Which is a good thing. In the US you can see some diesel-dyke feminist with spiked hair like an alarmed porcupine and hollering about what she thinks is machismo because she caught some guy leering at her tits. Mexican machismo isn't funny. It often involved broken jaws. Still does in the wilder parts.

You might think guys who know more about guns, engines, and questionable bars than about polishing doilies, or whatever you do with doilies, would be untouched by civilizing influences, and regard women as furniture or captive hookers. No, actually. I know lots of pilots, former door-gunners, cowboy divers, and generally very tough guys. They think women are nuts, but don't speak badly of them, even in private. Except gringas. Jonesy will gaze at an ambient lovely and opine wistfully that she could suck-start a leaf-blower. But he would never day it to her. He's just dreaming. He treats his wife with kindness and respect. But then, she's Mexican.

The Robot looks like a skull with skin stretched over it. Hollowed out, he'd make a good lamp shade. He has don't-fuck-with-me eyes that make you want to be his friend, or somewhere else. I've never figured it out. Some guys you look at and you know mayhem is readily available. It isn't a scowl, threatening manner, over-hanging orbitals, or angry voice. But you know. You just know. "Cops eyes," they have been called.

He talked about motorcycles he'd had, which was lots, and falling off them occasionally to no good effect on bad turns, and long lonely rides down to Florida on a Harley panhead to dive and hang out with people your mother wouldn't like at all.

The better forms of human detritus tend to travel in similar social tunnels. The Robot and I both knew the Last Chance Saloon, a biker bar at the top of the Florida Keys. My lunatic friend Stu and I had spent time there when we drove down to pass the turn of the millennium underwater, which we did at Davis Ledge, trying to drink, at forty feet, a bottle of rust-cutter champagne called Domme Bahd Stufe, or something similar. It didn't work too well.

A couple of hours and considerable Corona later, I'd heard about getting dropped off in distant lakes in Alaska to fish by a float plane that wouldn't come back for two weeks so you better be alive then. About the shark that swept in on an attack run in cloudy water and veered off when it realized that divers weren't in its food chain. About the bomb squad in DC that sent robots to investigate what seemed to be a bomb, but turned out to be bull sperm in liquid nitrogen. About cold rain over a disintegrating M60 tank on the mud ranges of Fort Hood. About....

I don't guess we saved the world or cured cancer. But I thought it was a pretty good way to spend a slow afternoon, way south of the border.

55 PRECEDENT O'BAMA, WEDDING BOMBS, AND OTHER GOOD NEWS

I'm going to slit my wrists. I've been reading the news again. I always want to slit my wrists when I do that. I know, I know: I'll get encouragement from readers. OK, then, I won't, just to spite them. Ha.

One story says that Americans owe some bizarre sum on the credit card and god knows how much on the McMansion and on the five-hundred horsepower riding mower with a mini-combine, backhoe attachment, and satellite GPS for mowing the half acre. I think I'm supposed to feel sorry for them. Actually I think they are a persuasive argument for eugenics.

I don't get it. What is wrong with these idiots? Debt is easy to avoid. Herewith some blinding wisdom: If you can't pay for it, don't buy it. You saw it here first, a percipient contribution to economic theory. Works like a charm, too. Or how about this? Don't buy more house than you can live in. Move over, Keynes, Ricardo, here I come.

Another story is about how banks are all unhappy because they've got bad loans. A probing question if I may (characteristic of this column): Who made the bad loans? Permit me another searing insight. If you lend money to people who can't pay it back, they won't. I know, I know, a difficult concept. Not something a Wall Street banker would know.

Thank god America isn't a third-world country. In Mexico, the radio station of the local university, and other commie fronts, grouse about la impunidad, impunity, meaning that high-ranking criminals never get punished. You know, like the GQ-cover psychopaths who brought about the savings-and-loan scandal, or Milken, Boesky, and Levine, or Enron, and now the impoverishment of half the planet. But what can you expect? Mexico is a very corrupt country.

What I think is, we need a mass hanging. But no. The culprits will just reshuffle into the administration of Precedent O'Bama and remain attached, tick-like, to the withering federal dugs. The rats in the rafters may not be savory, but they look out for each other.

But on to matters of more import than whether we have anything to eat. I read that the world has gone euphoric over Precedent O'Bama. Simultaneously, O'Bama wants to send more troops to Afghanistan. I'll give euphoria two more weeks. His chief virtues are that he isn't Bush and isn't McCain. When you have to choose between two candidates of whom each is worse than the other, you can bet life ain't gonna be ham hocks and home fries.

Next, I see that the military has bombed another wedding in Afghanistan, killing forty-one. I guess it's because civilians are easier to kill. They don't hide very well. Usually they are unarmed.

Anyway, on BBC World News I saw some gringo colonel, maybe called Greg Julian, explaining that it was the Taliban's fault when America bombs weddings. Most likely the plane had Taliban pilots. Recruiting is getting difficult, and I guess the Air Force has to take just about anybody.

But it wasn't the fault of the military. In thirty years of covering the Pentagon, the military never did anything wrong. That's a pretty good record. I know because they told me.

Anyway, Colonel Julian was impressive. He clearly had the makings of a future chief of staff. He was good-looking, delivered the word from corporate in grammatical English, and had the unnerving wholesomeness of a Christian Boy Scout. Definitely JCS material, depending only on his PowerPoint technique . He explained that the military goes to great lengths to avoid bombing weddings, that wedding-avoidance is practically an obsession, and they would try to keep from doing it too much in the future. I reckon it must have made any survivors feel good.

Funny, I too try to avoid bombing weddings, but I'm a lot more successful at it, despite a much smaller budget.

Now, I don't want to sound cynical or anything. Still, I'd like to know how the good colonel would look at things if his daughter, if he has one, were having her wedding and kerblooey! Daughter and forty members of the family and close friends suddenly become clotting goo over a fifty-yard radius and the bombers say, "We're sorry, kind of, but that wedding looked just like a troop concentration." Troop concentrations always feature a woman in a white dress holding flowers. It's what they teach at West Point.

Stray memory: I read once that bin Laden said he wanted to

suck the US into long drawn-out losing wars to bankrupt the country and end its influence over the Muslim world. I don't know why I thought of that. I need to focus better.

On to jollier topics, specifically federal porn. I find in Der Spiegel Online that Germany has decided against strip-search x-rays at airports. It's because Germany carries civil liberties and privacy to impractical extremes whereas we, more realistic, know that the most innocent-looking girl probably has a bomb hidden in her skivvies. Those cheesecake scanners doubtless cost only a million bucks each, a song, times all the gates in all the airports in the world. This establishes pretty clearly that no economic interest is involved.

I bet the guys at TSA (Tits Scanners, and Ass) fight over the job of monitoring that screen. Hooboy. Especially as resolution increases. (Pressing research idea: Are color x-rays doable? Bombs probably come in different colors.) Maybe the government could recoup the cost by selling instant prints on request when some hot-ticket babe from a cheerleading squad comes through. Her boyfriend might want them. The rest could go to marketing at cellulite reduction outfits.

Yet more glad tidings. A while back I read where the Chinese did their first space-walk. On another page it said that as usual the Chinese economy had grown at twelve percent or some such number, and then I found a website talking about how China was buying up all the natural resources of Africa. The US can't because it doesn't have any money. It owes it all to China. And that's because we borrowed from Beijing to make kinky nekkid-women scanners for ill-bred affirmative-action retreads at Homeland Security to look at, and bombs to drop on Afghanistan. Which doesn't make sense, because Afghanistan was pretty much rubble from the start. It's always been rubble.

I wish we had adult leadership like China has.

And now I hear that NSA is buying Bride magazine. Sounds like they're hunting. Hey, stay single, or wear Kevlar and disperse quickly. (OK, I may have made that part up. I'm not sure.)

I can't take any more of this. I really am going to slit my wrists. I swear it. Anyone need A-Positive? Send a bucket.

56 KILLING AMERICA'S KIDS.

No Big Deal. Hey, They Breed Fast in Tennessee

The web is covered in stink today because of a reporter for the Associated Press, Julie Jacobson, who photographed the death of a Marine whose legs had just been blown off. The kid was Joshua Bernard, a Lance Corporal of 21 years. When the photo appeared, Robert Gates, the Secretary of Defense [sic] furiously tried to get the AP to quash the photo. It didn't, to its everlasting credit. To quote one of many accounts on the web:

"Gates followed up with a scathing letter to Curley [of AP] yesterday afternoon. The letter says Gates cannot imagine the pain Bernard's family is feeling right now, and that Curley's 'lack of compassion and common sense in choosing to put out this image of their maimed and stricken child on the front page of multiple newspapers is appalling. The issue here is not law, policy or constitutional right—but judgment and common decency.'

I thought a long time before writing about this matter, and was not pleasant to be around. The photo resonated with me, as we say. You see, long ago, in another pointless war, promoted by another conscienceless Secretary, I too was a Marine Lance Corporal of twenty-one years. I too got shot, though not nearly as badly as this kid, and spent a year at Bethesda Naval Hospital. At this point I am legally blind following my (I think) thirteenth trip to eye surgery as a result of an identical foreign policy.

Big fucking deal. Shit happens. At this point I'm comfortable and doing fine. Don't cry for me, Argentina. The other kid is dead.

But that bothers me. And all of this perhaps gives me a certain insight into the matter that not all reporters have, nor all editors. It also makes me poisonously, bottle-throwing angry to think about another chilly professional bureaucrat, the Second Coming of McNamara, with less combat experience than Tinkerbell, sending kids to croak in weird places having nothing to do with the US.

But Gates. The words "decency" and "unconscionable" coming from him are fetid with hypocrisy. Gates was director of the CIA. "Intelligence" agencies are moral dirt, hated the world over for torture, murder, and destabilization of countries leading to hundreds of thousands of deaths. The KGB, Mossad, CIA, STASI, SAVAK—they're all the same. A man who presides over torture and murder should not speak of decency. He has none.

Nor is it easy to believe that Gates feels the slightest sympathy for the dead kid or for his family. If you don't want kids to die in Afghanistan, don't send them there. He does. How sorry can he be?

It could almost make you turn against the war. Some 6,000 American kids have died like this, the photographs carefully hidden by the press. The Pentagon has killed many, many more Afghan and Iraqi civilians, and the number of permanently disabled Americans is far higher. Today I find a column on Antiwar.com by Joe Galloway, whom I remember from UPI Saigon, entitled The War in Afghanistan is Not Worth Another American Life. I agree. Nor another Afghan life. They did nothing. Another headline notes that the Kondor Legion, the USAF, killed ninety-five Afghans in another witless air strike. These days, we are the Nazis.

Why then is he so angry at having the war photographed? Easy: Spin control. Spin is so very important in war these days. While America is only barely a democracy, still, if the public, the great sleeping acquiescent ignorant beast, ever gets really upset, the war ends. The Pentagon is acutely aware of this. It remembers its disaster in Asia. The generals of today learned nothing military from Vietnam—they are fighting the same kind of war as stupidly as before—but they learned something more important: Their most dangerous enemy is the America public. You. Me. Defeating the Taliban isn't particularly important, or even desirable. (No war means fewer promotions and fewer contracts). But while the Taliban cannot possibly defeat the Pentagon, the American public can.

Photographs are death to a war, boys and girls. They can asphyxiate a war faster than roadside bombs can even dream. Gates does not want the sprawling somnolent inattentive beast, the public, to see what his wars really are.

In wars, there are many enlightening things to see. For example, the Marine with a third of his face and half a lung, going ku-kuk-kuk as red gunch rolls out of his mouth and he drowns in his blood.

Ruined or dying teenagers whimpering the trinity of the badly wounded, Mother, wife, and water. The brain-shot guy jerking like an epileptic as he tries not to die. Ever see brain tissue from gunshot? I have. It makes a pink spew across the ground. Like strawberry chiffon.

Gates does not want you to see this. You would puke, buy a bottle of bourbon, and take to the streets. He knows it. CBS could end these wars in a week if it aired what really happens. Gates cannot afford to let the dam break. PR is all. Thus Bush forbade the photographing of coffins coming home, and the CIA ferociously resists the publication of photographs of torture. Professional sadists do things to people that would make you gag.

Then there are the enlisted men. In these hobbyist wars, and to an extent even in peacetime, it is crucial to keep the enlisteds from thinking. In some three decades of covering the military, I saw this constantly. If I went to Afghanistan today as a correspondent, I could argue in private about the war with the colonel. If I suggested to the troops that they were being suckered, the colonel would go crazy. Next to keeping the public quiescent, keeping the troops (and potential recruits) bamboozled is vital. If a high-school kid saw what awaited, if he saw the cartilage glistening in wrecked joints, he wouldn't sign.

Do I think that the press should publish such photos? Not yes but hell yes on afterburner. Every time an editor covers for the Pentagon, every time papers refuse to show the charred bodies still…slowly…moving, the dead children, the…never mind. The effect is to ensure that more kids will die the same way. And the press almost always does exactly this. We are a trade of whores and shills. Except that whores give value for money. The press kills our children.

Julie Jacobson sounds like that modern-day rarity, a reporter, as distinguished from a volunteer flack. Bless her. I used to wonder whether women could hack it as combat correspondents. I no longer do. (There are lots of them.) I used to refer to smarmy over-groomed bloodthirsty office warts as pussies, saying that they lacked balls. The anatomical reference no longer works. I note that Jacobson has more combat time than the aggregate for Bush II, Cheney, Rumsfeld, Rice, Obama, Biden, Gonzalez, Clinton, Perleman, Abrams, Kristol, Feith, Podhoretz, Krauthammer,

George Will, Dershwitz, and Gates. These men, if the word is appropriate, killed that kid. Jacobson just caught them in the act.

57 REALITY CHECK, MEXICO

I have been reflecting on the curious ideas of Mexico common in the US, the routine factual inaccuracy, and the clotted hatred existing among nativists represented by such as Fox News. Some of it is the natural intolerance of a naive Anglo population that has historically hated blacks, Amerindians (the only good one being a dead one), Italians, Irish, Poles, Jews, Japanese, and so on. Plus ca change. Yet I think that something more is involved, not so much a clash of civilizations as an incompatibility of cultures.

It is the difference between the Latin and the Anglo, the Protestant and the Catholic, the engineer and the painter, between the Nordic and the Italian. As you move northward through Europe, efficiency grows, orderliness rules, things feel scrubbed and well managed and comparatively there is much industriousness. At the same time color dies, the arts give way to practicality, emotion ebbs, leisure becomes suspect and the richness of life diminishes. Germany rules classical music of chill grandeur, and has oompah bands, but one cannot imagine a German writing Carmen. The condition becomes extreme in the US where the Protestant work ethic dominates, the view that labor is the purpose of life rather than just the means of paying for it.

On one hand, the northern peoples have produced almost alone the spectacular growth of science, technology, and industry from the Industrial Revolution to the present. The benefits have been enormous. On the other hand, the Italian Renaissance alone produced more of the arts, of painting, sculpture, and architecture than the northern, English-speaking world has yet managed. In the US, music has been way-a-a-y disproportionately the work of Jews, blacks, Cajuns, and Southerners who, like Latins, have been poor, inefficient, and artistically fertile.

For people raised in places settled by northern Europe, Latins seem lazy, their churches garish, their lesser concern with time and precision frustrating, their music wild and their celebrations chaotic. It is no accident that Carnival occurs in Rio, Mardi Gras in New Orleans, and neither in Indianapolis. By contrast, to Latins America seems sterile, uncultured, weirdly driven, impersonal and, ultimately, boring, with its bland suburbs and emotional restraint. Take your pick.

Now, reality in Mexico.

Despite the profound hopes of many, Mexico is not primitive. It runs a variety of airlines, good land-line telephone system, cell-phone service indistinguishable from anyone else's, and pretty good internet. Multitudes of dentists, trained in Mexico, draw Americans in what is now called medical tourism: You save enough on big jobs, such as several crowns, to pay for air fare and a week in the country. In the dental offices and hospitals I have seen, competence has been high, with all the usual ultra-sound, x-rays, computers, and the like. No doctor has endeavored to cure me by sacrificing a rooster.

But things are spotty. Mexico's national health care, while way the hell and gone better than nothing, is underfunded, overworked, and often doesn't have the equipment it wants. It isn't contemptible. When Natalia fell through a glass door and severed three tendons in her wrist, a surgeon in the public system sewed her back together, no charge, and the hand works fine. Countless such examples exist. Yet sometimes the big public hospitals are so swamped that stretchers lie in corridors. Care suffers. The private hospitals do not lack for resources.

While Mexico uses technology well, as do various Latin American countries, they do not invent it, never have, and show little likelihood of doing so. Why? Four explanations are common. Latin America is Catholic, it is Latin, it is exploited and oppressed by the United States, and it suffers low average intelligence because the Spanish interbred with genetically inferior Indians.

The explanation relying on American oppression doesn't work, although many South Americans believe it passionately. The US has a long history of nasty meddling in Latin America, as it does everywhere, but this has little to do with conditions in Latin America. The US did not cause the horrific and crippling corruption of Mexican society, nor the devastating birth rates of the past, nor the now-declining lack of interest in schooling. Not guilty, your honor.

Nor, as far as I can see, does the notion of low intelligence work. For one thing, Mexicans just don't seem stupid. The teenagers I see are as agile with computers as the American variety, stealing music and movies through proxy servers—*burlando los servidores*, spoofing the servers—chattering easily of quad cores and high-def video and using serious pirated software for sound and video editing. Vi and I talk to techs at Telmex about problems in configuring routers, and they know exactly what they are doing. I watch kids at the *Centro de Artes Audiovisuales* in Guadalajara expected to learn to use a digital SLR, fast, without the automatic functions. They do. It's not for dummies, I promise. News shows on television, university radio at U. Guad, editorials at newspaper around the country, Mexican authors I have read—all are at American standards.

I cannot imagine a more thundering torrent of truth than my impressions. Still, enthusiasts of IQ tests of my acquaintance constantly offer what appear to be scientific and mathematical evidence of the intellectual inferiority of most of the world. The effectiveness of these arguments profits mightily by careful selection of evidence. This is I think worth looking at briefly.

There is an organization, the OECD, that runs what are called the PISA tests of what students know in various countries. Some of the IQists, reading the scores, conclude that southern Italians, who make lower scores than northern Italians, are genetically less intelligent than northerners. Oh. But…but…if lower scores suggest genetic inferiority, well, I mean....I quote a friend, himself brown though not Latin, on the conclusion of south-Italian dim-wittedness.

"Fred: Interestingly enough, Mexico does better than Argentina. Wait a minute, isn't Mexico majority mestizo/Indian and Argentina 90+ percent white?? And black Trinidad and Tobago outscores Argentina as well as countries with substantial white populations (Brazil and Colombia). Italy, despite the drag from its southern regions, is outscoring Luxembourg and Austria. And Dubai (weren't the Arabs supposed by the in 80 range for IQs?) is on par with Russia and beats lily-white Serbia and Bulgaria.

Further, in Asian countries kids spend a huge percentage of their after school hours in various test prep and tuition classes. If they were genetically more intelligent, why on earth would they have to study more than kids in other parts of world? In other words, shouldn't they study less than or as much as the other kids and still have higher test scores?"

Uh, hmm, ah...*urg*. Note that the US comes in 12th on the list.

Yet, while Mexico advances on many measures of things countries want to advance on, as for example 5% GDP growth for 2010, the development is, again, spotty. You have large numbers of Indians who still live not too differently from their ancestors of centuries back. Large regions, as for example the Sierra Madre Occidental, remain backward and lawless. Spottiness shows in other ways. Cell phones, computers, and wireless come fast because they are easy to install. Sewerage and safe water arrive later because capital investment is high and the labor involved great. Thus Mexicans drink purified water bought in huge jugs.

Mexico is also thought to be a land of grinding poverty. No it isn't. GDP per capita is $9230. Egypt's is $2250, unless you use the CIA FactBook's figure of $13,800 for Mexico in 2010. Mexico has the world's fourteenth economy. It isn't Japan, but it isn't remotely Haiti, Pakistan, India, or Bolivia.

Mexico is widely believed to have a high birth rate, usually by people with a low thought rate. It did. It doesn't.

A birth rate of 2.1 children per woman is generally accepted as needed to keep a population stable. The United Nations puts the Mexican rate from 2000 to 2005 at 2.40, and from 2005 to 2010 at 2.2 1; i.e., low and dropping fast. The CIA's figures put the rates at 2.67 and 2.31, higher but hardly explosive. And dropping fast. Unicef puts annual population growth from 1990 to 2000 at 1.8%, from 2000 to 2009 at 1.2%. Note direction of trend.

Why do so many Americans believe that Mexicans are breeding like flies? Inattention, hostility, and because it was recently true. I know many Mexican women from families of eight to twelve children, who have exactly two of their own. Why the drop? Women's lib, says Violeta. Because girls go to school. Because both sexes have figured out that they can raise two well or fifteen badly. Because it is no longer culturally accepted that having large families is what one does. Because a family can have a decent standard of living, or fifteen kids, but not both. "If men ever had a baby," says one woman, "they wouldn't ask the question."

Mexico is also thought to suffer from machismo, to engage in the oppression of women. It did. But, while machismo remains among the lower classes to some extent, it is on a respirator, and the lines on the little green screens

58 BUT WE HAVE THE NARCO WARS

Things change. They change. I arrived in Mexico some seven years ago amid dire warnings from all and sundry that I would instantly die of foul disease, trampling by burros, and splashing sanguinary crime. All of this I regarded as nonsense, because it was. The State Department issued travel warnings and similar alarums, but State would regard Massachusetts as hazardous. There was little to fear. Expats traveled at will and walked the streets without concern.

Things change. While crime is hardly epidemic where we live, and in most places mostly involves narcos killing narcos, and takes place mostly away from the agringada regions rife with Americans, these days there is more of it. Before, you could walk home from a watering hole after midnight without worry. Now, no. There's not a lot of worry, but more than before.

The local people remain as decent as always, small towns tending to be law-abiding everywhere on the planet. The problem is the growing reach of the drug cartels, causing a weakening of the fabric of law. When one variety of violent crime gets out of control, every other kind more easily flourishes.

If Mexico were not next to the world's most ravening drug market, it would be a corrupt, but functioning and reasonably successful upper Third-World country. If this were not so, Mexico would not have the huge number of American who have come here to retire. But the country cannot withstand a drug bsuiness that, by a common figure, brings the traffickers forty billion dollars a year. The money means that the cartels can buy heavier armament than can the government, as well as buy heavier officials on either side of the border. (It is an American conceit that corruption exists only in other countries. Tell me another story, Grandpa.)

It is getting out of hand. The killing of policemen, judges, and mayors is now common. Journalists die in droves. After the murder of another of its reporters, El Diario, the major paper of Ciudad Juarez, published the following editorial, addressed to the drug lords:

"We bring to your attention that we are communicators, not mind-readers. Therefore, as workers in information, we want you to explain to us what you want of us, what you want us to publish or stop publishing, what we must do for our security.

"These days, you are the de facto authority in the city, because the legally instituted authorities have been able to do nothing to keep our co-workers from continuing to fall, although we have repeatedly asked this of you. Consequently, facing this undeniable fact, we direct ourselves to you, because the last thing we want is that you shoot to death another of our colleagues."

This is astonishing. It is worse. A blue whale singing Aida would be merely astonishing, but here we have the editors of the major newspaper of a substantial city stating candidly, with perfect clarity, that the *narcotraficantes*, not the national government, exercise sovereignty over the city. The federal government understandably denounced the editorial. No capital wants to be told that it does not control its territory. But this is exactly what the paper said.

Why is this happening? The root of the chain of causation is plain enough: that Americans want drugs, want them intensely, at almost any price—but the federal government doesn't want Americans to have drugs. Lots of gringos want dope: We are not talking of a few ghetto-blasted crack-heads and William Burroughs types sticking needles in their arms in rat-infested alleys. These don't have forty billion dollars. The users are college students, high-school kids, Ivy League profs, pricey lawyers, Congressmen, bus drivers, cosmetoligists, and American presidents (though they don't inhale). All God's chillun wants drugs. Or at least enough of them do to make fortunes for those who sell the stuff.

Let's admit it: Americans are drug-mad. Legal, illegal, smokable, injectable, edible—hit don't matter. They would inject plaster of paris if nothing better were available. When I was in Washington, at least half—at the very least, half—of the single women I knew for whom the clock ticked were on lithium, Depacote, Prozac, Xanax, Zoloft, all the gobbled M&Ms of the quietly unhappy. Shrinks regularly prescribed drugs for high-school girls miserable over divorce and uncertainty. Boys were forced to take Ritalin. My parents generation survived on Miltown and Equanil. In the Sixties, hippies took drugs. Now it's everybody. We have democratized chemistry.

But Mother Washington doesn't want Americans to have drugs. Nor does it want to imprison half of Yale for droppin,' poppin,' and tokin,' as we once said. In effect the feds protect the consumption (through low penalties and slight likelihood of being caught) while penalizing the sale, thus keeping prices high.

The War on Drugs is of course a farce, having accomplished less than nothing over a half-century. Somewhere the other day I saw a story saying that consumption in the US has just risen by seven percent. This is not surprising since, as a society decays, the escape market prospers. And, despite excited hype about having killed this or that drug lord, there is no hope, no hope at all, of eliminating a business that lets impoverished third-worlders drive BMWs.

None of this would matter if it weren't causing copious bloodshed in countries like Mexico, and threatening the anarchy that is often called "destabilization." Absent this creeping hecatomb clotting in the streets, everyone would be happy. The narcos would get their money, consumers their drugs, officials their bribes, and DEA types their salaries. All good. But the bloodhed exists.

Intelligent Mexicans of sound mind, to the extent that humans can approximate the condition, worry that all hell may break loose. Not "will," but "may." There is a sense here, as there is in the United States, that something is wrong, and that something will hapen. Mexico cannot defeat the traficantes. These are bad, bad boys, willing to ambush police convoys, kill federal judges, and rule towns. By comparison the Italian Mafia was a basket of puppies.

The US had better think about what it wants on its borders. As long as drugs are illegal, they will flow and the gringos will buy and the narcos will roll in dough. Nothing will stop or impede this. American colonels with steely gaze and firm handshakes and the comprehension of flatworms have told me that the Merida Initiative will rid Mexico of corruption, and then the Federales will clean house on the narcos. Is there an adult in the house?

I understand that Americans have no interest in Mexico other than to give jobs to illegals and then complain that they have them. And of course to buy drugs and then complain that Mexicans sell them. But a bit of attention, even of realism, might have its virtues. Afghanistan is somewhere else. Mexico isn't.

59 A BRIEF HISTORY OF THE UNITED STATES, FROM BEGINNING TO END

In 1492 Columbus rediscovered America, and the settlers, destructively exploiting its vast resources, achieved a success which they attributed to their own near-miraculous virtues, some of which they actually had: courage, rude vigor, industry, and an independent spirit. Shortly after, they emerged from WWII unscathed due to the military genius embodied in two oceans while competitors—Europe, Russia, China, and Japan—lay prostrate. America's intact military and an economy up and running allowed the establishment of a fairly benign empire and an astonishing commercial dominance, both being attributed to near-miraculous virtues and regarded as permanent.

They didn't see it coming.

Japan revived and began producing something it called a Toyota while Detroit, sure of its market, manufactured lousy cars that arrived falling apart, final assembly by owner. Germany revived. Communism still protected America from China, and no one foresaw that this would change. Airbus Industries appeared, but no one believed that it could compete with American know-how and engineering. It did. One by one American manufacturers of airliners took shelter in the military market until only Boeing was left, more or less equal to Airbus. But Americans knew that Europe was socialist and had no work ethic.

Before long Japan had completely devoured the market for consumer electronics, cameras, and suchlike. Ship-building went, except for builders catering to the captive military market. The steel industry left for foreign shores. Few noticed. Americans knew that their prosperity sprang from their near-miraculous virtues, which foreigners could never achieve.

Eventually China gave up on communism and became 1.3 billion smart, hard-working people who saw nothing wrong with the idea of becoming the world's dominant power. Brazil began making airliners and American airlines began buying them. Even India showed signs of life. Americans didn't worry because they knew that these funny countries couldn't compete with America's democratic values.

Manufacturing jobs began flowing to Asia, first a trickle and then a torrent. Americans didn't pay attention, not knowing exactly where Asia was. Anyway, those foreigners were comic little people with squinty eyes and ate with sticks. Who could take them seriously? Then design work and programming began emigrating eastward. American had invented the internet and now would pay the price. Intellectual capital had broken free from physical capital. Oops.

American industry largely ceased to exist, or at least ceased to be American. The big companies became free-floating international entities, adventitiously putting down roots wherever taxes were low and labor cheap, which wasn't America. An HP laptop now consisted of a CPU from Intel but made perhaps in Ireland, the motherboard, hard drive, power supply and case made in Taiwan, RAM and screen from Samsung, assembled in Taiwan or China, but the label said HP, so it was American.

The trade balance went sour, and then very sour. The country had long since become captive to consumerism both national and individual, "He who dies with the most toys wins" being a bumper-sticker anthem. At every level America began living on credit, but America's credit was good, which American's attributed to near-miraculous virtues which they no longer had, if they had ever had them.

As the economy invisibly declined, the military's budget grew and grew. The country could no longer afford it, but the Pentagon was so deeply embedded in the economy and Congress that the country couldn't stop affording it. The five-sided money hole spent on, an aging kept woman with no obvious purpose since, with the fall of the Soviet Union, America had no military enemies.

Consequences sometimes arrive tardily. After WWII, Zionists had conquered Palestine and begun mistreating its people in the manner of white South Africans at their worst. Muslims, of whom it later turned out there were quite a few, came to hate Zionists and, by extension, all Jews. Since America supplied the bombs that Israel used to kill Muslims, these came to hate the US. Thus 9/11. This was used as a pretext for war by hawkish wimps, now called Neocons. The conflicts were embraced by the Pentagon, which needed a raison d'etre in the face of the lack of enemies. The ensuing wars were enthusiastically supported by evangelicals, more Zionists, confused patriots, imperialists, military industry, and those who just wanted to kill some Arabs, any Arabs. President W. Bush with his eternal martial priapism and yokel grasp was just the man. The military budget now was about a trillion a year in a country that owed more money than it could ever repay.

Many things had changed since the arrival of Columbus and smallpox. Americans still imagined themselves as Marlboro Man, rugged individualists, though many had never actually seen a live horse. In fact the country had become a society of mass conformist consumerism with its tastes designed at corporate. America was still a land of opportunity, if you were an Ivy techy with an IQ in excess of 180, but everybody else was pretty much screwed. Most people lived in velvet serfdom, afraid of the boss and imprisoned by the retirement system. Few young males could any longer meet the physical requirements for induction. The Army softened training so they could appear to get through. So much for Davy Crockett.

Americans had become the Frightened People, afraid of terror, of Muslims, of an outside world they couldn't find or, in many cases, spell. The government used this bounty from heaven to justify rapid elimination of civil liberties, telling the public that it was to protect them. They still prided themselves on their democracy, without any longer having one, and on being a light to the world, which hated them. "The whole world hates us. What is wrong with the whole world?" they asked, deeply puzzled.

The looters came. In the past there had been an element of noblesse oblige, of concern for the nation, a sense among the upper classes that they ought to pay some slight attention to keeping the country alive while picking its bones. This changed. The country was now ruled by the tightly interlocking directorates of Wall Street, Congress, the upper reaches of the executive branch, and the big corporations, none of whose members had ever worked a night shift at Walmart while living in a rented trailer. The worst and brightest went to Harvard and then into i-banking. Thus the sub-prime adventure. This catastrophe was regarded as a cyclical correction instead of as the first notes of the knell.

By this time the country was acquiring the attributes of the

Third World. Impunity: financiers did not go to jail for financial crimes, nor generals for war crimes, nor congressmen for anything. National incapacity: The government handled natural disasters with the adroitness one might expect of Burundi. Intractable slums festered in the cores of its great cities. Over its age America had achieved greatly, done much that was admirable and much that wasn't, and now, overreaching, still convinced of its miraculous virtues, was perilously close to falling on its face.

60 MORALE TO THE LEFT, MORALE TO THE RIGHT, AND NOT A STOP TO THINK: HOW NOT TO WIN WARS

Ever wonder why the US military can't win wars? Why a few ragtag guerillas could send it running out of Somalia (Black Hawk Down)? Why one guy with a truck bomb could chase the Marines out of Lebanon? Why the attempt to rescue the hostages in Iran was such a disaster? Why the world's most expensive military can't win its unending wars against peasants with rifles? How is this possible?

Different jobs attract different personalities. The Mike Tysons of the world do not go into ballet, nor do the Mother Teresas become tank commanders. The career military attracts people who run from the merely abnormal to the frankly weird. For example, they place extreme value on ritual and ceremony, on ribbons and medals and colored things more appropriate to a Christmas tree than to a human being. They are authoritarian by nature, comfortable in a rigid, hierarchical, and conformist society that most of us would find equally unbearable and absurd. Suppose your boss told everyone in the office that they had to wear exactly the same clothes and stand at attention in the morning to that he could determine whether they had dressed themselves correctly. Militaries start with odd material.

Then they inculcate in themselves an exaggerated sense of their own powers, a sort of Terminator complex. This is done calculatedly in basic training when men are in impressionable late or, in the case of officers, extended adolescence. They absorb the notion of invincibility and it persists into adulthood.

Examples abound. When I was at Parris Island in a previous geological epoch, a large sign in Third Battalion conspicuously said, "The Most Dangerous Weapon in the World: A Marine with his Rifle." This didn't rise to the level of nonsense. Few Marines are as dangerous as a hydrogen bomb, and Marines in general are just pretty good light infantry, well-equipped as an expeditionary forces.

But you can't tell fresh young troops, "You're maybe a bit

above average, but the Afghans are much tougher people, having been raised fighting and living on dried goat-meat, and they know the terrain, whereas you will have no idea where you are and your equipment and tactics are badly unsuited for the region, so it's going to be hard slogging." Not optimal for recruiting. More profoundly, men in combat arms want to feel inexorable, deadly, the best. Whether they actually are doesn't occur to them until the war starts. A satisfying state of mind is what is wanted.

This preference for mood over reality runs through their careers. Constantly they are told that they are "the best trained, best equipped, most powerful and effective fighting force the world has seen." This is not a statement of fact but of mandatory enthusiasm. The Pentagon's record since WW II has been a sorry one. Further, effectiveness, training, and so on are relative to a particular situation: a force well-equipped for desert war against aging Iraqi armor is not necessarily equipped to fight guerrillas in Quang Tri or Helmand.

But soldiers, romantics pretending to be realists, do not think in these terms. And so you hear from them unending expressions of fierceness. "Crush their skulls and eat their faces," and "Oooo-rah!" The tee shirt of the 82nd Airborne said, "Death from above." (I saw a Marine cook whose shirt said, "Death from Within.") "The Marine Corps Builds Men," or did until feminists put an end to that. Now they are "The Few, the Proud." Well and good, but morale is no substitute for victory. (You can quote me on that.)

The relentless affirmation of their lethality leads to underestimation of the enemy. Before you stick your hand into a hornets' nest, it is well to examine the hornets. We don't. The Taliban are primitive mountain-crawlers with AKs. "No problem, sir! We can take them. We're the best equipped etc." In an ancient war of classical antiquity, the Vietnamese were held in contempt as rice-propelled paddy maggots. No problem, sir. We've got fighter planes and tanks and endless zip-wowees. Everything but understanding and curiosity.

Of course, Saigon is now Ho Chi Minh City. In like fashion, the French also got run out of Viet Nam, and from Algeria, the Russians from Afghanistan, the Israelis from Lebanon, in each case a trained modern military losing to angry and inventive amateurs.

The norm is a wild overestimation of one's own powers, disdain for the enemy, and inattention to tactical facts. Why? Not because soldiers are actually stupid, but because they prefer martial ardor to thought.

The compulsory belief that they are the best-trained, best-equipped etc. elides quickly into the can-do-ism of the US military. A lieutenant does not say, "Colonel, this is a half-assed idea you have and isn't going to work. Maybe you need to think a little more." No. He says, "Yessir! Can do, sir!" Thus the glandular optimism of "Failure is not an option!" when since World War Two it has become the norm, and "There is no substitute for victory," when losing and going home has proved serviceable, and, "The difficult we can do today; the impossible takes a little longer." Agreeably cocky, stirring, mindless, and rampant in the Pentagon. "Sir! Yessir! Can do, sir!"

In their elevated estimation of their powers, (which is not personal egotism) militaries routinely underestimate the difficulty and duration of their wars. The American Civil War, widely expected to end after First Manassas (or, as I think Yankees call it, Bull Run), turned into four years of ghastly bloodshed. In WW I the German general staff thought that the Schlieffen Plan, keep to the right, to the right, would end the war quickly, but it turned into four bloody and completely unexpected years. The Pentagon had no idea that Vietnam would turn into a long, ugly, losing war, nor that Iraq would present a struggle still not over, nor that Afghanistan would turn into the ten-year-and-counting monstrosity that it is. "Sir! Yessir! Can do, sir!"

Aggravating the sense of omnipotence is the possession of impressive weaponry. It is impressive, even the old stuff. The electronics, sensors, noises, flashes, the sheer technological mastery, the thrill of speed and roar—all appeal to the male love of power and controllable complexity. They do not elicit the crucial question, "Yeah, but how is it going to work in this war?"

In Libya one sees this touching innocence. Air power would save the day for the rebels. Can do, sir. Wasn't Libya open desert where air power should be decisive? The assumption apparently was the usual, that Gaddafi's forces were pathetic mugs who couldn't adapt. So the Mad Colonel's troops began riding in civilian cars and mixing with civilians and the war is now being

called a stalemate. Who would have though it?
    "Yessir! Can do, sir!" Yeah.

61 SLOUCHING TOWARD GUATEMALA: REFLECTIONS ON THE IMPOSSIBILITY OF GOVERNMENT

God it's wonderful—really diverting in a macabre sort of way, at least if you have a diseased sense of humor and enough Padre Kino red. Which I do. As I write the world's only delusional superflower, perennially in love with itself, navel-gazing as narcissistically as ever, ignorant, self-indulgent, gurbling like an insane relative in the attic and fondling electro-trinkets from Japan, is broke. Yes, we see a beautiful dive from the high board, two somersaults and a half-twist, into the Third World. And so richly deserved.

Congress, a collection of whores, con-men, and penny-ante sharpers from East Jesus, Nebraska, ponders the Great Question: Default now, and admit manfully to being the economic lepers everyone else already knows we are? Or raise the debt ceiling, keep spending like a spoiled Swarthmore sophomore with daddy's credit card, and collapse a bit later?

It's just lovely. The World's Greatest Economy holding out the begging bowl to China. "Alms? Alms for the poor?" Maybe I don't have enough Padre Kino after all. Maybe there isn't enough.

On the lobotomy box, congressmen come and go, not talking of Michelangelo, like mayflies but without the brains, calling each other names. They seem to think that they are in an off-year election. I mean, it's only the future of the country. What, me worry? What if a huge cosmic flyswatter came down on Cap Hill and turned them into barely historical smears? How the hell do you start a cosmic flyswatter?

The Republicans want to protect the wars, the rich, and the military companies. The Democrats want to protect the entitlements. Well, OK, I guess killing Afghans matters more than feeding Granny in Spokane. Unless of course you are Granny. Who really cares? I mean, how many "defense" contracts does she have?

But actually the Dems have the best of the argument of national security. Entitlements are our friend. Welfare is the price we pay for not having the cities burn. Mailbox money is our protection, not gaudy aircraft carriers like the USS Thundertrinket, zooom-kerpow.

It's the Empire, stupid. You want spending cuts? Easy, if you don't want to rule the world for three more years before going down history's cloaca. Pull out of Iraq, Afghanistan, Korea, Japan, and NATO tomorrow. Pull out. Pull out. Coitus interruptus. Stop wasting precious engineering talent and non-existent money on pointless funsy weapons of no utility: the F35, the Airborne Laser.

Come to think of it, don't bother. It's too late. The only sensible answer is cheap Mexican red. The US really is poised to enter Central America. You know, continental drift. It can't be stopped. South Korea and Finland among others are far more advanced in their internets. Health care in America is first-priced and second-rate. The country is thirty-third in infant mortality. Schooling would be pathetic if we could raise it to that level, the universities largely farces. The Russians and Chinese have manned space programs; we don't. Industry flees Gringolandia or has fled. The great moiling gerbiltry out there hasn't figured it out. Wait.

I hear babbling about "the recovery." Which recovery is that? There ain't none, boys and girls. There won't be one. We are not in a temporary recession or correction or what have you. We are going poor. The last dance just finished, and the band is leaving.

And it is self-inflicted. There is, I grant you, a pleasing monumentality about truly phenomenal stupidity. A certain brilliance is needed to be so witless. In this sense the American political system is a work of genius, relying on the principle of Sufficient Ditz-Rabbitry.

You don't need to fool all of the people all of the time. Enough of the people, enough of the time is entirely adequate. Lincoln knew this but, being a politician, didn't point it out. Here is the basis of what Americans believe to be a democracy. Curious: Mexicans know they have a corrupt government, but Americans don't. In the US, books are written about the scams and cons and rips practiced on the public. Few read them, though, and those who do already know what is in them. Enough of the people, enough of the time. If the talking heads on the blinking hamster-diverter don't talk about the swindles, the rubes never know.

The country is in fact ruled by the interlocking directorates of

Wall Street, Washington, and the media, Triamese twins joined at the head and aimed at sucking money from the easily fleeced. We're not talking Senior Civics and the Federalist Papers. It's straight drain-the-dullards. And it works. Boy does it.

Can you name anything in America today that is not a disguised fraud? Credit cards are not a convenience, but a way of luring suckers into borrowing crippling amounts of money at usurious interest. The sub-prime circus was carefully designed to do just what it did. There's the student-loan racket, and Big Pharma: A tiny bottle of ophthalmic salt water from Bausch & Lomb, called Muro, costs $23 in Washington, and about $6 in Mexico. That's our government, fixing prices that weren't broken. Pure Third World.

I dunno. What's going to happen when what's left of the cream-flow dries up? Maybe it's the Padre Kino, but...in the last depression of '29, most of the country was rural or close. People, many of them, lived on farms, and didn't need much money.

Today most of the population is utterly dependent on remote mechanized farms winch are dependent on supplies of gasoline and chemicals and then on trucks to take the crop to cities that, if the foregoing chain broke down, could not possibly support themselves. The discovery that food doesn't really come from Safeway will astonish.

I guess I'm paranoid, and no real unrest and disruption could really occur. I guess. I mean, probably. I think. And that's a good thing, because with so many people dependent on entitlements, to the extent that they can't eat without them, and everything dependent on intricate systems that can't handle chaos—hooboy. Think: What happens to skyscrapers if there's no electricity for elevators?

I say invest in drug cartels. Some say gold, but you can't smoke gold. When times get bad people want booze, grass, crack, scag, crank, Oxys, and maybe shrooms for the more advanced. Investment is low, and governmental interference has proved minimal.

I hope I'm crazy. I'd better be.

62 BAIL!: EYE-BALLING THE FIFTH CENTURY

When a country works reasonably well—when the schools teach algebra and not governmentally mandated Appropriate Values, when the police are scarce and courteous, when government is remote and minds its business and works more for the benefit of the country than for looters and special interests, then pledging to it a degree of allegiance isn't foolish. Decades back America was such a country, imperfect as all countries are, but good enough to cherish.

As decline begins, and government becomes oppressive, self-righteous, and ruthless yet incompetent, as official spying flourishes, as corruption sets in hard, and institutions rot, it is time to disengage. Loyalty to a country is a choice, not an obligation. In other times people have loved family, friends, common decency, tribe, regiment, or church instead of country. In an age of national collapse, this is wise.

A fruitful field of disengagement might be called domestic expatriation—the recognition that living in a country makes you a resident, not a subscriber. It is one thing to be loyal to a government that is loyal to you, another thing entirely to continue that loyalty when the Brown Shirts march and the government rejects everything that you believe in. While the phrase has become unbearably pretentious, it is possible to regard oneself as a citizen of the world rather than of the Reich.

Home schooling is an admirable form of disengagement for those who cannot physically expatriate. The primary schools once taught enough of reading and arithmetic, and little enough of mediocritizing propaganda, as to render them other than pernicious. Today, no. Here it is worth reflecting, contrary to governmental insistence, that schools are needless, at least for bright children. An intelligent child quickly reads several years ahead of his grade level, at which point school becomes only an obstacle. He will be savagely bored, regard his teachers as imbeciles, and learn nothing that justifies his being there but much that justifies being somewhere else. In the deepening twilight, home-schooling becomes almost a responsibility, a parallel to medieval monks copying Greek manuscripts.

Disengagement from the system of universities, or as I should say, "universities," is also advisable. This is true, first, because if you seek cultivation, to gain a grasp of such matters as history, literature, the arts and the sciences, you can do it better on your own. Professors serve little purpose other than to ensure that the student does his homework. If the student wants to study, he can do it by himself, and if he doesn't want to study, he has no business in a university.

Second, universities these days, with exceptions I hope, are citadels of intellectual darkness. They teach little, and chiefly serve to force the young to borrow backbreaking sums from colluding banks. The wasted time and phenomenal cost cannot be justified unless they provide some remarkable recompense, and they do not.

Universities largely prepare the student for a life of office work in some dismal institution, trapping him in the retirement system and making him a prisoner of the state. In a nation subsiding into the Third World, institutions cannot be counted on.

It makes more sense to become, say, a commercial diver, or a master auto mechanic. Or paramedic. The training costs less than piratical fifth-rate USOs (university-shaped objects). Both are interesting, challenging, and well-remunerated, which cannot be said of law for most who do not go into Wall Street. Crucially important, cars can be found everywhere, and such as oil companies the world over need divers. You are not tied to the United States, where the death rattle begins to be heard over the thump of the storm troopers' boots.

Disengagement from the consumerist zeitgeist is essential. Yes, I know. Distaste for a life dedicated to buying the unnecessary can seem a pose: "I, I, am of such lofty character that I do not dirty my philosophical hands with mere...things."

No. It is not a pose. In a time of economic retrogression, rejection of consumerism is utterly practical. And almost treasonous.

One might ask oneself, "What do I really need, and what things really matter to me? How much money do I really need, and how much am I willing to pay to get it?" Remember, you pay more for money than for anything else.

I once lived briefly in an old one-bedroom trailer set in a patch of pine woods near Farmville, Virginia. A brick barbecue came with it, and a large floppy pooch, apparently a mixture of Irish setter and whatever was around. The place was blessedly quiet. Birds and bugs aren't noise. When it rained I delighted in being almost in the storm, but dry. I think the whole shebang cost the owner five thousand dollars, including a well and septic system.

If you are thinking, "Why...no...I couldn't possibly live that way," you are probably right. But if I were doing it now, I would have staggering amounts of pirated music on today's monstrous memory sticks, a set of very decent speakers for a few hundred doomed green ones, a Kindle or the free computer version for reading books from Amazon if I had the money or Project Gutenberg if I didn't, and a fairly large flat screen for watching movies donated by uTorrent. Net cost: Under a grand.

Circumstances differ, yes. But you get the idea: Comfort, quiet, music, books, barbecue, undefined dog, storms, friends, for practically nothing. Mutatis mutandis, the principle applies almost everywhere.

It also fits well with Fred's Bifurcate Law of Economic Independence: If you can't pay for it, don't buy it; and if you don't need it, don't buy it. Therein lie the seeds of the utter destruction of America, but I'm not Wall Street's mother.

To labor the point a tad, where I live, near Guadalajara in Mexico, at least two friends are living quite comfortably on a thousand a month, to include beer, internet, and in one case substances crucial to the bloated salaries of DEA. Each has a tired truck, but no granite counter-tops or riding mower.

Another step toward independence is to disengage to the extent possible from the maintenance cycle. You are much better off in bad times if you can do the kind of plumbing, wiring, and auto maintenance that used to be commonly understood. This is easy to say, I know. Yet, if done, it gets you farther off the grid.

Again, circumstances differ and details vary. The principle remains: Disengage, cut your expenses, seek the interstices, and don't believe in anything unless you are sure it was your idea to believe in it. What is coming looks to be ugly. If so, it will be every man for himself, his family, his friends, and what principles he believes. The government doesn't give a wan, etiolated damn about you.

63 WHITE MEN: WOMEN CUTTING THE ROPE THAT SUPPORTS THEM

One constantly hears tedious squalling by the affirmative-action classes—chiefly blacks, females, and to a limited extent Hispanics—about evil white men, whom they want to evict from practically everywhere. The crusade is always described as moral. The pattern is to discover that, say, an engineering department consists almost entirely of white European men (WEMs). This is taken by everyone, including those who don't believe it but want to save their political hides, as prima facie evidence of discrimination.

Head-hunting lawyers pile on. The federal government threatens to cut off contracts. The firm hires whoever is thought to be suffering discrimination, and regards them as an operating cost.

The Chinese, Japanese, and Airbus hire the best available talent. Hmmm....

Now, while bashing WEMs is doubtless orgasmic for the vengeance-deficient, I suggest that it will be disastrous for the country. The bitter truth, obvious to Americans who read history— perhaps three Americans—is that WEMs have been responsible for practically everything that keeps us out of the Third World. Yes, I know. Those in the affirmative-action classes reading this will think I am engaging in obnoxious crowing, racism, male chauvinism, or something involving the word "deconstruction." No. I am engaging in economic prediction.

Reflect on the sciences and technology, where they arose, and who arose them (I say it's English, dammit). From sub-Saharan Africa: nothing. Latin America: almost nothing. India, China, Southeast Asia: very little. Women: almost nothing. Science and technology have been, and largely still are, a game of white European men.

Perhaps this will change. Many peoples—Koreans, Japanese, and Chinese among others—have the intelligence to play. Women may flower. India and China rise. Many Asians work in American labs. If one day they equal or surpass WEMs, the world will be a better place for it. To date, however, Japan is the only non-

European nation to amount to anything technologically.

The magnitude of the disparity between WEMs and the rest is easy to overlook in a country ignorant both of history and, usually, technology. Go to Peru, Mexico, or the high cold altiplano of Bolivia. You will find late-model technology well used: cell phones, internet, computers. But all of it came from elsewhere, and from WEMs. It still does.

Consider mathematics, the basis of physics and therefore of chemistry, electronics, and, most importantly in the US, video games. The Greeks invented geometry: real, serious, theoretically aware math. They didn't discover hyperbolic or elliptic geometry, which would have to await Lobachevsky and Riemann, but they smelled problems with Euclid's Fifth.

Males, sort of Greek-Arab-Indian, invented algebra, a monumental achievement but pretty much their last, and Indian males apparently came up with 0, neither obvious nor trivial (try long division in Roman numerals).

After that, it was a WEM racket. Newton and Leibniz more or less simultaneously invented calculus, with different notations but the same idea. Afterwards dozens of scintillating WEMs followed, only a few of them well-known: Galois (group theory), Gauss (practically everything), Fermat (of the famous and mysterious theorem), Laplace, Lagrange, Hamilton, Cantor, Boole, on and on. Without them, there would be no cell phones to cause death on the highways.

Pick your field: Engineering, aerodynamics, abstruse theory for computers (von Neumann, Minsky), even wacko stuff (Rupert Sheldrake). The atomic bomb and nuclear power were all invented by WEMs, largely Jewish. (The staff list at Los Alamos read like a Yeshiva yearbook.)

White European men probably are no smarter than all manner of Indians, Asians, Brazilians. Yet they somehow produce the science. American WEMs are biologically indistinguishable from those in Europe, yet until recently at any rate have produced more in the sciences.

Why? The best answer I can give is "culture." WEMs, certainly the American variety, have lived (this is changing fast) in a society that has allowed and cherished freedom, merit, adventurousness, merit, independence, merit, and competition. And merit. This sounds like ray-rah senior-civics propaganda, but is actually true.

It shows. The internet is an invention of American WEMs. The transistor, of William Shockley and his group. Microsoft, of Bill Gates. Intel, of Gordon Moore and Robert Noyce. Apple, of Steve Jobs and Steve Wozniak. Dell Computer, of Michael Dell. Public-key encryption, of James Ellis, Clifford Cocks, and Malcom Williamson at GCHQ in England and later of Rivest, Shamir, and Adelman of RSA Security. The World Wide Web, of Tim Berners-Lee, a Brit at CERN. Google, of Larry Page and Sergey Brin. Yahoo, of Jerry Yang and David Filo. The list could go on for another yard or so. Can the US afford to discourage such men in the name of low-IQ, eighth-grade, Koom Bah Yah politics?

No. Yet a lot of choleric billingsgate goes into denouncing WEMs and trying, fairly successfully, to root them out of the universities. The public schools are hostile to boys, attend to the dull at the expense of the bright, view high intelligence as pregnant with elitism, and prefer form to substance. Science is said to be inherently racist. This does not augur well for the country's future. The Chinese, I promise, do not strive for ever greater mediocrity.

I recently read an official of Siemens in America saying that it is hard to find American employees with the technical background to work in his company. In the United States? In like fashion, a woman who teaches in a major department of petro-geology complains that Nigerian—yes, Nigerian—students are better prepared mathematically than American.

This suggests, does it not, that America is living off the ghost of Christmas Past, and will shortly be using goods not just made in China, but designed in China, and then invented in China.

Things stir beyond the frontiers. If we are not to swirl down history's drain while singing We Shall Overcome, perhaps we should begin again to pay attention to ability. It is one thing, and a good thing, to insist on equality of opportunity. Them as can cut the mustard should have access to mustard. But affirmative action, meaning the hiring of those who would not be hired on their merit, lowers competitiveness in a world that is not going to cut the US any slack. White European men have been far away and gone the world's most bounteous fountains of the sciences. Maybe we should keep them, even encourage them. The deliberate enstupidation of the schools to favor the unable, to make those who can't or won't look as if they could or have, is auto-Kevoirkian governance.

If those who detest white European men can do better, they should. Show me. I am waiting. Meanwhile, let them eat goose who do not like golden eggs.

64 WHITE TRASH AND THE AMERICAN EXPERIENCE: A PEOPLE SELDOM SEEN

Tell you what: them as has interest in Americana would like this documentary. If you want an expedition into the bottom layers of the American social experiment, down where even catfish won't feed and everything you think is good isn't there, try The Wild and Wonderful Whites of West Virginia—Google it—Boone County to be exact. Here you have a well-done account of a dying breed, Appalachian white trash, at its finest. (In the title, "White" is a family name, like Reed, not a racial designation.)

It resonates with me somehow. I was born in Crumpler, an unincorporated coal camp up the holler from North Fork, in McDowell County, but McDowell and Boone are the same place, or were—ugly poor, beaten down by ruthless coal companies that don't care about anybody or anything, awful schools, no future, black lung, men crushed by slate falls. It's better now than it was, though. Some better.

The life of the mines and mountains bred strange people, like Jesco White the Dancing Outlaw, Jesco being an Elvis look-alike and probable psychopath, and Deeray White and Sue Bob and Darky, people your mother wouldn't want you to play with because they play with guns and knives and Xanax, coke, and Oxycontin. Some sniff gasoline, which even in the Sixties would have been thought excessive.

White trash was a whole, grett big, motingator part of America, and still is more than most people imagine. Most people that read things on computers, anyway. The history books talk about the virtuous and largely imaginary Boy Scouts, the Kit Carsons and Tom Jeffersons and a sea of rude but hardy and decent pioneers, courageous and independent saints who made this country from scratch. Sure, and I'm the Tooth Fairy. The people who believe this haven't been down the dirt roads to the thirty-year-old trailer with the broken washing machine in the yard and Bobby Ann, sixteen and pregnant, slouched on the steps in dirty shorts.

The truth was a bit different from what the high schools tell you. There were lots of mean, shiftless sonsofbitches, colorful God knows, who stayed drunk on busthead and beat each other into cripples or knifed or shot, and didn't think anything of it really. You don't know what trouble is till you've been in the wrong pool hall in some forlorn mountain town and the locals look for an excuse to beat you half to death with a pool stick. They don't need much excuse.

White trash made up a lot of the Confederate Army, collard-green poor from the pine barrens. You still see them, the crackers of Florida, the residual bad seed n Appalachia. They live on welfare, thievery, a little armed robbery. The women run to fat, the men often lean and savage. The gals will knife you as quick as the men. Don't ever lean on these folk, unless you've got serious insurance.

Those are the Whites of Boone County, exactly. They are hard people from hard lives and they have hard faces that would scare the bejesus out of decent people without having to say a thing. They don't fear the law because they are used to jail. You might call them pathetic from a distance, but you wouldn't do it to their faces. Not more than once.

Not too many of them are left, and that's a good thing.

In the film you have Jesco holding a knife to his wife's throat and telling her that if she don't stop cooking him those sloppy, slimy eggs he'll slit her. There's the woman who slashed a man's hand in a dispute and then, thinking that he was a big sucker and it might not go well if he got hold of her, stabbed him for real. They are slow-talking, heavy on drugs, sometimes seeming brain-damaged, in and out of jail.

Yet they are not inhuman. There is an insidious appeal to these lying, fat, promiscuous, drug-befogged outcasts, an attraction that few might admit to but—it exists. They are trapped, but their trap is different from those of most of us. If you go every live-long day to a meaningless job in a federal-wall green cubicle, if you are bored at home, afraid of the boss, a prisoner of the retirement plan, crippled by the mortgage on a house you don't really like, over-regulated—then you could feel a sneaking envy of these raffish pariahs who say "Screw you and your goddam regulations. Put'em where the sun don't shine. We're gonna party."

You wouldn't want to be one of them. They live in shacks, don't read and maybe barely can, and ain't what most of us would want to be—at least, not reglar.

But...but...a big cooler full of cold ones in a bedraggled clearin, outside someone's old trailer, no cops, no laws, no rules, a couple of pickups gunning it and sliding around in the yard and everybody whooping and carrying on and you can tap a kidney against a tree because nobody gives a damn....

Mostly I guess they are fairly miserable. Leastways the ones I've known could distinguish between McDowell and paradise. But at least they're miserable on their own terms, and I'm not sure they are any more miserable than the rest of us.

You can't romanticize white trash. Not really. So if one day you see this film, call it free-lance anthropology. But watch the Whites in a roadhouse that nobody respectable would ever go to with country music blowing the shingles off and the women dancing dirty but nobody cares. Wild and crazy and everybody knows everybody and you can forget that somebody you knew just got fifty years for attempted murder.

There's music in them, the raw country sound that has been mellowed out and domesticated by Nashville, and a curious mountain ethos that I can feel better than describe. Jesco's backwoods dancing is worth the price of admission by itself.

The Whites don't represent West Virginia as it is today. They're in it, and it's in them, but while much of the state is still poor, its people are generally decent. Bluefield is both safer and friendlier than Washington. Charleston a year ago when I was there with Joe Bageant was delightful. Crumpler sleeps on, good-natured, not changing much. My grandfather's egg-yolk yellow house is still next to the country store at the top of the hill. But if you are a history reader, and want to know how things were in the days of Devil Anse Hatfield and Ran'all McCoy, and still are in pockets, Wild an Wonderful is right on the money.

65 THE NEO-FREDWINIAN SYNTHESIS: TROUBLE AT THE MIND-MATTER INTERFACE

This will bore most people to the point of throwing themselves from a high bridge. I can't help it. The Devil made me do it.

The theory of evolution does not stand alone. It is part of a vast synthesis which fits all of existence into a coherent whole:The Big Bang, the formation of stars and planets, the chance appearance of life in primeval seas, the evolution of that life, the Pyramids, Space Shuttle, and Renoir. It is an imposing intellectual edifice, mechanistic, easily comprehended, self-assured, with only the details to be worked out. Or so we are told.

This agglomeration of everything under one theoretical roof appeals powerfully to minds that need an overarching explanation of everything. The great intellectual divide perhaps is not between those who believe one thing and those who believe another, but between those who need to believe something—I am tempted to say believe almost anything—and those who are comfortable with uncertainty and even the unknowable. Adherents of Christianity, atheism, scientism (as distinct from science) and classical evolutionism fall into the first category; the agnostic of every sort, into the second. Unshakable belief seems to alleviate unease with the unfathomed, the anxiety that naturally comes of not knowing where we came from, or why, or whither.

In the following, unfairly but conveniently, I use "scientist" to mean the sort who needs to think that all of existence is understandable, if perhaps not yet understood. The distinction between "understandable" and "understood" is crucial. The scientist (again, of the sort I speak of) regards existence as one might regard a difficult and unfinished crossword puzzle. The puzzle may be challenging. The solver may have struggled for days to find a seven-letter word meaning "ancient Sumerian perfume bottle." But he knows that the puzzle can be solved, that there is an answer, and he understands the rules of crossword puzzles. The scientist sees the universe as he would see the puzzle. It is only a matter of time, he thinks, until everything is understood.

This is very different from seeing the world as profoundly mysterious, as in many ways being beyond our understanding, as containing questions that have no answers.

And so he sees everything as mechanical, as physics. The Big Bang, if any, was a monumental eruption following the laws— "fitting the descriptions of" might be a better phrase—of physics. Chemistry, a subset of physics dealing with the interactions of atoms, next came into play and then, with the advent of life, biochemistry, a subset of chemistry dealing with reactions in living things. Evolution, the study of the interactions over generations of those physical systems we call life with each other and their physical environment, is thus itself a subset of physics. According to this view, nothing happens, or can happen, that does not accord with physics.

This approach, mechanistic and deterministic, works well as long as the observer is not taken into account. Astrophysics predicts with near exactitude the motions of planets. Solid-state physics describes accurately the behavior of electrons in microcircuits. In textbooks of biochemistry one reads of stereochemistry and charged groups and catalysis and so on that in fact describe what happens. It all works.

Grave problems arise when you take the observer—the scientist, you, me—into consideration. The obvious first problem is that of consciousness. Your brain is a complex structure undergoing complex reactions, but all of these reactions follow the laws of physics. Yet nonetheless you are conscious. Is this something outside of physics? If so, then we have the sciences on one hand, and Something Else on the other, and the question becomes how they interact. Or is consciousness a physical variable, like gravitation? If I give you a large injection of Demerol, you will lose consciousness, and the biochemical mechanism can be given—but that doesn't explain what consciousness is.

Then there is the vexed question of volition. The end points of physical systems are determined by the starting conditions: The final positions of balls on a pool table depend entirely on the initial velocity of the cue ball, elasticity, coefficient of friction, and so on. The same determinism applies to chemistry: mix identical quantities of identical chemicals under identical conditions, and you get statistically identical results. If this weren't true, chemical engineers would be in a helluva fix.

So how can you choose to do one thing instead of another? Why is your "decision" not completely determined by the starting configuration of your brain? This is certainly true of computers which, given the same program and the same inputs, will always produce the same results.

Evolutionists espouse the mechanistic and deterministic view, though more as metaphysics than science. Selective pressures, plausible though not measurable, defined, or confirmed, push evolution in certain directions. Much of it is wonderfully questionable, but we will pass over this. The evolutionist, again meaning the sort for whom evolution must explain all human behavior, falls into difficulties when he considers humanity.

Consider morality. For the evolutionist, everything must be explained in terms of maximizing the production of offspring so that, for example, honesty serves to promote cohesion in hunting bands, making them more efficient and therefore having more children. Right and wrong do not exist, nor Good and Evil, as these have no meaning within evolutionism unless they can be tied to fecundity.

Which leads the evolutionist into logical swamps. I have asked such people why I should not make a hobby of torturing to death the genetically feeble-minded. In evolutionary terms, killing them is a good idea, as it reduces the diversion of resources in maintaining them and raises the average intelligence of the group.

How they are killed has no evolutionary importance, and in any event executing them with a blowtorch would consist merely in substituting certain chemical reactions for others: Pain has no existence in physics.

Of course if I actually did such a thing, the evangelists of scientism would be horrified. They are not immoral. They just can't explain why they are not.

The other place where evolutionism breaks down is in human reproduction. All through evolutionism runs the idea of maximizing reproduction. Women have big breasts to attract men so that they can make more babies. Men are big and strong so that they can get the women and make more or better babies. People cooperate in bands so they can stay alive and make more babies. On and on.

Yet now we have whole societies which by choice are not having babies. Japan, Italy, Spain, Russia, Germany and so on are breeding at below replacement. In Mexico the birth rate falls like a rock, even though nutrition has improved and health is better. The drop is easily explained in human terms. Why do you, the reader, not want fifteen children? The same answers apply in Mexico. Interestingly, the drop in procreation is steepest among the most intelligent , educated,and wealthy—that is, among those most able to support large families. There is no evolutionary explanation. When I ask, I encounter silence or vague mumblings about how there must be some mutation or, well, something.

True believers are true believers. You cannot re-program a door knob.

66 SMITING THE IN-FIDDLE: AND MALT DOES MORE THAN MILTON CAN, TO JUSTIFY GOD'S WAYS TO MAN

Cyburg, Tennessee—The Reverend McBilly Osfeiser strode to the rostrum of of the Full Bible Perfect Word Baptist Church, a frame building reeking of plainess and Protestantism. He was a tall man, with the sharp facial planes and hard visage of a desert patriarch about to kill something. The congregation shrank in their pews. He was a man who brooked no sin, and no sinners, whom he consigned to eternal damnation, and thought they were getting off light. He looked fiercely about, and spoke:

"Brethren, I come before you to preach the word of God, for these be evil times, and the children of Israel, and yea the parents and grandparents, even unto their heirs and assigns, are sore beset by the tribe of Mohammed, and Beelzebulb, and Luciferin and Luciferase. In the name of God we must gird our loins, whatever exactly gird means, and smite the followers of Allah, and suffer them not to live, neither child nor mother with child nor suckling babe. Their lands shall be accursed and nothing there shall prosper, neither tares nor the wild ass; thus saith the Lord God, the God of Israel, the god of love and mercy.

"Today we shall begin our sermon with the story of Samsung and Delilah, in the book of Hezechiah, chapter fourteen, verses nine through twenty-seven, in the reign of Herod Agrippa. In that time Israel was sore beset by the Malachites and the Catamites, even the Stalactites and Stalagmites, and the Assyrians of Kng Areopagitica with many chariots threatened the city of Solomon. But Samsung spent three days and three nights fasting and praying, and sacrificed a sheep, and it was good in the eyes of the Lord. In the morning he went forth and slew them all, cutting through them with sling and samothrace as one scything wheat until not a Stalagmite was left standing. Thus he saved the Lord's city.

"Today, brethren, we of Christ face the same test of our faith. In Afghanistan, as we speak, the Mohammedan Taliban build mighty forces which they will use to conquer all of Christendom and enslave us, having gotten here mysteriously.

"The powers of the darkness are many and patient, and the Mohammedan awaits to make our wives and daughters into harem slaves. It is well said that if we do not slew them there, or perhaps slay them, they will slew us here, or a slew of them will slay a slew of us there, maybe here, or they will...whatever. Remember the second book of Malthusians, when Chay-suss expelled the Gadarene Swine from the woman afflicted with leprosy, "Rebus sic stantibus," he said. "Carthago delenda est," which is the Latin for "Get the back whence thou camest, and thy towel."

"I urge you, brethren, to support our Christian troops who with magnificent courage are killing the heathen with drones strikes from thousands of feet while sitting in Colorado. To those weak in faith, who say that we are killing innocent women and children, I say unto ye, women are the source of all Taliban and thus must be military targets. If we destroy arms factories, should we not destroy Taliban factories? As the mighty warrior Jay-suss would want, we will smite them, and leave them bleeding and dying, and wailing over their broken children, blinded and crushed and burned, that they might learn to walk in the ways of righteousness.

"And now, brethren, I want to introduce you to one of our own warriors for Christ, Willy Bill Bedford, who is just back from the heathen land of Afghanistan, and wounded—wounded, brethren!-- smiting the in-fiddle for Jay-suss. Willy Bill, will you come up and testify?"

Willy Bill was a big, chunky kid with a sloping forehead you could have used to bank a turn in a motorcycle race, and about every other tooth was missing so he looked like a piano keyboard. His left arm was in a cast. "Willy Bill," shouted Reverend Osfeiser, "Tell your brothers and sisters in Jay-suss how you been doing the Lord's work."

Willy Bill seemed uncomfortable but he sort of scrunched up his courage and said, "Yeah, well. OK, Reverend. Well, we was out in Litani Province and there was twelve of us in a Humvee with 'bout a thousand rounds each of seven-six-two and a sack full of Bibles an'...."

The reverend roared, "And tell the brethren why you had Bibles, the inerrant perfect word of God, with you!"

"Oh, yeah. We belong to Bible Spreaders, we try to bring

Muslims to know Jesus, you know. BS is real important to us, so we always...."

"You hear that? Bringing souls to God!"

"Well, we came to Awali, that's this village, maybe three hundred sand-nig—Taliban and their kids, all dirty and livin' in mud huts because they don't love Jesus and the kids there beg for something to eat because they don't know that beggin' ain't right. Well, we told them to get away and smacked them around a little because they might be suicide bombers, you know, and you could just tell the grown-ups hated us for our religion and our freedoms and all, and then we heard a rifle go off. Well, they ain't supposed to have rifles. So the lieutenant called in a air strike and a couple of sixteens came in, and whoom, they just smacked the livin' dog-snot out of those fuckers and....."

"Now, Willy Bill, don't be using language like that. Do you think Jay-suss talked that way? It's a sin."

"I'm sorry, Reverend. I won't do it again. I don't want to commit no sin. Anyway, it was a good strike, killed almost everybody although a few was left screamin' and makin' a fuss and women was huggin' kids or what was left, I mean, how much sense does that make? I guess they learned their lesson. So we went through and left Bibles on top of some of the dead ones so whoever found them would come to Jesus and then I fell off the Humvee and broke my arm."

At which the Reverend McBilly Osfeiser shouted, "Hosannah! Praise the Lord! While we have sat here, living a life of ease, Willy Bill, Cyburg's own Willy Bill, has smote the in-fiddles, and saved our precious daughters from being in harems, though perhaps not in back seats, and saved our holy Tennessee, where we are free and snakes have handles and the God of Wrath rules as he did with Noah in the Sinai!"

I need a drink.

67 A POLITY OF CASTRATI: SOPRANO NATION

"All of the world's problems are products of the male ego," said a swaggering bulldagger she-cop in *Law and Order* the other night. Average gringa. Actually, only some of the world's problems, as for example wars, are products of the male ego.

Of course, a curmudgeonly man—though I don't know any of these—might respond, "Woman, everything that keeps you and your sisters from squatting in caves and crushing lice is a product of the male brain."

Which is true.

It is curious: Women seem to have no idea how profoundly they depend on men, and not just to fix thingy-whiches that make cars go. The pattern is that men invent and women use. Men invented cars, and women learned to drive them, usually without having the foggiest idea of how they work. Men also invented refrigerators, television, aircraft, hair-dryers, and tampons. Since women with few exceptions do not think technically unless they have to, they are unaware of the inordinate amount of inspired brainwork that led over millenia to computational fluid dynamics, band theory, the double helix, and TCP/IP.

We hear much triumphalism from women these days about the "male malaise," the poor performance of boys in class, their depression and inattention in school, their declining presence in the universities. Why are these thing happening?

It is not that girls are doing better. They have always been dutiful, have pasted pictures neatly into projects, and have done their homework on time. Rather the boys have gone downhill. Why?

Much of it I think results from the relentless imposition of female values on all of society. Once, boys were boys and girls were girls. Now all must be girls, or nearly so.

This matters. Males value freedom over security; women, security over freedom. Men love venturing into the wild, whether in Silicon Valley or unexplored jungles, if any; women do not. Men are fiercely competitive; women, concerned with order and comity. Men are physical, enjoying, even needing, rough sports;

women are not. To a man of my generation the country today is unbearably controlled, restricted, safe, and feminized.

This ought to be worrisome, even to women. When men are free, they prosper. Time and again, bright males drop out of college and found Google, Microsoft, Dell, Yahoo, FaceBook, Intel. They go at it with single-minded determination and not a whole lot of humility. This balls-to-the-wall ethos, wing it and see what happens, screw the PhD, eighteen-hour days of frantic programming on Jolt Cola and Cheetos, we'll slit the competition's throat with this new app—this is guy stuff. Men like these have made life comfortable enough that feminists have time to complain. Constantly.

The qualities that make life bearable for males have been squeezed out of society by angry women. In the schools, dodgeball is violence, and must be replaced by a cooperative game led by a caring adult. If a third-grader draws a soldier, he is led out of school in hand-cuffs. If he is bored to suicide by some witless gal from a "teacher's college," he is drugged. This compulsory niceness is sheer female passive-aggression against males. It works.

The anger of women is real, easily noticed in the frequent snotty remarks and the portrayal on television of men as boobs and louts. Yes, there are among women exceptions and degrees. The anger remains. Why?

I suspect that that the reason is the abrogation of the implicit no-compete clause that once existed between the sexes. In the past, boys were certain things and did certain things; girls were other things and did other things. The girls didn't drag race against the boys, or think of challenging them at basketball. A girl would try to be valedictorian, but she saw herself as competing against other contenders, not the male sex.

Then came femlib. Women now explicitly saw themselves going head-to-head against men as a sex. It wasn't a wise fight to pick. Women of ability went into all manner of fields and performed well, as doctors, dentists, editors, reporters, and so on. But it wasn't enough. Since they were competing not as individuals but as a sex, it was crucial to them that women equal men arithmetically in everything. They couldn't.

In sports it ws hopeless. If there is an Olympic sport other than perhaps nymphette gymnastics or synchronized swimming in which women best men, I am unaware of it. NASCAR would dearly love to have female drivers to encourage women to buy tickets,but it can't find any who amount to anything; Formula One is worse.

Intellectually things were not so stark. Bright women abounded, and it was easy—thank god, think bright guys—to find women who were smarter than almost all men. Yet it remained that males outperformed females by a large margin on the SAT math section and by a lesser margin, but still a margin, on the verbal. The imbalance occurred on GREs, National Merit, and tests of IQ. Worse, at higher and higher ranges of intelligence, the men outnumbered the women by larger and larger amounts. This is settled science among psychometricians. It is also the glass ceiling. It was, further, the impetus behind affirmative action.

Affirmative action theoretically was intended to give the under-performing classes initial entry, after which they were expected, or said to be expected, to catch up. In fact it quickly became the equivalent of a golf handicap on the able.

Since affirmative action is patronage exchanged for votes, and unrelated to ability, we began to see female ambulance crew who, though perfectly good medically, could not carry stretchers. There were—are—female fire-persons who can neither carry the unconscious nor handle hoses.

Women had found that they could get by political means what they could not on their merits. While many women could compete at most levels on their ability, not enough could do it to produce the desired arithmetic equality. Ah, but women are the backbone of a consumerist society, the buyers, the shoppers. Thus television began pitching ads to women, and telling women what they seem to want to hear, namely that men are dull-witted slugs. Cop shows became populated by unsmiliing pistol-toting robo-dyke detectives who confused chronic PMS with manhood. While surveys show that women know less about politics than do men, they vote in larger numbers, and thus could demand special preference. Here we are.

It isn't going to stop. The country daily becomes more authoritarian, watched, feminized, regulated, and pervaded by disguised hostility that seeks to avenge itself on others.

Advancement today depends on race, creed, color, sex, and national origin instead of an ability and drive. In the schools boys will continue to be drugged, repressed, and made into puerile eunuchs.

The question becomes: Where is this leading? What does feminization accomplish? What can we expect of a nation run by and for women?

Fewer wars, just possibly. Declining international competitiveness as schools focus on therapy instead of integration of hyperbolic functions. Miserable little boys gagging down totalitarian niceness and Ritalin. Young men who see no point in going to fifth-rate universities rigged against them. And boredom. Oh god, the boredom.

68 ON PATRIOTISM: EXAMINING THE FIRMWARE OF WAR

Patriotism is everywhere thought to be a virtue rather than a mental disorder. I don't get it.

If I told the Rotarians or an American Legion hall that "John is a patriot," all would approve greatly of John. If I told them that patriotism was nothing more than the loyalty to each other of dogs in a pack, they would lynch me. Patriotism, they believe, is a Good Thing.

Of course the Japanese pilots who attacked Pearl Harbor were patriots, as were the German soldiers who murdered millions in the Second World War. The men who brought down the towers in New York were patriots, though of a religious sort. Do we admire their patriotism?

Of course not. When we say "John is a patriot," we mean "John is a reliable member of our dog pack," nothing more. The pack instinct seems more ancient, and certainly stronger, than morality or any form of human decency. Thus, once the pack—citizenry, I meant to say—have been properly roused to a pitch of patriotism, they will, under cover of the most diaphanous pretexts, rape Nanking, bomb Hiroshima, kill the Jews or, if they are Jews, Palestinians. We are animals of the pack. We don't admire patriotism. We admire loyalty to ourselves.

The pack dominates humanity. Observe that the behavior of urban gangs—the Vice Lords, Mara Salvatrucha, Los Locos Intocables, Crips, Bloods—precisely mirrors that of more formally recognized gangs, which are called "countries." Gangs, like countries, are intensely territorial with recognized borders fiercely defended. The soldiers of gangs, like those of countries, have uniforms, usually clothing of particular colors, and they "throw signs"—make the patterns of fingers indicating their gang—and wear their hats sideways in different directions to indicate to whom their patriotism is plighted. They have generals, councils of war, and ranks paralleling the colonels and majors of national packs. They fight each other endlessly, as do countries, for territory, for control of markets, or because someone insulted someone. It makes no sense—it would be more reasonable for example to divide the market for drugs instead of killing each other—but they do it because of the pack instinct.

Packery dominates society. Across the country high schools form basketball packs and do battle on the court, while cheerleaders jump and twirl, preferably in short skirts (here we have the other major instinct) to maintain patriotic fervor in the onlookers. Cities with NFL franchises hire bulky felons from around the country to bump forcefully into the parallel felons of other cities, arousing warlike sentiments among their respective fellow dogs.

Fans. Fans, I meant to say.

Such is their footballian enthusiasm that they will sometimes burn their own cities in delight at victory or disturbance at loss. Without the pack instinct, football would hardly matter to them at all.

It's everywhere. The Olympics, the World Cup, racial groups, political parties—Crips and Bloods, all.

Part of patriotism is nationalism, the political expression of having given up to the pack all independence of thought. Patriotism is of course incompatible with morality. This is more explicit in the soldier, a patriot who agrees to kill anyone he is told to kill by the various alpha-dogs—President, Fuehrer, emperor, Duce, generals.

Is this not literally true? An adolescent enlists, never having heard of Ruritania, which is perhaps on the other side of the earth. A year later, having learned to manage the Gatlings on a helicopter gunship, he is told that Ruritania is A Grave Threat. Never having seen a Ruritanian, being unable to spell the place, not knowing where it is (you would be amazed how many veterans of Viet Nam do not know where it is) he is soon killing Ruritanians. He will shortly hate them intensely as vermin, scuttling cockroaches, rice-propelled paddy maggots, gooks, or sand niggers.

The military calls the pack instinct "unit cohesion," and fosters it to the point that soldiers often have more loyalty to the military than to the national pack. Thus it is easy to get them to fire on their own citizens. It has not happened in the United States since perhaps Waco, but in the past the soldiery were often used to kill striking workers. All you have to do is to get the troops to think of the murderees as another group.

If you talk to patriots, particularly to the military variety, they will usually be outraged at having their morality questioned. Here we encounter moral compartmentation, very much a characteristic of the pack. If you have several dogs, as we do, you will note that they are friendly and affectionate with the family and tussle playfully among themselves—but bark furiously at strangers and, unless they are very domesticated, will attack unknown dogs cooperatively and kill them.

Similarly the colonel next door will be honest, won't kick your cat or steal your silverware. Should some natural disaster occur, he will work strenuously to save lives, at the risk of his own if need be. Yet he will consciencelessly cluster-bomb downtown Baghdad, and pride himself on having done so. A different pack, you see. It is all right to attack strange dogs.

The pack instinct, age old, limbic, atavistic, gonadal, precludes any sympathy for the sufferings of outsiders. If Dog pack A attacks intruding dog pack B to defend its territory, its members can't afford to think, "Gosh, I'm really hurting this guy. Maybe I should stop." You don't defend territory by sharing it. Thus if you tell a patriot that his bombs are burning alive thousands of children, or that the embargo on Iraq killed half a million kids by dysentery because they couldn't get chlorine to sterilize water, he won't care. He can't.

The same instinct governs thought about atrocities committed in wartime. In every war, every army (correctly) accuses the other side of committing atrocities. Atrocities are what armies do. Such is the elevating power of morality that soldiers feel constrained to lie about them. But patriots just don't care. Psychologists speak of demonization and affecting numbing and such, but it's really just that the tortured, raped, butchered and burned are members of the other pack.

I believe I'll have some Padre Kino red. A bunch of it.

69 THE INEXPRESSIBLY, UNTHINKABLY OBVIOUS: SOMBER THOUGHTS ON RACE AND ETHNICITY

I have just read Jared Taylor's new book, *White Identity*. The title might lead one to expect racial ranting, but there is none. It is a good read. Jared deals thoughtfully with America's changing racial and ethnic make-up and the probable consequences. He is usually painted as a hate-monger who regards his bed sheets as evening wear, wants (as Lincoln did) to send blacks back to Africa, shoot Hispanics, and blame Jews for sun spots and loose fillings. Alas, he fails to perform. The book is no more extreme than Pat Buchanan, well documented, and utterly incorrect politically. His crime is asking questions one mustn't because the answers come up wrong.

For example, he doubts the existence, and the desirability, of racial integration, as very distinct from desegregation. It hasn't worked, he says.

Isn't this obvious? I ask my readers, most of whom are white, how many close black friends do you have? When did you last have them over for dinner? We talk mixing. We don't do it.

I lived a couple of decades in Washington, DC, a city then mostly black, and had many white liberal friends. They believed they believed in multiculturalism, but they—we—lived in an overwhelmingly white world: white restaurants, friends, bars, clubs, dances. I can't remember even once being in an establishment in which the majority, or anything close to it, were black. Whites associate with whites, blacks with blacks. That's how it is.

Jared points out that most of what we think we are supposed to think about race and ethnicity isn't true. He notes the mandatory refrain, "Diversity is our strength," and asks, exactly how is it our strength? I have myself wondered. Name five ways diversity has made the country stronger (without mentioning ethnic restaurants or music).

Um...ah...well...ah...urg.

The book is a curious one in that most of it is obvious though one mustn't say it. Does not diversity just cause trouble, almost everywhere? As much as one might want it to lead to comity, it doesn't. Consider: Shiites and Sunnis, Irish Protestants and Catholics, Hutus and Tutsis; blacks, whites and Hispanics in the US; Turks and Kurds; Tamils and Sinhalese in Sri Lanka, Turks and Armenians; Indians and Ugandans; Turks and Germans; Muslim and the French; Muslims and Dutch; Jews in many places; Christians and Muslims in Sudan; Chinese and Indonesians, and so on for pages. None of these groups is evil, but none mix well. Usually they kill each other.

A staple of political correctness is that groups eventually merge into happy indistinguishable citizens. Occasionally, yes, if the groups are similar and want to assimilate: The Irish and Italians in the US did. Jared points out that, whatever one might wish, it usually doesn't happen. Sunnis and Shiites have been around since the seventh century. They celebrate diversity by exchanging car bombs. In the US, neither blacks nor Amerindians have assimilated to the dominant European culture, nor have the cultures blended.

Jared notes that the US now has fifty million Hispanics, or sixteen percent of the population, expected to rise soon to twice that, as well as thirteen percent of blacks. Now, since I live in Mexico, have a Mexican wife, and speak Spanish at home, it will be difficult to nail me with racial hatred of Hispanics. Nor do I hate blacks. But…is this going to work? Or are we going to end up with three mutually hostile countries in one land? The possibility is real. Several states, including California, have Hispanic majorities, which means that shortly they will have Hispanic governments. If the majority vote as a bloc—bingo.

Aggravating the problem is that the people who most believe that we will eventually be one big happy family are those with the least experience. They have never been in the huge, hopeless, festering slums of Detroit, Chicago, Newark, Washington, on and on and on. These are awful, culturally isolated, and not getting better. If there is an answer, no one has found it.

Americans hardly notice the cost of diversity, as they have never known anything else. Jared was born in Japan to missionary parents, went to Japanese schools, and speaks Japanese. He makes the point that in Japan there is virtually no diversity, and therefore no civil-rights acts, no forced busing, no governmental agencies counting how many of whom one hires, no voting-rights laws, no affirmative action and resulting anger. An employer simply hires the best qualified candidate. And the Japanese do not burn their cities in racial rioting.

We are what we are, a mixed nation, but need we make things worse? Unrestricted immigration may let us feel good about ourselves, but does it really have a happy ending? One may well wonder what will follow when half of the country is either black or Hispanic.

Further, when some groups are economically and academically way below the dominant culture, hostility and separatism become almost assured. As Jared points out, blacks and Hispanics are on average scholastic disasters. In the schools the gap in achievement is large between white and black, and has proven resistant to everything: Head Start, forced busing, integrated class rooms, segregated class rooms, affirmative action, schools run entirely by blacks, or entirely by whites, and so on. Hispanics in the US are not doing a whole lot better. If the shortfall doesn't change, it won't matter whether it is genetic or cultural in origin.

The implications, discussion of which is verboten, are not trivial. The US depends on and rewards deployable intelligence, particularly on IQs bordering on the scary, as in 180 and up. The clearest examples are in Silicon Valley, many of them from the physics department at Stanford or Harvard. These men—almost all are men—have given the US its dominance in technology. They are not just bright, like the valedictorian in your high school. They are off-scale, almost another species.

If you follow the computer/internet racket, you know that they are overwhelmingly white, Jewish (a subset of white, granted), Chinese, Asian Indian, Korean. The black and Hispanic proportion is close to zero if not actually zero. This isn't because of racial discrimination. Santa Clara runs on raw brains, and doesn't care what package they come in. Google would hire a giant clam if it could program well enough.

Sez me, this is not going to lead to cheery Kum Bah Yah harmony. As the country becomes a two-tier society—it already is, but as the second tier grows rapidly in size and political potency—how is this going to work?

Jared will disappoint many by not making exterminationist

recommendations. But if you want a clear exposition of what is happening, he's worth a read.

70 HOW WE WERE: A RURAL MEMOIR

I peaked early. It happened in tenth-grade English in King George High, in rural King George County, Virginia, in 1962. The teacher had asked us to write the beginning of a short story, which she would read aloud to the class for criticism. I wrote about an Indian fur-trapper named Three Feathers in Quebec who at the local trading post bought traps made by Bob Ferguson, an English Canadian. But it seemed that competition had come in the form of a French-Canadian named Jock Lerou, which I thought sounded French, who made stronger traps. Mrs. Souder duly read my effort to the assembled studentry:

"Do you want Bob's traps?" the store owner asked Three Feathers.

"Three Feathers no want Bob's traps. Three Feathers want twelve Jock's traps...."

Like I say, life has since been mere, dull, and pedestrian, without savor. You can't go up from the top.

The county was forested, abutting on the Potomac River, with muddy Machodoc Creek, catfish rich—in that part of Virginia, three-quarters of a mile wide is a creek—emptying into the river. At sixteen we sailed along winding wooded roads at night in ailing jalopies that remembered compression as an octogenarian remember the ardors of youth. We had guns, fishing poles, deer and, blessedly, almost no adult supervision. We parked endlessly in the deep woods with the nicest girls on this or any other planet, and...again...no supervision! Adults assumed we had sense enough not to kill ourselves. Rather to our surprise, we did have it.

If we wanted to paddle half a mile into the Potomac in a canoe and jump overboard to swim, we did. Sunlight. Brown water. Sparkling waves slapping against aluminum hull. Nobody knew where we were, or cared. No life guard. No Coast-Guard approved "floatation device." We didn't need one. It would have taken a major federal program to drown us.

We had less sense that a blue-tail fly in a moonshine jar, but it didn't seem to hurt us any. Steve Hunt and I once made a ramshackle raft by putting four inner tubes under the corners of a sort of platform knocked together from packing crates. Unfortunately one inner tube had a robust leak. We set from bravely from the boat dock at Dahlgren Naval Proving Ground on the Potomac, where we lived, Steve paddling, me working the bicycle pump....

The rural South was car country. We thought cars, breathed cars, drove cars, or at any rate drove wheel-born ruins resembling cars. They were necessary in a county where anywhere you might want to be was miles from where you were. A car was a heraldic emblem, codpiece, bar, salon, identify and, far more in hope than in practice, love nest. Flashing past each other in the night, we recognized each by the merest glimpse of tail fin. And we talked cars, endlessly.

"Saddy night, saw Bobby in that fitty-sedden Chev he got, ba-a-a-a-ad mo-sheen, oh man, 283, log manifold, three-quarter Isky, magneto ignition, solids, lake pipes an' cut-outs, phone flow, ported and polished, bored out like buckets, Sun tach, udden udden udden sceeeeeeeeech."

Decrypted, this meant that we had seen, or hadn't and were lying about, a 1957 Chevrolet so hopped up as to go fast and noisily, briefly, before throwing a con rod through the oil pan. "Phone flow" is four-on-the-floor, a totemic form of gear shift, hopefully involving a Hurst narrow-gate shifter. It was good juju.

King George shared the gun culture of the South. All the boys had shotguns and rifles. I'd estimate we could have overpowered the average Central American army. The first day of deer season was a school holiday since the teachers knew the boys and Becky B. weren't coming anyway. Guns were thought a natural part of life. No one cared. You walked around with them.

I remember a frigid winter night when my friend Rusty and I went to shoot rats at the dump near Colonial Beach. He had his twelve gauge, I my prized Marlin lever-action .22. We drove my '53 Chevy, a disintegrating wreck in two-tone dirt brown, and ooched down the dirt road through woods to the dump, lights off so as not to alarm the rats, Rusty sitting on the right fender. Ice in frozen puddles crackled under the tires. We could hear rats squealing and knocking tin cans down the garbaged slopes. I switched on the lights, Rusty snap-shot Blam! Blam! And fell of the fender onto his head with the recoil.

Becky and Rusty eventually married. It actually made sense, but they did it anyway.

Gun culture, yes, but nobody shot anyone, or thought about it. The boys were hardy and muscled from chopping cord wood and "lifting hay," heaving bales into trucks collecting them in the field. They were not delicates. You could get smacked in the mouth if you chose to start a fight, but nobody would have kicked an opponent in the head or picked up a length of rebar or ganged up. It wasn't how we were.

We lacked many of the appurtenances of modernity. Anorexia and bulimia, for example, of which we had never heard. The girls were entirely sane and didn't know what Prozac was, since it wasn't yet. The boys often did have attention-deficit disorder—we called it "boredom," and cured it by finding something interesting to do. Hyperactivity disorder? When you play three hours of fast-break pick-up basket ball after school, plus phys ed, and spend most of your life in the water or on it, or on a bike, you don't have time to be hyperactive.

They say global warming doesn't exist, but it was sure colder then, and twenty high school kids would drive to Payne's Hill or various ponds to sled and ice skate, no adults, life guards, surveillance cameras, nothing, just snow and ice and stars, and we'd hoot and holler and slide until most had gone home and you were alone in the night with the ice creaking glooonk, and the wind coming up, and it was a different world.

Now, I can't say that we always had good judgement. One day Franklin Green and I decided to explore Pepper Mill Creek, at the bottom of a sharp valley on Route 206, in my canoe. When we got there, the creek turned out to be more a rivulet. It was also so convoluted that the canoe couldn't turn its corners, so we got out and lifted it around turns. The underlying problem was a lack of water. Sometimes just sitting in the canoe grounded it. Stubbornly we continued, stopping often to sit in the canoe and drink Pepsis.

Finally the creek, if such it was, debouched into a wide plain of wet mud covered in marsh grass. We found that we could stand in the canoe, stick our paddles in the mud, and pole along. Once I did this and the canoe shot out from under me, leaving me up the paddle without a creek. It was a new concept in unwisdom.

The only drugs we knew about came mostly from Anheuser

Busch. We often got them from a country store I shall not name, as it may still exist, but would have sold beer to a nursing babe. We were not a particularly drunken lot, usually. The first time I ever drank, some country boys and I went to a road house where you could get adults to buy you booze. I didn't like the taste of beer, so I got a bottle of evil, sticky red wine such as you might use to seal a driveway. Later the boys began chugging beers at one swig in pursuit of a manhood barely visible on a remote horizon. Not to be outdone, I chugged...but even now I can't bear the thought....

And now, somehow, we are sixty-five. How did that happen?

71 BAD TIME IN BALTIMORE: A TIME FOR ATTENTION

I found on the Drudge Report yesterday a cell-phone video of yet another attack against whites by feral blacks in the cities, in this case Baltimore, where in a McDonald's two black females kicked a white girl into convulsions, presumably due to brain damage. It seems there was a dispute over precedence for the rest room.

You can see the video at the site of the American Renaissanc, www.amren.com. AmRen is regarded as racist, and is, but consists mostly of articles from legitimate newspapers. It doesn't make up its facts. The comments at the bottom are interesting in that they represent the response to the beating by a large part of the American population. Most don't post such thoughts where the thought police can find them. They think them, and express them to friends.

Things are bad out in the world, with blacks openly furious at whites and a whole lot of whites quietly so in return. It isn't a recipe for domestic tranquility. A price will be paid.

Two things stand out about the video. First, cell phones with video cameras built into them are changing the landscape of journalism. All teenagers and most adults now carry video cameras, the difference being that the teenagers know how to use them.

This is not unimportant. Note that such siege howitzers of the media as the BBC frequently run shaky, wobbly, low-res footage of such things as Syrian police beating people, or of citizens dying of bloody head wounds. These can be embarrassing enough to affect policy, and make it harder for repressive governments to control the press. It is now a crime in parts of the US to photograph a policeman; here, as in Syria, governments move to hide the behavior of their "security forces." This is why China censors the internet, and Washington very much wants to. When the Egyptian public erupted, the government immediately shut down the net. It is interesting that Obama wants an "internet kill switch."

The other salient point of the beating in Baltimore is that the

Drudge Report, a huge, huge, huge site, posted the video under a banner headline almost as huge. I don't know Matt Drudge, and so can't speak to his motives, but he had to know that posting video of godawful beating of a white girl by blacks is Something One Doesn't Do.

Various voices ask, Was it racial? Of course it was. You don't beat someone into convulsing brain-damaged semi-consciousness over precedence in a line for the bathroom. Ravening homicidal hatred is needed. Welcome to the ghetto.

This sort of thing is not uncommon. In a previous life as a police reporter I encountered or knew of many instances, always of a gang of blacks beating hell out of a white, and in a manner to do serious damage. The maidens in the video wanted to hurt the girl, wanted to hurt her badly, and continued kicking her dangerously when they had her helpless. It is one thing to punch someone's lights out, another to kick him repeatedly in the head.

Always the media respond by describing the attackers as "teenagers" and "youths," and by burying the story as quickly as possible. When I was writing my Police Beat column for the Washington Times, any mention of racial hatred disappeared during editing.

Ignoring the hatred is not going to serve anyone well, black or white. In the Cook County Jail in Chicago, I once interviewed a Three Star Perfect Elite, if my memory of the title serves, a high-ranking man in the Vice Lord, a black gang. These were and probably are a serious gang. Why, I asked him, do black gang-bangers spend so much time killing other blacks?

"We'd rather kill whites, but we know we'd lose," he said, stone cold. This disappeared in editing.

This is not remotely the sentiment of blacks in general, but of the decaying, jobless, culturally isolated slums. If if it boils over, which is entirely possible, nobody is going to like it. More accurately perhaps, a few blacks and whites would very much like it, but it would be hideous to decent people. You don't solve a problem by hiding its existence.

Why do the media hide the attacks? I suspect that underlying the circumspection is a half-aware realization that if whites really knew what was happening, some might respond in kind, in which case God help the nation. Having no better idea what to do—I don't either—journalists figure to keep the lid on and hope the problem goes away, which it won't. The whole business smells of trouble.

Further, journalism is a rigorously conformist profession. You know what you have to say you believe. You say it. Joe Sobran once defined public opinion as "what everybody thinks everybody else thinks." Exactly.

And the press corps in Washington lives in a hothouse, insulated from the rest of the country, for most of which they have contempt. They pride themselves on racial correctness yet, in a city the majority of which is black, they have only a few black friends unresembling those of the urban badlands of Northeast, and you never see them in restaurants and clubs where most patrons are black. Many seem to want to protect blacks from criticism. They don't report reality because they don't see it. What does this accomplish?

Thus if you point out that black schools in the cities are terrible, an assertion with which every black columnist in the US would agree, many journalists will furiously argue that it isn't true—not quite calling you a racist, but very nearly. And so nothing changes.

Stray thought: What would you think of an oncologist who insisted that your tumor didn't exist?

I wonder how wise this wanton inattention probably isn't. The United States has a grave racial problem that isn't getting better. The problem is not the black middle class, which is about like any other, but the dangerously angry underclass of the graveyard cities—Newark, Detroit, DC, Chicago, Trenton, Dade, Richmond, Atlanta, on and on. I've spent many nights in such places. It's ugly. And it's explosive. Depending on your politics, you can blame blacks, whites, God, terrorists, or sunspots, none of which changes anything.

Psychology trumps politics. We can do the liberals-vs-conservatives dance, call each other racists, howl and yowl and pose and prance. What fun. But a spring is being wound. The economy declines, auguring cuts in social subsidies and perilous unrest. burned. It can burn again. The hatred is still there. If there is a solution to the racial disaster, we had better find it.

72 BAGEANT MOVES ON: WE DON'T LAST, AND THERE'S NO WARRANTY.

With Joe, on left, in Ajijic. A better companion there never was.

Jocotepec, Mexico—Joe lived awhile down the lake. We would visit him of an afternoon, Vi and I, and find him, a bear of a man, bearded mountain Buddha, writing on the porch of his one-room place in Ajijic. Always he wore his old fishing vest, in which I suspect he was born, and sometimes he carried a small laptop in one of its pockets. Usually we adjourned to the living room, which was also the bedroom, dining room, and salon. He would fetch bottles of local red, or make the jalapeño martinis he invented— there was a bit of mad chemist in him—and we would talk for hours of art, music, the news, politics, and people. Especially people. Sometimes he grabbed one of the guitars from the wall and sang blues, at which he was good. I guess growing up dirt poor in West Virginia puts that kind of music in you.

Joe could fool you. He talked slow and Southern, lacked pretensions, and you could talk to him for weeks without realizing how very damned smart he was.

One day we dropped in and he said he had just found that he had cancer. It went fast. He died yesterday.

Most who have heard of him have done so through his books, *Deer Hunting with Jesus* and *Rainbow Pie*. books *Deer Hunting* is a curious work, a sleeper, that you can read the first time without noticing that it deserves a high place in American letters. He tells of that huge class of unnoticed people in America, the white underclass of a thousand small towns and countryscapes, of Winchester, Virginia where he lived and by implication of Waldorf, Maryland and King George, Virginia and, well, all over the Carolinas and the Cumberland Plateau and…everywhere. America thinks it is a middle-class country. It isn't. Joe knew.

You wouldn't see it at first as sociology. Sociology is supposed to be written in drab, repetitive, half-literate, numbingly narcotic prose that would make an anvil beg for mercy. Joe was more Twain. Never eat cocktail weenies out of the urinal, he said, no matter how high the betting gets, while talking of people working whole lives in jobs without benefits or retirement and generally getting screwed. He had no patience for smug commentators in Washington who talked at half a million bucks a year of how America was a land of opportunity if only you worked hard. It isn't. He knew it. So did I, having grown up in rural King George County, Virginia, where the same people lived. He was exactly right.

He lived largely, coming out of the mountains and spending a year at the Corcoran School of Art, and drifting west where his immense talent had him spending a lot of time with Hunter Thompson and the giants of the era and writing for all manner of publications. He believed deeply in booze and recreational drugs, which in those years was perhaps not a view unique to him. Shortly before his death he told Vi and me about having met some local Mexican folk here of Indian antecedents and going up in the hills one night to do mushrooms, and lying out half the night watching the stars swirl and dance. He lived for years on an Indian reservation without electricity, worked as an editor for Military History magazine, likewise for an agribusiness magazine flogging pesticides, and told horrendous stories about what we actually eat. He was miserable at Military History, but needed to live.

He went to the internet, driven to write for whatever reasons drive people to write, and got found by Dan Greenberg, the literary agent. Agents, and publishing houses in New York, are generally characterized by a lack of knowledge of writing, writers, America, and books, but Greenberg was lax in observing the traditions of his trade. He asked Joe to write a book. Which Joe did.

The consequences were odd. Deer Hunting became immensely popular in…Australia. It sold well in…England. It was translated into Spanish, twice, in Spain and…Argentina. Argentina? Joe was invited to 10 Downing Street, did countless radio interviews in Australia, a book tour in Italy. Rainbow Pie would go into German and Italian. It was by comparison ignored in America. Something is very wrong somewhere. I'm not sure what.

Maybe New York just doesn't like rural people, or doesn't know that there are any. And there was certainly a rural flavor to the man. Seeing a young woman with piercings in her nose and ears and God knows where-all, he commented that she seemed to have fallen face-first into a tackle box. His politics may have confused the chattering classes. Joe was the least racist guy who ever lived, but he wrote about the white poor, whose very existence runs against hallowed doctrine. He was also explicitly in favor of the Second Amendment, noting that ninety pounds of dressed venison matters a whole lot to many families. These are families that reviewers of books have never heard of.

Joe described himself as a redneck socialist, and was. He was profoundly concerned with the fate of the people he wrote about, those who worked hard all their lives and ended up with nothing. Funny: I've never met a socialist who didn't care about others, or a capitalist who did. The truth is that a great many decent people are on the wrong side of the intelligence curve, don't come from families that send their young to university, and can't protect themselves from the corporate lawyers and bought legislatures.

It wasn't a pose. He really and truly, honestly, demonstrably and implausibly, had no interest in money. He lived for some time in Hopkins Village in Belize, a seaside community of black, downscale garifuna and, when some money began to come in from Deer Hunting, regularly gave it away to help the locals. He didn't have a sainthood complex. He just didn't care. He wanted books, a guitar, friends, internet, wine, and occasional substances not approved of by DEA. No pretenses. Drop acid, not names.

When he had to choose between horrible surgery of dubious prospect, and just saying, "Nah," he said "Nah." Joe was going to start Spanish lessons with Vi once he got past the paperwork of Rainbow Pie, but I guess that's not going to happen. We'll miss the throaty blues and mountain ballads, the discovery that Edward Hopper was our favorite painter, the jalapeño martinis barely drinkable though they were, and swapping tales of wild times and odd places. And the sheer good-hearted intelligence of the man.

It was great, brother. Hope to see you again in a few years.

73 FRED REED RACONTE JOE: THE FRENCH TRANSÑATION

Jocotepec, Mexique

Joe a vécu un certain temps près du lac.

Nous allions le voir, Vi et moi, et nous trouvions un ours, un bouddha montagnard barbu, en train d'écrire sur le pas de la porte de sa maison à une pièce à Ajijic. Il portait son vieux gilet de pêcheur, qu'il avait déjà, d'après moi, le jour où il est né.

En général, nous rentrions dans la pièce à vivre, qui servait aussi de chambre, de salle à manger et de salle de séjour. Il sortait des bouteilles de picrate local ou nous préparait des martinis au piment jalapeño de son invention – il y avait chez lui un peu du savant fou – et nous parlions pendant des heures d'art, de musique, de l'actualité, de la politique et des gens. Surtout des gens. Parfois, il attrapait une des guitares accrochées au mur et se mettait à chanter du blues, qu'il chantait bien. Je suppose que quand on est né dans la misère en Virginie Occidentale, c'est une musique qu'on porte en soi (voir la vidéo ici).

Joe avait le don de bluffer les gens. Son accent traînant du Sud, sa simplicité, on pouvait parler des semaines avec lui sans se rendre compte qu'il était sacrément intelligent.

Un jour, il est passé me voir. M'a dit qu'il venait d'apprendre qu'il avait un cancer.

C'est allé vite. Il est mort samedi.

La plupart de ceux qui le connaissaient l'ont connu à travers ses livres : Deer Hunting with Jesus : Dispatches from America's Class War , et Rainbow Pie : A Redneck Memoir.

Deer Hunting parle de cette immense classe de gens qui passent inaperçus en Amérique, le sous-prolétariat blanc des petites villes et des zones rurales de Winchester, Virginie, où il avait vécu, et par voie de conséquence, de Waldorf, Maryland et de King George, en Virginie et puis des Carolines et du Plateau de Cumberland … et de partout ailleurs.

L'Amérique pense qu'elle est un pays de bourgeois.

C'est faux. Joe savait ça.

On ne peut pas dire qu'il s'agisse de sociologie. La sociologie est censée être rédigée dans une prose répétitive, semi-analphabète, soporifique et abrutissante à faire crier grâce à une enclume. Joe, c'était plutôt Twain.

"Ne mangez jamais des saucisses cocktail servies dans un urinoir", disait-il, "quelle qu'en soit la mise, en parlant des travailleurs qui passent leur vie à faire des boulots sans prestations sociales ni retraite et qui se font en général baiser".

Il n'avait aucune patience avec les journalistes suffisants de Washington qui touchent un demi-million de dollars par an pour dire que l'Amérique est un pays qui offre ses chances à tout le monde, pour peu qu'on travaille dur.

C'est faux. Il le savait. Moi aussi, qui ai grandi dans le comté de King George en Virginie, où il y avait le même genre de population. Il avait tout à fait raison.

Il a eu une vie bien remplie. Descendu de ses montagnes, il avait passé un an à l'Ecole des Beaux Arts Corcoran (Corcoran School of Art), puis il était parti vers l'ouest où il avait côtoyé Hunter Thompson et les géants de l'époque, et écrivant pour toutes sortes de publications. Il vouait un culte à la picole et aux drogues récréatives, dont il n'était probablement pas le seul adepte, à l'époque.

Peu avant sa mort, il nous a raconté, à Vi et à moi, qu'il avait rencontré des Mexicains du coin d'origine indienne et qu'il avait grimpé une nuit dans la colline pour ramasser des champignons et était resté allongé une partie de la nuit à contempler les étoiles qui tournaient et dansaient au-dessus de sa tête.

Il avait vécu sur une réserve indienne sans électricité, avait été rédac' chef du magazine Military History, et également pour un magazine d'agrobusiness qui fourguait des pesticides, et racontait des histoires horribles sur ce que nous avons réellement dans nos assiettes.

Il était très malheureux à Military History, mais il fallait bien vivre.

Et, puis, il a commencé à écrire sur Internet, poussé à écrire pour on ne sait quelles raisons poussent les gens à écrire sur Internet, et a été découvert par Dan Greenberg, l'agent littéraire.

Les agents et les maisons d'éditions à New York se caractérisent, en général, par une ignorance des auteurs, de l'écriture, de l'Amérique et des livres, mais Greenberg mettait peu d'ardeur à observer les traditions de sa profession. Il avait demandé à Joe d'écrire un livre. Ce qu'il avait fait.

Le résultat a été surprenant.

Deer Hunting a eu un succès fou en … Australie. Il s'est bien vendu en … Angleterre. Il a également été traduit en espagnol, deux fois, en Espagne et en …. Argentine. l'Argentine ?

Joe a été invité deux fois au 10 Downing Street, a été interviewé à la radio en Australie des milliers de fois, a fait une tournée de promotion de son livre en Italie.

Rainbow Pie a été traduit en allemand et en italien. Comparativement, il n'a eu aucun écho en Amérique. Quelque part, il y a quelque chose qui ne tourne pas rond du tout. Je ne sais pas trop quoi.

Peut être bien qu'à New York on n'aime pas les paysans, ou qu'ils ne savent même pas que ça existe. Et c'est sûr, il y avait du paysan en Joe. (…).

Il était ouvertement en faveur du Deuxième Amendement (qui garantit pour tout citoyen américain le droit de porter des armes, NDT), parce que, disait-il, une quarantaine de kilos de ragoût de chevreuil, c'est très important pour beaucoup de familles. Et ces familles-là, les critiques littéraires n'en ont jamais entendu parler.

Joe se présentait comme "socialiste redneck". Ce qu'il était.

Il s'inquiétait sincèrement du sort des gens dont il parlait dans ses livres, ceux qui travaillaient dur toute leur vie et qui se retrouvaient sans rien. Bizarre : je n'ai jamais rencontré de socialiste qui ne s'inquiétait pas du sort des autres, ni de capitaliste qui s'y intéressait.

La vérité, c'est que beaucoup de gens bien sont du mauvais côté de la courbe de l'intelligence, ne sont pas issus de familles qui envoient leurs enfants à l'université et ne peuvent pas se défendre contre les avocats du capital et les élus corrompus.

Ce n'était pas de la frime. C'était vrai, sûr et certain et vérifié : l'argent ne l'intéressait pas.

Il avait vécu un certain temps à Hopkins Village au Belize, où vivait une communauté noire de Garifunas misérables située au bord de mer, et, quand il a commencé à recevoir de l'argent de la vente de Deer Hunting, il le distribuait pour aider la population locale.

Il ne se considérait pas comme un saint. Simplement, il se

fichait complètement de l'argent. Ce qui l'intéressait, c'était les bouquins, une guitare, les amis, Internet, du vin et des substances non approuvées par La Drug Enforcement Administration (DEA). Il n'y avait aucun snobisme chez lui.

A Vi et à moi, il nous manquera toujours le blues guttural, la découverte qu'Edward Hopper était notre peintre préféré, les martinis au piment jalapeño, aussi imbuvables étaient-ils, et les histoires que nous nous racontions de moments épiques et de lieux insolites.

Et l'intelligence du cœur et de l'esprit de cet homme.
The End
###

ABOUT THE AUTHOR

Fred Reed, a Marine veteran of Viet Nam, NAUI Master Scuba Diver, former long-haul hitchhiker and later international correspondent for *Soldier of Fortune*, spent nine years as a police reporter for the *Washington Times* of Washington, DC, riding weekly with the cops in bad places and many cities. He has written for many stations of the literary cross, such as the Washington Post, Harper's, Playboy, and Army Times, and for many years was a military columnist for Universal Press Syndicate. He currently lives in Mexico, near Guadalajara with his wife, Violeta Gonzalez, and several useless dogs.

www.ingramcontent.com/pod-product-compliance
Lightning Source LLC
Chambersburg PA
CBHW070634290526
45790CB00001B/94